Inspection, testing and commissioning

Malcolm Doughton and John Hooper

CENGAGE Learning

Australia • Brazil • Japan • Korea • Mexico • Singapore • Spain • United Kingdom • United States

Inspection, testing and commissioning
Malcolm Doughton and John Hooper

Publishing Director: Linden Harris
Commissioning Editor: Lucy Mills
Editorial Assistant: Claire Napoli
Project Editor: Alison Cooke
Production Controller: Eyvett Davis
Marketing Manager: Lauren Mottram
Typesetter: S4Carlisle Publishing Services
Cover design: HCT Creative
Text design: Design Deluxe

British Library Cataloguing-in-Publication Data
A catalogue record for this book is available from the British Library.

ISBN: 978-1-4080-3995-3

Cengage Learning EMEA
Cheriton House, North Way, Andover, Hampshire, SP10 5BE, United Kingdom

Cengage Learning products are represented in Canada by Nelson Education Ltd.

For your lifelong learning solutions, visit **www.cengage.co.uk**

Purchase your next print book, e-book or e-chapter at **www.cengagebrain.com**

Printed in Malta by Melita Press
1 2 3 4 5 6 7 8 9 10 – 14 13 12

Dedication

This series of studybooks is dedicated to the memory of Ted Stocks whose original concept, and his publication of the first open learning material specifically for electrical installation courses, forms the basis for these publications. His contribution to training has been an inspiration and formed a solid base for many electricians practising their craft today.

The Electrical Installation Series

Legislation: Health and Safety & Environmental

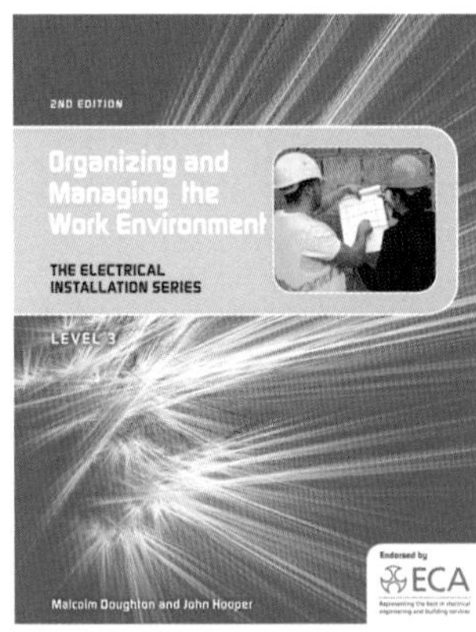

Organizing and Managing the Work Environment

Principles of Design Installation and Maintenance

Installing Wiring Systems

Planning and Selection for Electrical Systems

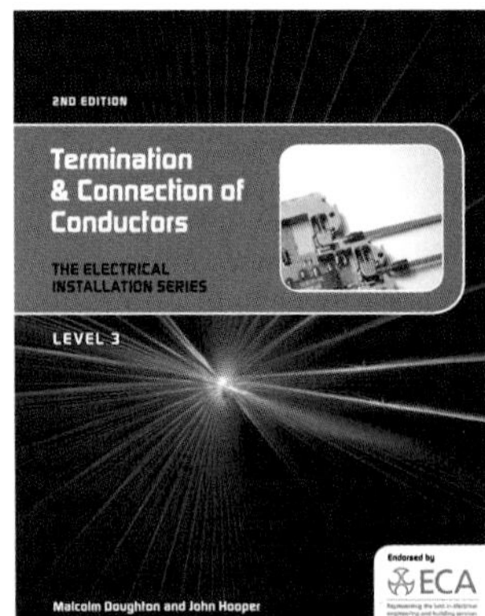

Termination and Connection of Conductors

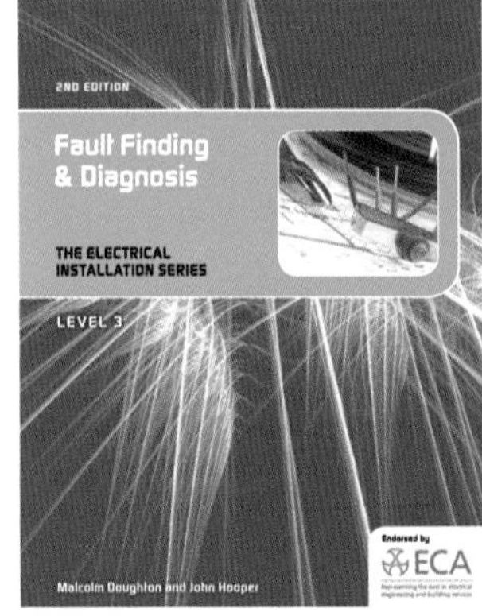

Fault Finding and Diagnosis

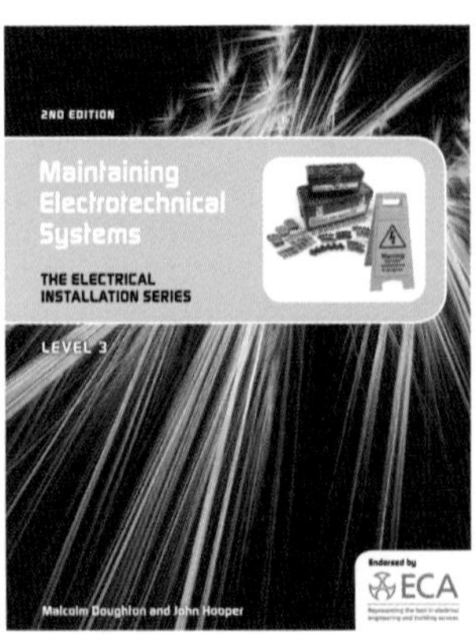

Maintaining Electrotechnical Systems

Contents

About the authors

Malcolm Doughton

Malcolm Doughton, I.Eng, MIET, LCG, has experience in all aspects of electrical contracting and has provided training to heavy current electrical engineering to HNC level. He currently provides training on all aspects of electrical installations, inspection, testing, and certification, health and safety, PAT and solar photovoltaic installations. In addition, Malcolm provides numerous technical articles and is currently managing director of an electrical consultancy and training company.

John Hooper

John Hooper spent many years teaching a diverse range of electrical and electronic subjects from craft level up to foundation degree level. Subjects taught include: Electrical Technology, Engineering Maths, Instrumentation, P.L.C.s, Digital, Power and Microelectronic Systems. John has also taught various electrical engineering subjects at both Toyota and JCB. Prior to lecturing in further and higher education he had a varied career in both electrical engineering and electrical installations.

Acknowledgements

The authors and publisher would like to thank Chris Cox and Charles Duncan for their considerable contribution in bringing this series of studybooks to publication. We extend our grateful thanks for their unstinting patience and support throughout this process.

The authors and publisher would also like to thank the following for providing pictures for the book:

Brady Corporation
HSE
Ideal Industries Ltd.
IET
Kewtech
Martindale
MK Electric
Olimat

A special thank you to the ECA for providing the examples of Electrical Certificates and to Megger for supplying equipment for images in this book.

Every effort has been made to contact the copyright holders.

This book is endorsed by:

Representing the best in electrical engineering and building services

Founded in 1901, the Electrical Contractors' Association (ECA) is the UK's leading trade association representing the interests of contractors who design, install, inspect, test and maintain electrical and electronic equipment and services.

www.eca.co.uk

Study guide

This studybook has been written and compiled to help you gain the maximum benefit from the material contained in it. You will find prompts for various activities all the way through the studybook. These are designed to help you ensure you have understood the subject and keep you involved with the material.

Where you see 'Sid' as you work through the studybook, he is there to help you, and the activity 'Sid' is undertaking will indicate what it is you are expected to do next.

Task

Familiarize yourself with the requirements of BS 7671, Section 526 Electrical Connections before you continue with this chapter.

Task A 'Task' is an activity that may take you away from the book to do further research either from other material or to complete a practical task. For these tasks you are given the opportunity to ask colleagues at work or your tutor at college questions about practical aspects of the subject. There are also tasks where you may be required to use manufacturers' catalogues to look up your answer. These are all important and will help your understanding of the subject.

Try this

List five factors that must be considered before carrying out an insulation resistance test.

1 ____________________

2 ____________________

3 ____________________

4 ____________________

5 ____________________

Try this A 'Try this' is an opportunity for you to complete an exercise based on what you have just read, or to complete a mathematical problem based on one that has been shown as an example.

Remember

On larger boards it may be necessary to use a link and if this is the case the resistance of the link wire should be included in the null process.

Remember A 'Remember' box highlights key information or helpful hints.

RECAP & SELF ASSESSMENT

Circle the correct answers.

1 A minor works certificate does NOT include a record of:

a. System earthing arrangement
b. External earth fault loop impedance
c. Circuit protective device
d. Circuit earth fault loop impedance

2 The tick boxes used to identify the use of an Electrical Installation Certificate do NOT include:

a. A new installation
b. An alteration to an existing installation
c. An addition to an existing installation
d. A replacement of an accessory

Recap & Self Assessment At the beginning of all the chapters, except the first, you will be asked questions to recap what you learned in the previous chapter. At the end of each chapter you will find multichoice questions to test your knowledge of the chapter you have just completed.

Note

The $R_1 + R_2$ test will not confirm the polarity of radial socket outlet circuits where the test is carried out from the socket fronts and a visual confirmation of polarity is required.

Note 'Notes' provide you with useful information and points of reference for further information and material.

This studybook has been divided into Parts, each of which may be suitable as one lesson in the classroom situation. If you are using the studybook for self tuition then try to limit yourself to between 1 hour and 2 hours before you take a break. Try to end each lesson or self study session on a Task, Try this or the Self Assessment Questions.

When you resume your study go over this same piece of work before you start a new topic.

Where answers have to be calculated you will find the answers to the questions at the back of this book but before you look at them check that you have read and understood the question and written the answer you intended to. All of your working out should be shown.

At the back of the book you will also find a glossary of terms which have been used in the book.

A 'progress check' at the end of Chapter 6, and an 'end test' covering all the material in this book, are included so that you can assess your progress.

There may be occasions where topics are repeated in more than one book. This is required by the scheme as each unit must stand alone and can be undertaken in any order. It can be particularly noticeable in health and safety related topics. Where this occurs read the material through and ensure that you know and understand it and attempt any questions contained in the relevant section.

You may need to have available for reference current copies of legislation and guidance material mentioned in this book. Read the appropriate sections of these documents and remember to be on the lookout for any amendments or updates to them.

Your safety is of paramount importance. You are expected to adhere at all times to current regulations, recommendations and guidelines for health and safety.

Inspection, testing and commissioning

Material contained in this unit covers the knowledge requirement for C&G Unit No. 2357-307 (ELTK 06).

This studybook may also prove beneficial to students undertaking the C&G Award in the Initial Verification and Certification of Electrical Installations (2394) and the C&G Certificate in Fundamental Inspection, Testing and Initial Verification (2392)

Inspection, Testing and Commissioning considers the principles, practices and legislation for the inspection, testing, commissioning and certification of electrotechnical systems and equipment. It covers the regulatory requirements and procedures for completing the inspection and the safe testing and commissioning of electrical installations. It also covers the procedures and requirements for the completion of electrical installation certificates and related documentation.

You could find it useful to look in a library or online for copies of the legislation and guidance material mentioned in this unit. Read the appropriate sections and remember to be on the lookout for any amendments or updates to them. You will also need to have access to manufacturers' catalogues for wiring systems, tools and fixings.

Before you undertake this unit read through the study guide on pages viii-ix. If you follow the guide it will enable you to gain the maximum benefit from the material contained in this unit.

1 Principles and regulatory requirements for safe isolation

Carrying out and ensuring safe isolation is an essential part of an electrician's work. For this reason the requirements for safe isolation appear in a number of the units of the national occupational standard. This chapter considers the requirements for safe isolation in relation to the activities of inspection and testing for initial verification.

LEARNING OBJECTIVES

On completion of this chapter you should be able to:

- State the requirements of the Electricity at Work Regulations (1989) for the safe inspection of electrical systems and equipment.
- Specify the correct procedure for completing safe isolation.
- State the implications of not carrying out safe isolations to:
  - Self
  - Other personnel
  - Customers/clients
  - Public
  - Building systems (loss of supply).

- State the implications of carrying out safe isolations to:
  - Other personnel
  - Customers/clients
  - Public
  - Building systems (loss of supply).
- Identify all Health and Safety requirements which apply when inspecting, testing and commissioning electrical installations and circuits including those which cover:
  - Working in accordance with risk assessments, permits to work and method statements
  - Safe use of tools, equipment and measuring instruments
  - Provision and use of personal protective equipment (PPE)
  - Reporting of unsafe situations.

Part 1 The Electricity at Work Regulations

This chapter considers the requirements of the Electricity at Work Regulations for inspection and testing, and the requirements for safe isolation of electrical circuits and installations to enable electrical work to be carried out safely.

Whilst working through this chapter you will need to refer to the Memorandum of Guidance to the Electricity at Work Regulations and the Health and Safety Executive's HSE Guidance Note GS 38, Electrical test equipment for use by electricians.

Note

The Memorandum of Guidance to the Electricity at Work Regulations and the Health and Safety Guidance Note GS 38, Electrical test equipment for use by electricians are available as free downloads from www.hse.gov.uk.

Legal requirements

The Electricity at Work Regulations (EWR) is the principal legislation relating to electrical activities in the workplace. It places duties on all those involved in terms of the work activities and the actions of the individuals.

The two main requirements we shall consider are those relating to the construction of the installation and the safety and actions of the operatives.

With regards to the installation construction, all electrical installations are to be constructed so that they are safe for use and can be maintained, inspected, and tested and altered safely. Compliance with the requirements of BS 7671 will generally result in the installation complying with the statutory requirements of EWR. This is the most common method used to achieve compliance with statutory requirements.

The requirements for the operatives are that they:

- Are competent to carry out the work they undertake
- Ensure the safety of themselves and others in so far as is within their control.

Competence

This series of studybooks considers the requirements of competence for the construction of the electrical installation. This particular studybook considers the competence requirements specifically related to the inspection and testing of electrical installations before they are placed in service. This calls for the knowledge and understanding of the requirements of the electrical installation and the inspection and testing to ensure the installation meets these requirements and is safe to put into service.

Safety

This is essential during the inspection and testing of the electrical installation, and Regulation 4(3) of EWR requires that '*work on or near an electrical system shall be carried out in such a manner as not to give rise, so far as is reasonably practical, to danger*'. This means the safety of the inspector and anyone in the vicinity or within the premises must be safeguarded. The requirements for safety can be achieved by following appropriate procedures for inspection and testing as detailed in this studybook.

One of the main risks associated with working on electrical installations and equipment is that of electric shock. Regulation 14 of EWR refers to working on or near live conductors. This regulation is one that is classed as 'reasonably practicable' which allows a risk assessment to be undertaken.

Working on or near live conductors should only be undertaken where:

- It is unreasonable under all circumstances for the equipment to be dead
- It is reasonable for the work to take place on or near live conductors
- Suitable procedures have been taken to prevent injury.

In the majority of cases work on or near live equipment can be arranged so that isolation is possible and therefore the danger is removed. There are some activities which will require work on equipment which is live such as during the testing of electrical installations.

The inspection, and much of the testing, is best carried out with the supply isolated to remove the danger. During the course of our electrical installation work there are many occasions where we will be required to work on a circuit or installation which has been placed in service. This is often to allow us to make alterations or additions to the installation or a circuit. When undertaking such work it is important to ensure that the part of the installation we are going to work on is safely isolated from the supply.

Task

1 State two requirements of EWR for the personnel carrying out work on electrical systems.

2 List the three conditions which must exist to justify the decision to work on or near live equipment.

Part 2 The need for safe isolation

Safe isolation does not simply mean making sure that the supply is switched off; it also includes making sure that it is not inadvertently re-energized.

Figure 1.1 *Safe isolation is required*

Many of the activities we undertake require safe isolation to enable us to work safely and this action will have implications for building systems, other people and ourselves. Similarly, failure to carry out safe isolation will also have its implications and perhaps it would be as well to consider these first.

Failure to safely isolate

The most obvious implication of the failure to safely isolate when working on electrical installations and equipment is the risk of electric shock to ourselves and others.

The effect of electric current on the bodies of humans and animals is well recorded. The values quoted here are generic and so should be taken as general guidance. A current across the chest of a person in the region of 50 mA (0.05 Amperes) or more is enough to produce ventricular fibrillation of the heart which may result in death. As the average human body resistance is considered to be in the region of 1 KΩ (1000 Ω) with a voltage of 230 V then the current would be in the region of 0.23 A (230 mA). That is over 4.5 times the level needed to cause ventricular fibrillation.

When working on the electrical installation or equipment we often have to expose live parts which, if not safely isolated, pose a serious risk of electric shock. Other people and livestock within the vicinity of our work will also be able to access these live parts and may not have sufficient knowledge and understanding to avoid the dangers involved.

Where electrical work is carried out in public areas this risk is further increased as the installation and equipment may be accessed by anyone: adults, children and animals. The failure to safely isolate presents a very real danger.

Figure 1.2 *Failure to isolate may have serious consequences*

Electric shock also carries the danger of electrical burns which occur at the entry and exit points of the contact and within the body along the path taken by the current. These burns can be severe and whilst the casualty may survive the electric shock the damage, some of which may be irreparable, can be considerable. Whilst an electric shock may not be severe or fatal there is a risk of further injury as a result of a shock. Injuries which may occur include falls from steps and ladders, injury from machinery and vehicles all of which are caused by the involuntary reaction when a person receives an electric shock.

To ensure these dangers are removed, safe isolation of the installation, circuit or equipment is essential.

The failure to isolate can also affect the building and structure. Failure to isolate introduces a risk of arcing where live parts are exposed. This may occur between live parts at different potentials (Line to Neutral and between line conductors) and between live conductors and earth.

When an arc is produced electrical energy is converted into heat energy and the level of discharge energy results in molten conductor material being present in the arc. This presents a real risk of fire, and isolation of the circuit(s) by operation of the protective device will not extinguish a fire started in this way.

Note

The battery used to power a wristwatch can produce enough energy in a spark to cause an explosion or fire in a flammable or explosive atmosphere.

In the case of a fault, including one which does not result in an electric shock or fire, the supply should be disconnected automatically. In this case, the circuit or installation may be disconnected unexpectedly. The building systems may be switched off resulting in loss of data, failure of heating or ventilation, lighting and power.

In severe cases we may also lose the building and life protection systems such as fire alarm systems, sprinklers, smoke vents, firefighters' lifts and the like. It may also result in the loss of lighting and ventilation to internal areas that have no natural light or ventilation.

This may result in considerable expense to the client and damage to the electrical equipment and buildings. The loss of lighting can cause other dangers to persons within the building resulting in trips, falls and injuries from machinery and equipment.

Safe isolation

Carrying out safe isolation is essential to safeguard against the dangers we have identified above but there are a number of implications which must be considered.

Before we isolate we need to consider the effect this will have on persons, the building and the equipment and services. We need to determine the extent of the installation which needs to be isolated to carry out our work safely. There are certain actions which will need the whole installation to be isolated and others where the isolation of one or more circuits may be all that is necessary.

Figure 1.3 *Safe isolation will affect others*

The isolation of the complete installation has serious implications for the users of the installation as electrical equipment and lighting will not be available for use. This means that the timing and duration of the work must be carefully considered and discussed with the user to minimize disruption.

This will also affect our operation as there will be no supply available for lighting or power tools. So we will need to consider task lighting and power for our work and it may be necessary to arrange a temporary supply for the client's equipment.

Where any safety services or alarms may be affected we need to consider the consequences of isolation. For example, burglar alarms may be linked to the police or a security company and the loss of supply may result in a response visit. If this is a false alarm the client may be charged for the wasted visit. Similarly, a fire alarm isolated from the supply may cause an alarm to be triggered which could cause the fire service to respond.

In addition there are a number of other building services which may be affected including time locks, door access systems, bar code readers and tills, security cameras and public address systems.

Figure 1.4 *Safe isolation may affect safety services and alarms*

Isolation of individual circuits may also cause inconvenience to the client and the requirements will need to be discussed to ensure that any disruption is kept to a minimum. In any event we must always obtain permission before we isolate.

In certain instances it may not be possible to carry out some or all of the work during normal working hours. In these cases arrangements will need to be made with the client to ensure that access is permitted. This may require the client to provide staff to attend, for security or access purposes, during the period when the work is carried out.

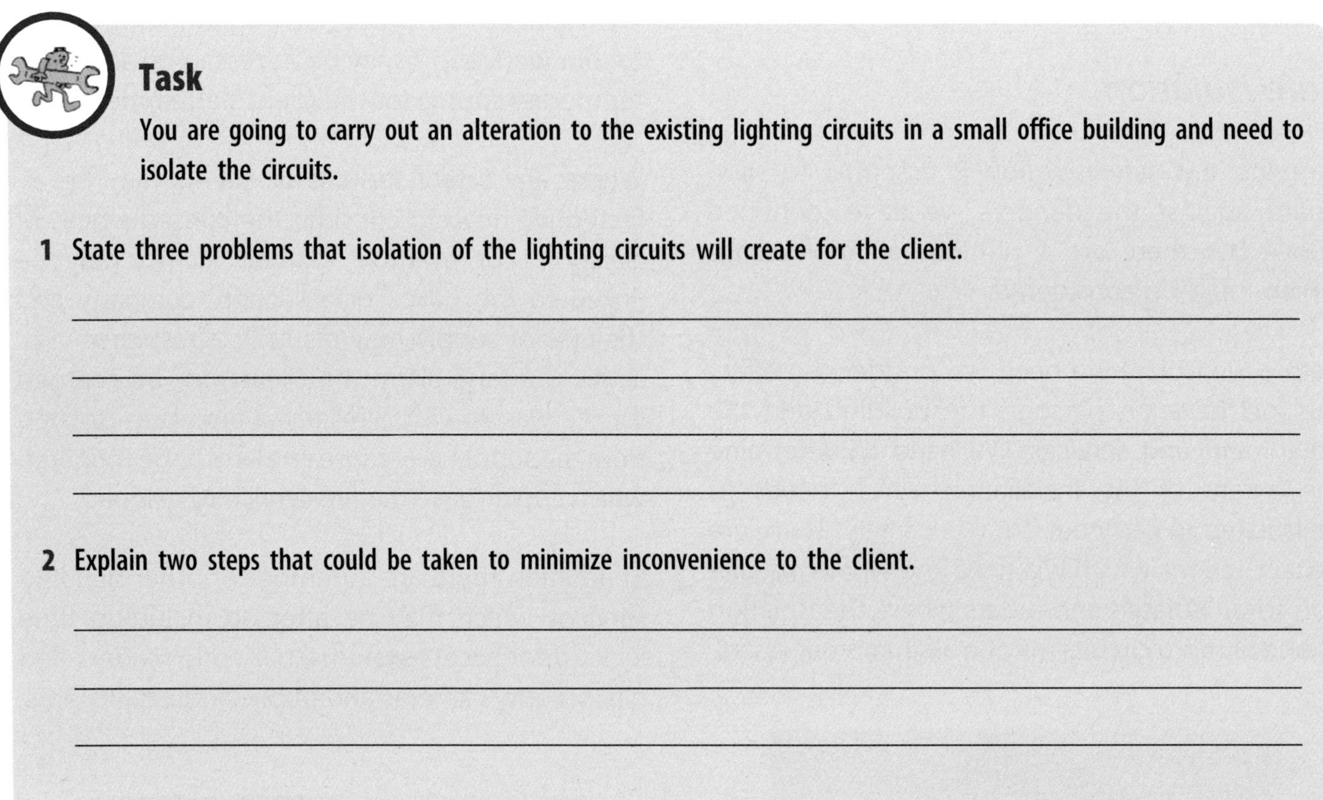

Task

You are going to carry out an alteration to the existing lighting circuits in a small office building and need to isolate the circuits.

1 **State three problems that isolation of the lighting circuits will create for the client.**

2 **Explain two steps that could be taken to minimize inconvenience to the client.**

Part 3 Safe isolation procedures

The key to safety is to follow the correct procedure(s) throughout the isolation process. Let's consider a situation where we are going to carry out an addition to a lighting circuit in a workshop. We need to carry out the safe isolation of the single circuit so that we can work on it safely.

Before we can begin to work on the addition we must safely isolate the circuit from the supply. This particular circuit is protected by a BS EN 60898 type B circuit breaker (cb) in the distribution board located at the origin of the installation.

Figure 1.5 *Safe isolation*

Before we can begin we must first obtain permission to isolate the circuit. This must be obtained from the person responsible for the electrical installation (the duty holder), **not** just any employee. As we are going to be isolating the supply the duty holder must ensure that the safety of persons and the operation of the business is not going to be compromised. To do this the area to be affected and the duration of the isolation should be explained to the duty holder to help in making the decision.

Once we have been given permission to isolate the circuit we must correctly identify the particular circuit within the distribution board. Where there are a number of lighting circuits it is important that we isolate the correct circuit. Providing the distribution board has been correctly labelled and the appropriate circuit charts are available this should be relatively straightforward.

There are proprietary test instruments which allow the identification of a circuit before it is isolated. These rely on being connected to the circuit when they then transmit a signal through the circuit conductors. A second unit is used to sense the signal at the distribution board to identify the fuse or cb. The sensitivity of the unit can be adjusted to give a clear and reliable indication of the circuit to be isolated.

This works well with circuits which include a socket outlet as the sender unit can be readily plugged into the circuit. However, where the circuit does not include a suitable socket a connection would need to be made to live parts. This introduces a higher risk to the operative as, due to the purpose of the device, the circuit will not be isolated. In these circumstances the operation would require two persons, one to operate the sensing unit and the other to make the connection to the circuit using test probes complying with GS 38. Extreme care is required when accessing the live terminals to make this connection and it should only be carried out by skilled persons using suitable equipment.

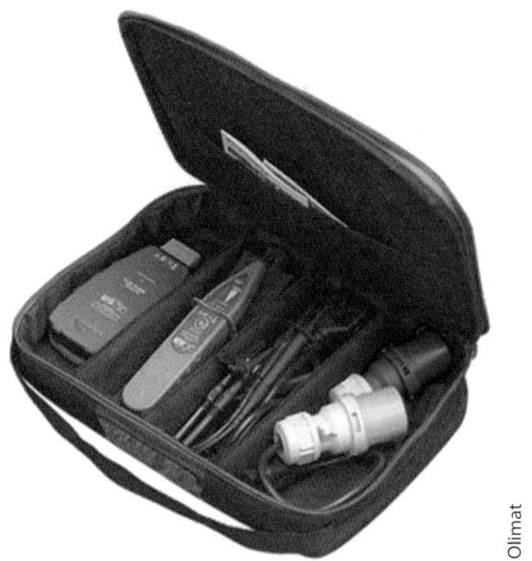

Figure 1.6 *Typical circuit identification or fuse finder instruments*

Having correctly identified the circuit the cb is switched off, isolating the circuit from the supply.

An appropriate locking off device is then fitted to the cb to prevent unintentional re-energizing of the circuit. There are a number of proprietary devices available for this task and they all perform the same function, which is preventing the operation of the cb. In most cases a separate padlock is inserted through the locking off device to prevent unauthorized removal. This secures the cb and a warning label should also be fitted to advise that the circuit should not be energized and that someone is working on the circuit. Typical lock off devices and labels are shown in Figures 1.7 and 1.8.

Re-produced with the kind permission of IDEAL INDUSTRIES LIMITED

Figure 1.7 *Typical lock off kit*

Figure 1.8 *Lock off in position*

Having safely isolated and locked off the circuit we must now confirm that the circuit is indeed isolated from the supply. To do this we will need an Approved Voltage Indicator (AVI) together with a proving unit, as shown in Figure 1.9. The term AVI refers to a voltage indicator which meets all the requirements of Health and Safety Guidance GS 38.

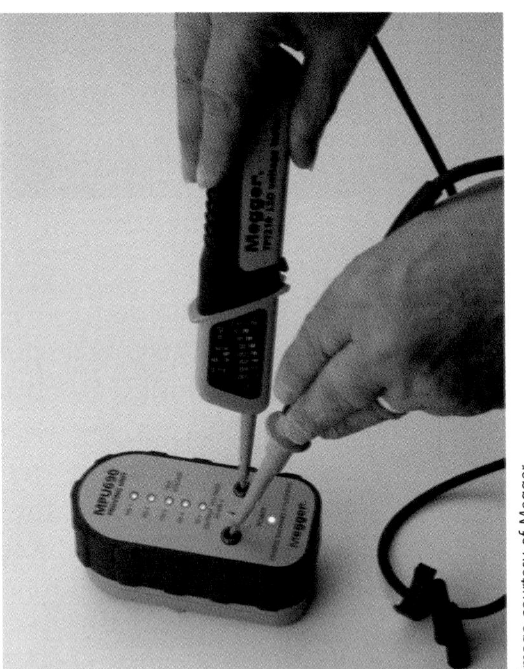

Image courtesy of Megger

Figure 1.9 *Typical proving unit and Approved Voltage Indicator*

In this instance we are going to remove the cover from a ceiling rose on the circuit at the point where we are going to start the alteration and confirm that it is actually isolated. The first step, having removed the cover, is to confirm that the AVI is functioning using the proving unit. The output produced by the proving unit should cause all the LED indicators to light showing that they are all functioning correctly.

As this is a single phase lighting circuit we will need to confirm isolation by testing between:

- All line conductors and neutral (loop line terminal and switch line terminal operating the switch to confirm in both switch positions)

- All line conductors and earth (loop line terminal and switch line terminal)
- Neutral and earth.

And there should be no voltage present at any of these connections.

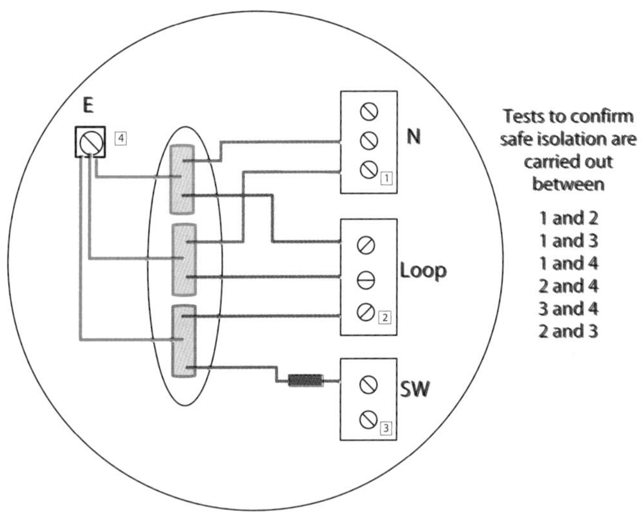

Figure 1.10 *Tests for safe isolation at ceiling rose*

Finally we must confirm that the AVI is still working. To do this we will use the proving unit again and all the LED indicators should light when the AVI is tested. This process will have confirmed that the circuit we are going to work on is isolated from the supply.

It is always advisable, when removing accessories to carry out work, to further check at each accessory that isolation is achieved. It may be that a luminaire or accessory which appears to be on the circuit is actually supplied from elsewhere.

For example, it is not uncommon to find a downstairs socket wired from an upstairs circuit and once the downstairs circuit is isolated it would be logical to assume that all the ground floor sockets are isolated. Similarly, where two circuits supply the same area, such as the ground floor of a dwelling, then it is not always obvious which sockets are supplied on which circuit.

Summary procedure for circuit isolation

1. Seek permission to isolate
2. Identify the circuit to be isolated
3. Isolate by switching off cb or isolator
4. Fit locking device and warning label
5. Secure area around accessory to be removed (barriers)
6. Remove accessory
7. Select an AVI
8. Confirm AVI complies with GS 38
9. Confirm the operation of the AVI using a proving unit
10. Test between all live conductors
11. Is circuit dead? If not go back to 2
12. Test between all live conductors and earth
13. Is circuit dead? If not go back to 2
14. Confirm AVI is functioning using proving unit.

Isolation of a complete installation follows a similar procedure but in this case we are isolating the supply to the whole installation or all the circuits supplied from a particular distribution board.

When isolating a number of circuits it is important to discuss with the duty holder the areas that will be isolated and determine any special requirements related to any of the circuits which will be isolated.

If we are to confirm safe isolation of a three phase distribution board then there will be a number of additional tests to be carried out as identified in Figure 1.11.

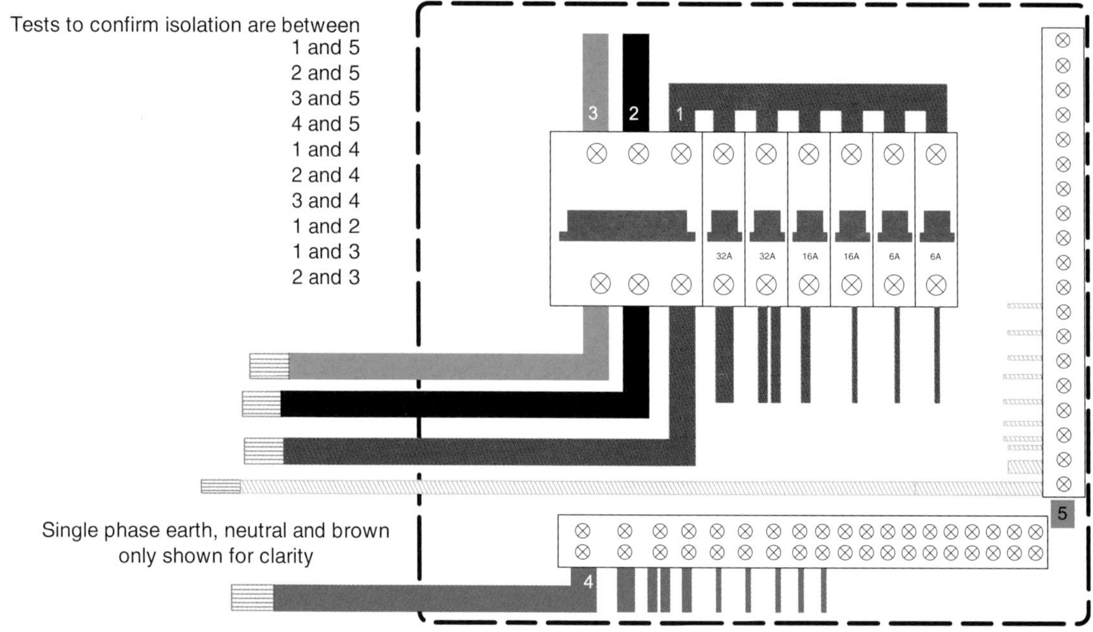

Figure 1.11 *Three phase points of test for isolation*

Summary procedure for distribution board isolation

1. Seek permission to isolate
2. Identify the distribution board to be isolated
3. Isolate by switching off main isolator
4. Fit locking device and warning label
5. Remove distribution board cover to access live terminals
6. Select an AVI
7. Confirm AVI complies with GS 38
8. Confirm the operation of the AVI using a proving unit
9. Test between all live conductors
10. Is circuit dead? If not go back to 2
11. Test between all live conductors and earth
12. Is circuit dead? If not go back to 2
13. Confirm AVI is functioning using proving unit.

Note

A safe isolation flow chart is included at the end of this chapter for your reference. You can copy this and put it with your test equipment as an aide memoire.

Remember

When we consider proving the operation of the AVI we can use a known live supply or a proving unit. When isolating a distribution board it is possible to use the incoming supply to the isolator to prove the AVI is functioning before and after we test for isolation. This is not possible when isolating a single circuit and so a proving unit is essential for circuit isolation.

Remember

All items of test equipment, including those items issued on a personal basis, should be regularly inspected and, where necessary, tested by a competent person.

Task

A three phase motor is to be replaced and needs to be isolated and disconnected to allow this to take place. Describe, using the terminal block information shown in Figure 1.12, the procedure to be carried out to confirm safe isolation of the motor. The local isolator has been locked in the off position and the motor terminal cover removed.

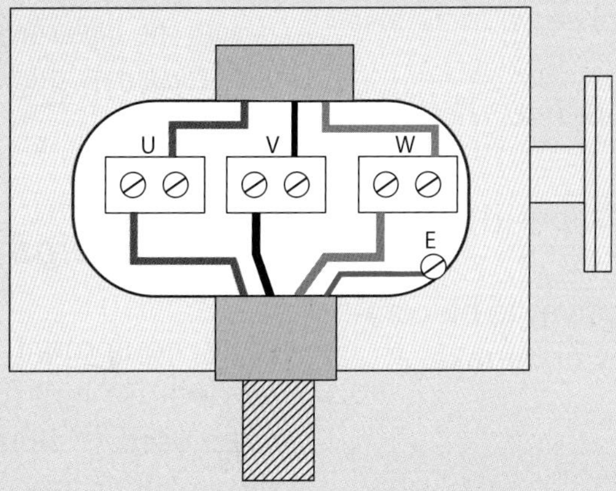

Figure 1.12 *Three phase motor terminals*

Part 4 Health and safety requirements

Complying with the applicable legislation, standards and codes of practice when inspecting and testing electrical installations is essential.

The legislation which we must observe includes:

- The Health and Safety at Work (etc.) Act (1974) and
- The Electricity at Work Regulations (1989).

Both these acts require the operatives to be competent to carry out the work they undertake.

Remember

A competent person is defined by the Construction (Health, Safety & Welfare) Regulations 1996 as; 'Any person who carries out an activity shall possess such training, technical knowledge or experience as may be appropriate, or be supervised by such a person.'

A number of regulations and codes of practice have been introduced under the Health & Safety at Work (etc.) Act. Any of these regulations or codes of practice which are applicable to the inspection and testing, or to the environment in which it is undertaken, will need to be complied with when inspecting and testing electrical installations.

BS 7671 and IET Guidance Note 3, Inspection and Testing identify the need for competence and when carrying out inspection and testing the requirement includes the use of suitable and appropriate test instruments. This requires the inspector to be fully versed in the inspection and testing process and with the knowledge of the capability and limitations of the test equipment.

Note

The statutory and health and safety requirements are considered in greater detail in both the *Legislation* and *Termination and Connection of Conductors* studybooks in this series.

Tools, equipment and instruments

Work equipment should be suitable for its intended use and for the conditions in which it is to be used. It should be maintained in a safe condition and inspected periodically to ensure that it remains safe for use. Records should be kept of the inspections carried out on the equipment.

An employee is required by law to:

- Not interfere with tools, equipment, etc. provided for their health, safety and welfare
- Correctly use all work items provided in accordance with instructions and training given to them.

Test instruments are to be regularly calibrated and records of ongoing accuracy must be kept to confirm the instruments continue to give accurate test results.

The function requirements and use of the test instruments are covered in later chapters of this studybook. Instruments should be treated with respect and it is important to remember that we rely on them being in good condition and to provide accurate readings. These results are used to determine whether the installation complies with the current requirements and is safe to put into service.

When testing electrical installations where voltages in excess of 50 V ac are involved, the test leads should comply with the requirements of HSE Guidance Note GS 38, Electrical test equipment for use by electricians. Test leads are subject to wear and tear and they should be checked regularly to ensure they are in good condition and comply with GS 38.

Personal Protective Equipment (PPE)

Inspection and testing is no different to any other activity in respect to the requirements for PPE. Wherever PPE is provided for an activity it must be used and maintained in good condition. Generally speaking the PPE needs are based upon other activities and requirements of the location in which the work is carried out. Safety glasses are one item of PPE equipment which should be used when carrying out testing as the risk, should an error be made, is of material produced from arcing entering the eyes.

Reporting of unsafe situations

Any unsafe situations identified during the inspection and testing of an electrical installation should be reported to the responsible person without delay. Any items which require immediate action and are within your control should be remedied. The reporting of unsafe situations does vary from one company to another and the requirements are covered in more depth in the studybook *Termination and Connection of Conductors*.

Task

Using the information in HSE Guidance GS 38, list the requirements for test leads and probes for test equipment used for electrical installations.

Congratulations, you have now completed Chapter 1 so correctly complete the following self assessment questions before you carry on to the next chapter.

SELF ASSESSMENT

Circle the correct answers.

1 Safe isolation is carried out on an installation prior to installing new luminaires to an existing lighting circuit. One of the consequences of this action is:

a. Use of the installation will be restricted
b. The installation will function normally
c. The user is not inconvenienced
d. An increased shock risk

2 The locking off of an isolator for safe isolation allows the electrician to:

a. Have control of the isolated part of the installation
b. Leave the building without a supply until work is finished
c. Use unskilled labour to keep costs down
d. Maximize the inconvenience to the user of the installation

3 A socket outlet circuit has been identified, isolated and locked off at the distribution board. One of the sockets has been removed from the socket box and tests indicate there is no voltage present. The final action to be taken before working on the circuit is to:

a. Disconnect the conductors
b. Confirm the AVI is functioning
c. Remove the remaining socket outlets
d. Notify the client the circuit is isolated

4 The maximum exposed tip on the probes of an AVI used to confirm safe isolation is:

a. 2 mm
b. 3 mm
c. 4 mm
d. 5 mm

5 In order to be considered as competent to work on an electrical installation a person should possess appropriate training, technical knowledge or experience. Alternatively the person should:

a. Only work on equipment made dead
b. Only work on live equipment when told to do so
c. Be careful when working on existing circuits
d. Be supervised by a competent person

Safe isolation flow chart

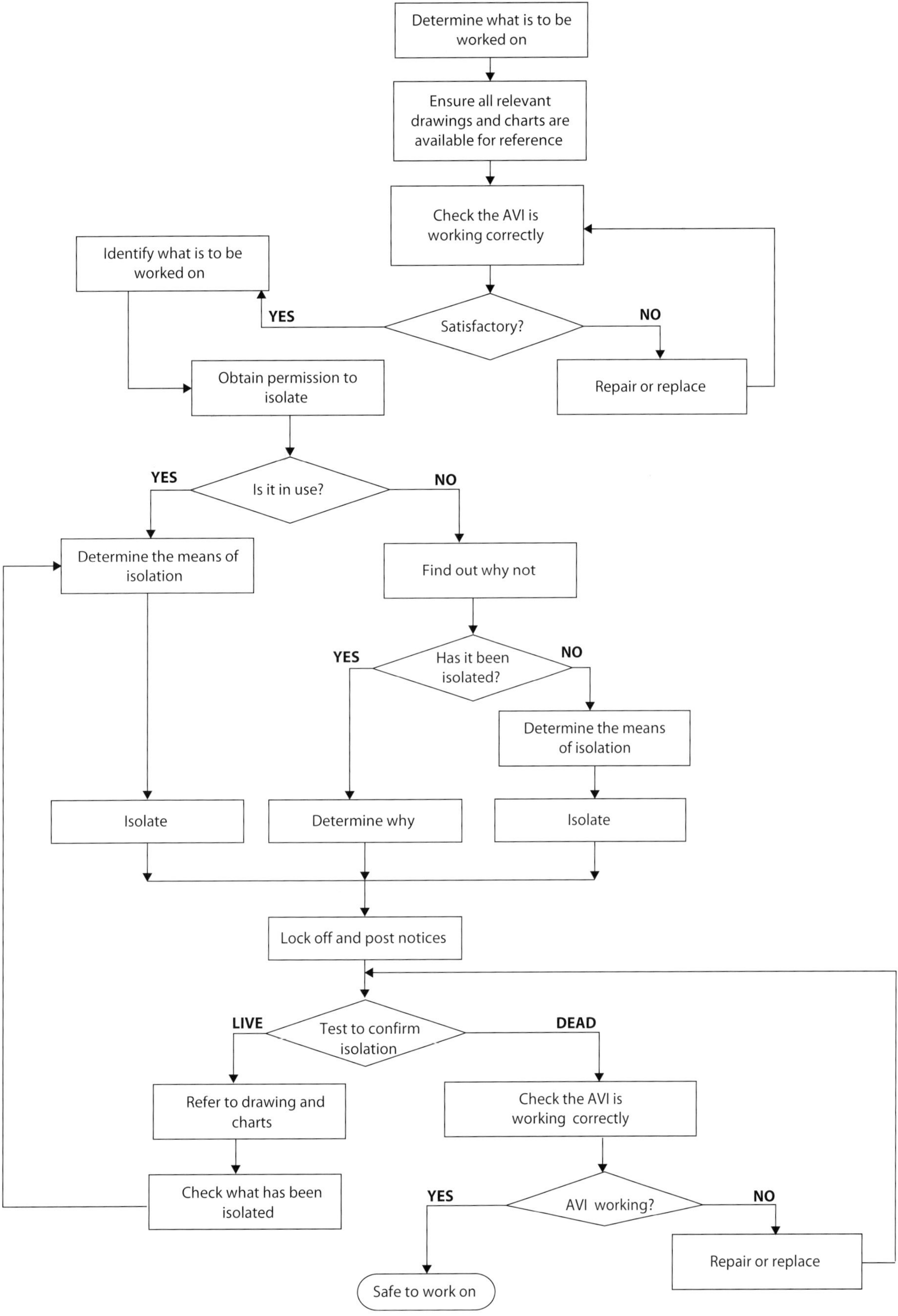

2 Principles and regulatory requirements for inspecting, testing and commissioning

RECAP

Before you start work on this chapter, complete the exercise below to ensure that you remember what you learned earlier.

- The Electricity at Work Regulations require work on or ___________ an electrical ____________ to be carried out so as not to give rise, so far as is ____________ practicable, to ______________.
- Working on or near __________ conductors should only be undertaken where it is ________________ under ________________ circumstances for the equipment to be ________________.
- Whilst an electric _________ may not be severe or __________ there is a risk of further ____________ as a result of a shock.
- Isolation of individual circuits may cause inconvenience to the ___________ and any ______________________ should be kept to a minimum.
- Before carrying out _____________ isolation we must first obtain _____________ from the ___________.
- An _______________ Voltage Indicator refers to a voltage indicator which meets ____________ the requirements of Health and Safety Guidance ____________.

- Tests to confirm ______________ isolation are carried out between all ______________ conductors and all ________________ conductors and ______________.
- All test equipment should be __________ inspected and, where necessary, __________ by a _____________ person.
- An employee is required by ___________ to not interfere with tools and ___________ provided for their health, ____________ and welfare and to use all work items provided __________ in accordance with __________ and training given to them.
- Safety __________ should be used when testing due to the _________ of __________ material entering the eyes.

LEARNING OBJECTIVES

On completion of this chapter you should be able to:

- State the purpose of initial verification and periodic inspection of electrical installations.
- State the requirements for initial verification and periodic inspection of electrical installations.
- Identify and interpret the requirements of the relevant documents associated with the inspection, testing and commissioning of an electrical installation including:
  - Electricity at Work Regulations 1989
  - BS 7671
  - IET Guidance Note 3.
- Specify the information that is required to correctly conduct the initial verification of an electrical installation in accordance with BS 7671 and IET Guidance Note 3.

Part 1 Purpose of inspection and testing

This chapter considers the principles and regulatory requirements for inspection, testing and commissioning of electrical systems. This includes the application of these requirements to the initial verification of electrical systems.

Whilst working through this chapter you will need to refer to the Memorandum of Guidance to the Electricity at Work Regulations, BS 7671, Requirements for electrical installations and IET Guidance Note 3.

Inspection and testing may be carried out at a number of stages during the life of an electrical installation. The main stages for any electrical installation are on construction (initial verification) and periodically during its lifetime (periodic inspection).

The purpose of these two events is:

- **Initial verification:** to verify that a new electrical installation complies with the design and is safe to place into service.
- **Periodic inspection:** to determine whether an existing electrical installation complies with the current requirements and is safe to remain in service.

Whilst this is a rather simplified view of these two forms of inspection and testing, it serves as an indication of the purpose of each.

A more detailed interpretation is necessary to appreciate what is actually involved in these two different types of inspection and test.

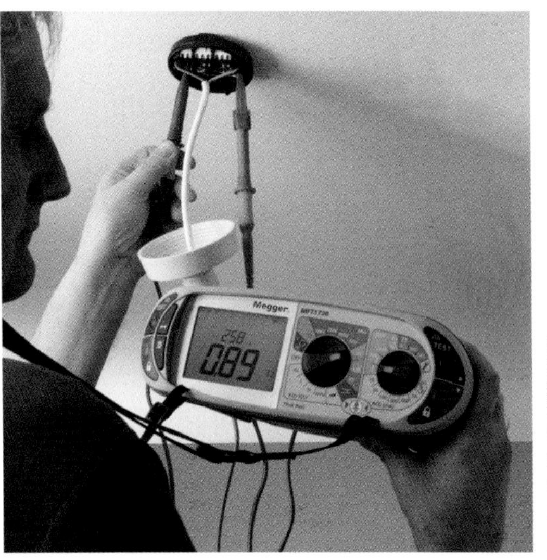

Figure 2.1 *Multifunction test instrument*

Initial verification

This is carried out to ensure that any new electrical installation meets the design criteria. An installation should be designed to comply with all the current requirements of the Electricity at Work Regulations and BS 7671. Where the design deviates from the requirements of BS 7671 the designer must confirm that the electrical installation is no less safe than it would be if it met all the requirements.

The process of initial verification is to confirm that the installation has been installed in accordance with the design and requirements of the building regulations. The building regulations cover the requirements in respect of the building structure and there are a number of approved documents published with the regulations. These give guidance on the requirements for such areas as structure, fire safety and conservation of fuel and power.

Note

More detailed information on the requirement of the building regulations is given in the *Legislation: Health and Safety & the Environment* studybook in this series.

The inspection (and where it is necessary) testing, of a new electrical installation begins with the construction stage to confirm that the cables and equipment are installed in accordance with the:

- Design
- BS 7671
- Manufacturer's instructions
- Building regulations

and that the installation and equipment are not damaged so as to cause danger, and all equipment and materials used are to appropriate British Standards.

This inspection and testing process continues throughout the construction and into the commissioning process until the installation has been confirmed as compliant and safe to put into service.

During initial verification, all the inspection and appropriate tests relevant to the particular installation must be carried out and the results verified as compliant before the installation can be placed into service. Any defects or non-compliances must be corrected before the installation can be handed to the client.

The designer, constructor and the inspector all sign a declaration that the work for which they are responsible is in accordance with the requirements and take responsibility for their work.

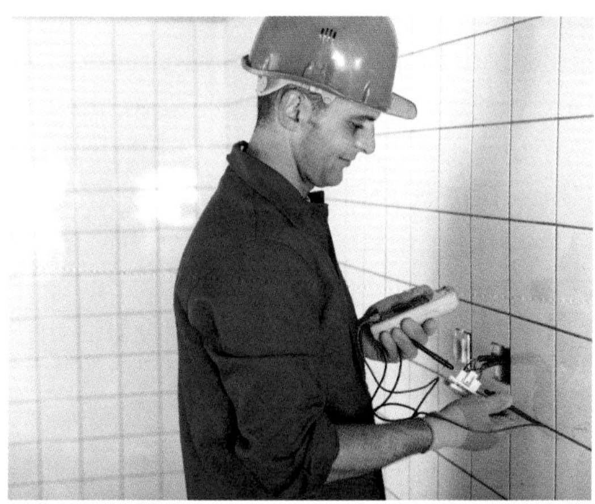

Figure 2.2 *Initial verification of a new installation*

Alterations and additions

Alterations or additions are often made to an installation during its lifetime. These may involve relocating existing parts of the installation or adding new sections or circuits. In any event, care has to be taken to ensure that the original design has not been changed in such a way as to make the installation less safe. Any alteration or addition must meet the current requirements of BS 7671, although the whole installation does not have to be brought up to the current requirements. To confirm this, the new work and any associated wiring must be inspected and tested to confirm that it complies. This constitutes an initial verification of the new work.

Periodic inspection

The Electricity at Work Regulations also places a responsibility on the Duty Holder; the Duty Holder is the person who is responsible for the electrical installation. It is the Duty Holder's responsibility to ensure the safety of those using the electrical installation. Regulation 4 of EWR states: '*As may be necessary to prevent danger, all systems shall be maintained so as to prevent, so far as is reasonably practicable, such danger.*' The Duty Holder for the electrical installation may not be electrically trained and therefore unable to make a judgement on the safety of the installation.

One method of satisfying the statutory obligation is to have a periodic inspection of the electrical installation undertaken. Just having the inspection carried out and a report does not meet the obligation. The Electrical Installation Condition Report (EICR) should identify any non-compliance with the installation, thus allowing the Duty Holder to arrange the appropriate remedial action.

A periodic inspection may be carried out for a number of reasons including:

- Compliance with the current edition of BS 7671
- Licensing, insurance, mortgages and the like
- Compliance with statutory regulations
- Following a change of use, an increase in the load, or as the result of environmental effects such as flooding.

The periodic inspection considers the condition of the existing installation and its compliance with current regulations, irrespective of when it was originally installed.

The extent of the periodic inspection and any limitations on the activities to be undertaken are agreed with the client and any interested third parties before the inspection begins. The report records the compliance of the installation and identifies for the client any action that needs to be taken to bring the installation to the required standard. The report does not identify remedial work but the areas of non-compliance and the urgency of the action to be taken.

Figure 2.3 *Existing electrical installation*

The inspector is responsible for producing an accurate report and identifying the condition of the installation within the agreed extent and limitations. The inspector does not take responsibility for the installation construction or provide a warranty for the installation.

On completion of the periodic inspection an Electrical Installation Condition Report is issued to the client detailing the findings and results of the inspection and test.

The inspector needs to be able to consider the installation and:

- Determine whether the installation is still safe for use
- Identify any non-compliances and deviations
- Determine the appropriate classification codes for these observations
- Identify whether improvement is required.

This means that the inspector needs to be able to distinguish between the current requirements and those applicable at the time of the original construction of the installation. The inspector must also be able to assess whether the installation methods used are acceptable even when carried out in a different way to that which the inspector feels appropriate. This difference is often referred to as custom and practice where there are a number of methods of achieving the same result. The true requirement is: does it meet the current requirements of BS 7671 and, if not, does it represent a danger to the user? If it does represent a danger then the inspector must classify this using a code to identify the urgency of the remedial work.

The periodic inspection of an electrical installation requires considerable experience in electrical installations and does not form part of the qualifications for which this series of studybooks is designed. The process of periodic inspection is therefore not considered in this studybook.

Task

Familiarize yourself with the requirements for Initial Verification and Periodic Inspection and Testing identified in Part 1 of BS 7671 before continuing with this chapter.

Part 2 Documentation

In much the same way that a vehicle technician needs reference manuals, data and documentation when servicing a car, so documentation and publications are required during the inspection and testing of an electrical installation.

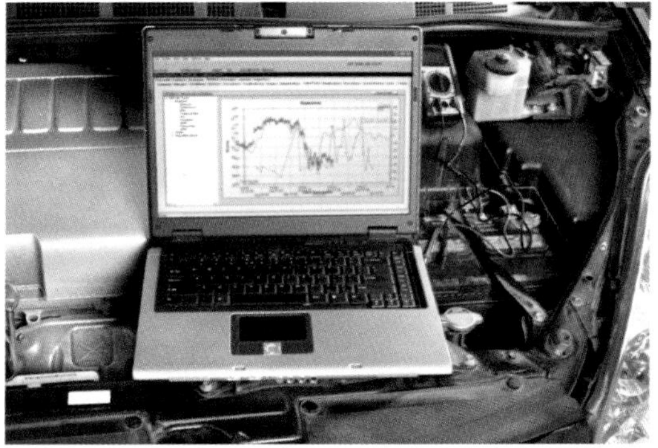

Figure 2.4 *Documentation is required when servicing a car*

The documentation requirements for inspection and testing can be considered in two categories. First there is the documentation and information which is required by the inspector in order to carry out the inspection and testing. Then there is the documentation that is produced by the inspector following the inspection and testing.

Documentation required before initial verification

The following documentation associated with the installation is required before the initial verification can take place:

- Specification
- Design data
- Drawings
- Commissioning procedures

For complex installations this information is generally to be provided to the client in the form of an operation and maintenance manual which will include all the installation details and manufacturers' information. The certification for the initial verification will be added later to this before it is passed to the client. The information contained in these documents is necessary to enable the inspector to carry out the initial verification.

In addition to the specific information for this particular installation the inspector will also need to have an understanding of the

Figure 2.5 *Documentation is required when commissioning an installation*

requirements of the relevant statutory, non-statutory, technical information and guidance material applicable to the work and installation.

This documentation includes:

The Electricity at Work Regulations (EWR): Regulation 16 places a duty on the inspector to be competent to carry out the inspection and testing. The regulation states that:

> *No person shall be engaged in any work activity where technical knowledge or experience is necessary to prevent danger or, where appropriate, injury, unless he possesses such knowledge or experience, or is under such degree of supervision as may be appropriate having regard to the nature of the work.*

In addition to the requirements placed upon the inspector, EWR also requires the installation to be constructed so that it:

- Is safe for use
- Can be maintained safely
- Can be inspected and tested safely
- Can be added to or altered safely.

There is no requirement in the statutory documentation for certification to be issued, simply that the above points are achieved. The certification is used extensively to demonstrate that this requirement has been met. Whilst not specified in the statutory documents it is essential to show that the statutory requirements have been achieved for both the client and the electrical contractor.

BS 7671: compliance with the requirements of BS 7671 is generally considered to ensure compliance with the requirements of EWR and there is a statement to this effect in the preface of BS 7671 under the title 'Notes by the Health and Safety Executive'.

Memorandum of guidance on the Electricity at Work Regulations 1989

Guidance on Regulations

HSE

Figure 2.6 *Memorandum of guidance on the Electricity at Work Regulations*

Part 6 of BS 7671 identifies the requirements for inspection and testing and Appendix 6 includes model forms for the certification of electrical installations and the results of inspection and testing. In addition to providing guidance on the design and construction of the installation it also provides information as to how the inspection and testing should be carried out. It does not, however, provide guidance on the actual procedures for carrying out the tests. This is given in more detail in IET Guidance Note 3 Inspection and Testing.

Guidance Note 3 (GN3): this document is produced by the Institution of Engineering and Technology to provide additional guidance on the procedures for inspection, testing and certification of electrical installations. It contains information on many of the procedures and the verification of acceptable values. The documents for the certification of electrical installations contained in GN3 are based upon the model forms in BS 7671 and are available from the IET website as a free download PDF.

Note

The model forms for the certification of electrical installations can be downloaded as a PDF from www.theiet.org.uk.

Documentation produced during initial verification

The initial verification of an electrical installation is to be recorded and to do this there are standard forms of certification available and variations of these are produced commercially. The standard forms of certification are given in Appendix 6 of BS 7671 and these include the minimum information that is to be recorded. Many of the commercially available forms include some additional information but this is acceptable as long as they contain at least the information in the standard forms.

IET Guidance Note 3, Inspection and testing includes model forms for certification which are based on the standard forms in BS 7671.

The forms which may be used to certify the initial verification of an installation include:

Minor Electrical Installation Works Certificate: used to certify alterations or additions to a single circuit.

Electrical Installation Certificate: used to certify installations which include a new circuit or circuits or where a number of circuits have been added to or altered. This requires schedules to be completed and attached to the certificate.

Schedule of Inspections: this records the results of the inspection of the electrical installation.

Schedule of Test Results: records the details of the circuits and the results of the tests carried out.

These documents are completed and the original given to the client and a copy retained by the inspector.

Form 1 Form No: ..../1

ELECTRICAL INSTALLATION CERTIFICATE
(REQUIREMENTS FOR ELECTRICAL INSTALLATIONS - BS 7671 [IET WIRING REGULATIONS])

DETAILS OF THE CLIENT
.... Post Code: ....

INSTALLATION ADDRESS
....
.... Post Code: ....

DESCRIPTION AND EXTENT OF THE INSTALLATION Tick boxes as appropriate

Description of installation:

Extent of installation covered by this Certificate:

(Use continuation sheet if necessary) see continuation sheet No: ....

New installation ☐
Addition to an existing installation ☐
Alteration to an existing installation ☐

FOR DESIGN, CONSTRUCTION, INSPECTION & TESTING
I being the person responsible for the design, construction, inspection & testing of the electrical installation (as indicated by my signature below), particulars of which are described above, having exercised reasonable skill and care when carrying out the design, construction, inspection & testing hereby CERTIFY that the said work for which I have been responsible is to the best of my knowledge and belief in accordance with BS 7671:2008, amended to .... (date) except for the departures, if any, detailed as follows:

Details of departures from BS 7671 (Regulations 120.3 and 133.5):

The extent of liability of the signatory is limited to the work described above as the subject of this Certificate.

Signature: .... Date: .... Name (IN BLOCK LETTERS): ....

Company: ....
Address: ....
.... Postcode: .... Tel No: ....

NEXT INSPECTION
I recommend that this installation is further inspected and tested after an interval of not more than .... years/months.

SUPPLY CHARACTERISTICS AND EARTHING ARRANGEMENTS Tick boxes and enter details, as appropriate

Earthing arrangements	**Number and Type of Live Conductors**	**Nature of Supply Parameters**	**Supply Protective Device Characteristics**
TN-C ☐ TN-S ☐ TN-C-S ☐ TT ☐ IT ☐	a.c. ☐ d.c. ☐ 1-phase, 2-wire ☐ 2-wire ☐ 1-phase, 3-wire ☐ 3-wire ☐ 2-phase, 3-wire ☐ other ☐ 3-phase, 3-wire ☐ 3-phase, 4-wire ☐	Nominal voltage, U/U_0 [(1)] .... V Nominal frequency, f [(1)] .... Hz Prospective fault current, I_{pf} [(2)] .... kA External loop impedance, Z_e [(2)] .... Ω	Type: .... Rated current..............A
Other sources of supply (to be detailed on attached schedules) ☐	Confirmation of supply polarity ☐	*(Note: (1) by enquiry, (2) by enquiry or by measurement)*	

Requirements for Electrical Installations:IET Wiring Regulations 17th Edition (BS 7671:2008 incorporating amendment no 1: 2011)

Figure 2.7 *Model form Electrical Installation Certificate*

Task

Familiarize yourself with the Notes by the Health and Safety Executive in the preface to BS 7671 before continuing with this chapter.

Part 3 Information required

Before the inspection and testing of a new installation can begin there is certain information which must be available to the inspector. Some of this information is necessary for the safety of the inspector and those persons in the premises at the time of the inspection and test. Other information is necessary so that the inspector knows precisely what it is that is to be inspected and tested.

In the case of a complete new installation this would seem to be quite straightforward and be the whole electrical installation. On smaller installations this may be the case but often there are other specialist contractors involved and certain parts of the installation may be their responsibility. These include emergency services, lifts, Heating, Ventilation and Air Conditioning (HVAC) systems and the like. Uninterruptable Power Supplies (UPS) systems and standby generators are often carried out by specialist contractors.

In the case of alterations and additions this may be even harder to determine and so the inspector needs to know what exactly is to be inspected and tested.

What information the inspector requires relates to the installation supply and the installation construction and we shall look at each in turn.

Characteristics of the supply

This information is identified in BS 7671 Chapter 31 in Sections 311, 312 and 313 and we shall use these as the reference for the information.

Maximum demand and diversity

The maximum demand is the total load which may be drawn by the installation at any one time. This is the total sum of the connected loads which is determined by the designer of the installation. The designer may apply diversity to the maximum demand which is basically determining the maximum load that is likely to be drawn at any one time. This process results in a reduced maximum demand.

The process requires a good knowledge of the installation and how it will be used and consideration is made of the load function. The type of circuits will also determine the level of diversity which can be applied so some circuits are subject to no diversity whilst others may attract a considerable diversity. The number of circuits of each type will also affect the amount of diversity which can be applied so the more circuits of a type the more diversity can be applied.

The inspector needs to be aware of the maximum demand of the installation and this should be provided by the designer.

Conductor arrangement and system earthing

The conductor arrangement relates to the number of live conductors of the supply to the installation. There are a number of variations of live conductors and the most common in general use from the District Network Operator (DNO) are:

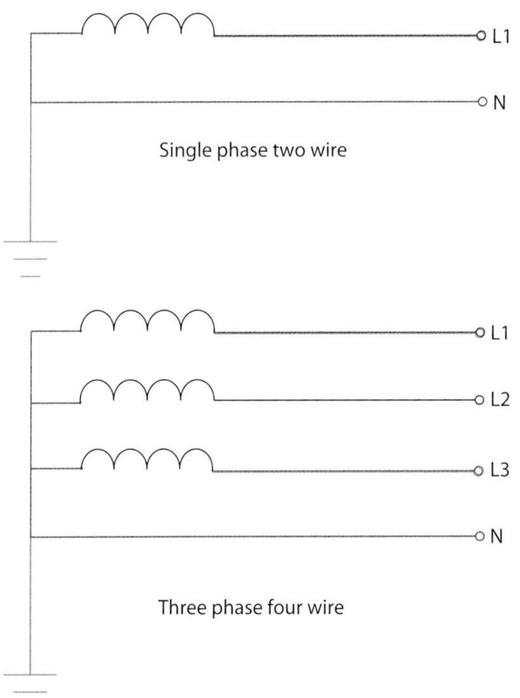

Figure 2.8 *Single phase two wire and three phase four wire*

The earthing systems available from the DNO are:

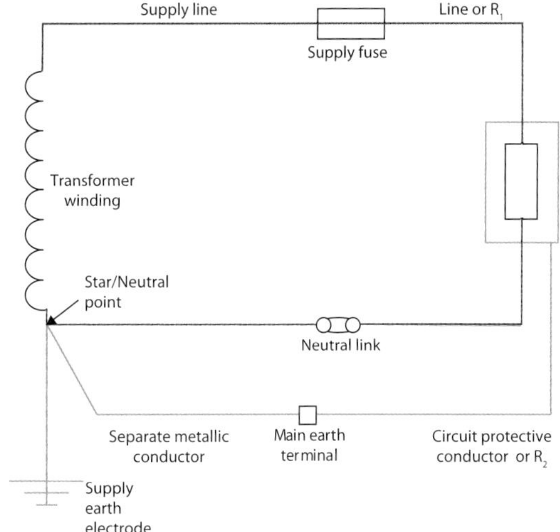

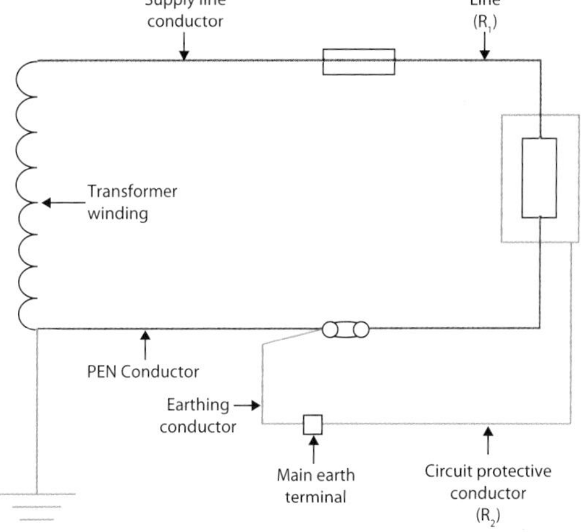

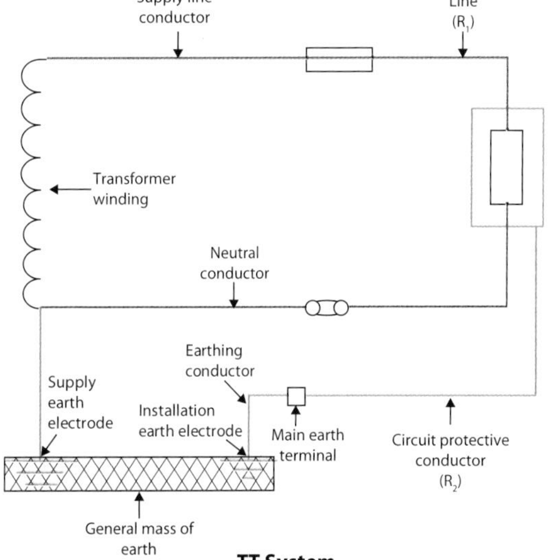

Figure 2.9 *The DNO supply systems*

Task

Familiarize yourself with the types of supply identified in BS 7671 before continuing with this chapter.

Remember

The system letters define the type of system and this will determine the requirements to ensure compliance with BS 7671.

The letters are used to identify:

First letter is the relationship of the system to earth:

- **T**: a direct connection of one point to earth, usually the neutral.

Second letter is the relationship of the exposed-conductive-parts of the installation to earth:

- **T**: connection of exposed-conductive-parts to earth independent of the earthing of the power system, usually an earth electrode
- **N**: direct electrical connection of the exposed-conductive-parts to the earthed point of the power system by a conductor.

Final letter is the arrangement of neutral and protective conductors:

- **S**: protective function provided by a conductor separate from the neutral conductor
- **C**: neutral and protective functions combined in a single protective earth neutral (PEN) conductor.

There are a number of other combinations of supply conductors which are identified in Part 2 of BS 7671.

The inspector needs to be aware of the type of earthing arrangement and the number of live conductors which form the supply for the installation. This will affect the type of installation earthing and bonding arrangements, the tests and expected test results.

The supply characteristics

This information is available from the DNO and it should be provided to the inspector on request and at no charge.

Nominal voltage: this has to come from the supplier as, due to the fact that the supply voltage fluctuates, it cannot be measured. From the DNO the standard ac voltages (U and U_0) are 400/230 V.

Nature of current and frequency: this also has to come from the supplier as, like the voltage, frequency of the supply does fluctuate. From the DNO the standard supply current is ac at 50 Hz.

Prospective fault current: this may come from the supplier and would be the prospective short circuit current at the origin of the installation. The standard value quoted by the DNO is 16 kA but this is the highest value likely on the system. The fault current at the origin can be measured as part of the initial verification to obtain a more accurate value.

External earth fault loop impedance: this may also come from the supplier and would be the highest value expected on their system. The standard values given by the DNO are

TN-S: 0.8 Ω and TN-C-S: 0.35 Ω. This may also be measured at the origin of the installation to obtain a more accurate value.

Suitability of the supply for the installation: this includes whether the DNO can provide a suitable supply for the installation including the maximum demand that can be taken from the supply. This is not the maximum demand of the installation but whether the DNO can provide this demand.

Overcurrent device at the origin: the type and rating of the overcurrent device at the origin is significant as the inspector will need to confirm that it is suitable for the maximum demand and that it can safely disconnect the prospective fault current at the origin of the installation. This will also determine the cross-sectional area (csa) of the main tails for the installation.

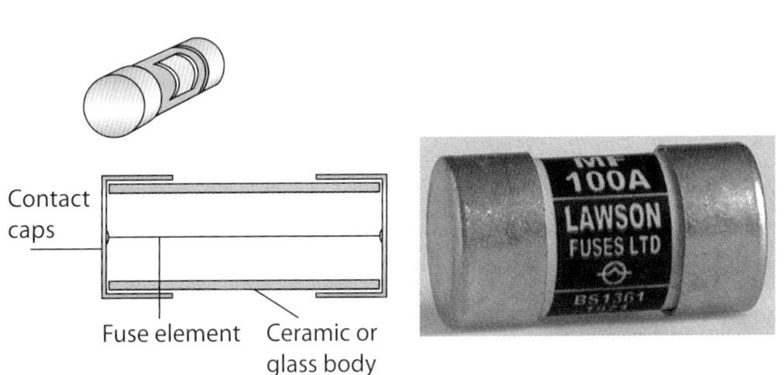

Figure 2.10 *Typical DNO fuse at the origin of a dwelling*

This information will be required whether the installation is supplied by the DNO or a private supplier or generator. If there are uninterruptable power supplies then this information will also be required from the manufacturer of this equipment.

In addition to the information related to the supply for the installation the inspector will also need to have information relating to the installation itself.

Diagrams, charts or tables

Certain information relating to the installation is necessary for an inspection to be carried out safely and accurately. This requirement is stated in BS 7671 and the type of information that is considered necessary is:

Circuit equipment vulnerable to test: there are certain items of equipment such as dimmer switches, RCBOs, photocells and motion detectors and surge protectors which may be damaged by some of the tests carried out and these need to be identified in order that suitable measures can be taken to prevent this damage.

Type and composition of circuits: the information here relates to the way in which the installation has been divided into circuits and should detail the type and composition of the circuits including:

- Points of utilization
- Number and csa of conductors
- The type of cable
- The installation method.

Identification of devices: the identification of the devices which perform the functions of:

- Protection
- Isolation
- Switching, and
- Where they are located.

Methods of protection: the methods of providing basic and fault protection are required by the inspector together with the method of achieving automatic disconnection of supply (ADS) where this method of protection is used. The compliance of the installation with these requirements is to be confirmed and therefore this information is essential for the inspector.

For simple installations this information may be provided on a Schedule of Test Results or distribution board chart.

As we discussed earlier the inspector also needs to know the scope of the installation to be inspected and tested.

Task

A new electrical installation in a small retail unit is to be inspected and tested before it is placed into service. List all the information that you will require before the inspection and test can begin, from the:

a Distribution Network Operator.

b Designer of the installation.

Try this: Crossword

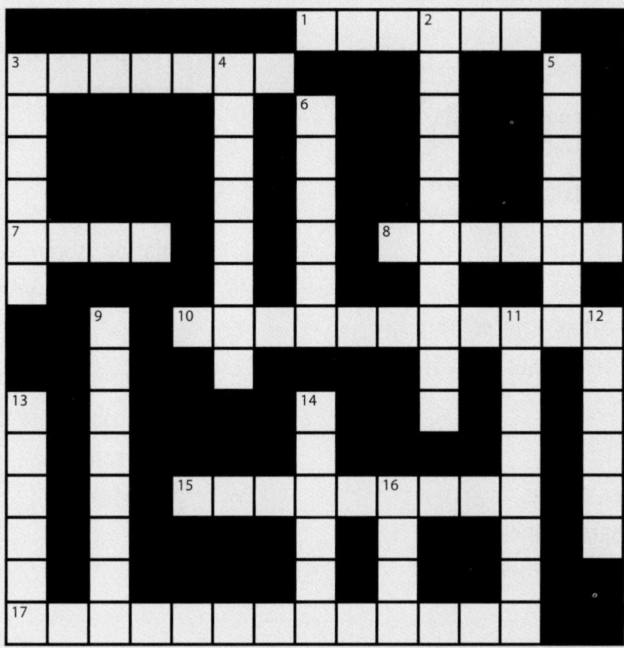

Across

1 If part of the installation is this it will require urgent attention (6)

3 The type of verification carried out on a new circuit (7)

7 This results from a hazard (4)

8 A hazard will create this (6)

10 An Electrical Installation ... is issued after 3 across (11)

15 You must be this to work on electrical systems (9)

17 Collective name for the forms of certification (13)

Down

2 One of these changes the electrical installation (10)

3 Possible outcome of 8 across (6)

4 The type of voltage indicator to be used (8)

5 What we do before testing is carried out (7)

6 One of these may be required to work on complex installations. (6)

9 The type of inspection carried out on an existing installation (8)

11 Installing another light on to an existing circuit is one of these (8)

12 We need to exercise great care when we do this to live terminals (6)

13 The way in which we do something (6)

14 An electrical installation condition ... is issued after 9 down. (6)

16 Could be an exam or a process. (4)

Congratulations, you have now completed Chapter 2 of this studybook. Complete the self assessment questions before you go on to the next chapter.

SELF ASSESSMENT

Circle the correct answers.

1 The purpose of initial verification is to confirm that an electrical installation complies with the design and:

a. Is safe to put into service
b. Includes sufficient socket outlets
c. Does not require any maintenance
d. Provides the client with a guarantee

2 A periodic inspection is carried out to confirm the condition of:

a. A new electrical installation
b. An existing electrical installation
c. An alteration to an existing circuit
d. An addition to an electrical installation

3 The three principle non-statutory reference documents for inspection and testing of an electrical installation are the Memorandum of Guidance on the Electricity at Work Regulations, BS 7671 and IET Guidance Note:

a. 1
b. 2
c. 3
d. 4

4 One characteristic of the DNO supply which cannot be measured is the:

a. External earth fault loop impedance
b. Prospective fault current
c. Voltage
d. Polarity

5 The letter S in the TN-S system indicates that the installation is connected to the system earth at the supply transformer by:

a. A metallic conductor
b. A suitable resistive path
c. A combined neutral and earth conductor
d. The soil between the installation and transformer

3

Inspecting electrical installations

RECAP

Before you start work on this chapter, complete the exercise below to ensure that you remember what you learned earlier.

- Initial verification is to verify that a ____________ electrical installation complies with the _________ and is _________ to place into _________.
- Periodic inspection is to determine whether an ________ electrical installation ________ with the ___________ requirements and is ___________ to ___________ in service.
- Any addition to an _____________ electrical installation must meet the _____________ requirements of BS 7671, although the ___________ installation does ___________ have to be brought up to the _____________ requirements.
- Periodic _____________ of an electrical installation requires considerable _____________ in electrical installations.
- The Electricity at Work Regulations require an electrical installation to be _____________ and ______________ so that it is safe for ______________.
- The documents which may be issued following initial verification include the __________ Electrical Installation Works _______________, the Electrical Installation _______________, a Schedule of ___________ and a Schedule of ___________.

- Maximum demand is the maximum __________ load for an installation. __________ may be applied to this based on the __________ of installation and its use.
- The supply characteristic information required by the inspector for an initial verification includes the type of system __________ and the type and __________ of the protective device at the __________ of the installation.
- The three types of supply system available from the DNO are __________, __________ and __________.
- Diagrams and __________ should contain information on equipment __________ to testing, the circuit __________, the csa of the __________ and __________ conductors and the rating of the __________ devices.

LEARNING OBJECTIVES

On completion of this chapter you should be able to:

- Identify the items to be checked during the inspection process for given electrotechnical systems, equipment, and their locations as detailed in BS 7671.
- State how the human senses can be used during the inspection process.
- State the items of an electrical installation that should be inspected in accordance with IET Guidance Note 3.
- Specify the requirements for the inspection of:
  - Earthing conductors
  - Circuit protective conductors (cpcs)
  - Protective bonding conductors (main and supplementary)
  - Isolation
  - Type and rating of overcurrent protective devices.

Part 1 Requirements of inspection

This chapter considers the principles and regulatory requirements for the inspection of electrical systems. This includes the application of the inspection requirements to the initial verification of electrical systems.

Whilst working through this chapter you will need to refer to BS 7671, Requirements for electrical installations and IET Guidance Note 3 (GN3) Inspection and Testing. IET Guidance Note 1 (GN1), Selection and Erection may also prove useful.

Inspection will be carried out from the very start of the construction of an electrical installation and completed immediately before the final testing of the installation during the initial verification.

The inspection process we shall consider here relates to the initial verification of an electrical installation. The requirements for inspecting existing electrical installations as part of a periodic inspection will include some of these items. As the periodic inspection should cause as little interference or dismantling as is necessary there will be some limitations to the inspection. For new installations there are no exceptions; all the items relevant to the particular installation are to be inspected.

Figure 3.1 *Inspection is an essential part of quality and safety for a new installation*

There is a misconception that the inspection process is purely visual but this is not the case. All the human senses, with the exception of taste, may be used when inspecting electrical systems. In the case of our initial verification the most common senses to use are those of sight and touch.

Most important, although not a true sense, is 'common sense' which needs to be applied throughout the inspection process. For example, some of the inspection will need to be carried out during the construction and that can include some simple activities such as secure terminations. Parts of the electrical installation, such as the cables and containment systems, may be concealed once the building is completed. These will need to be inspected before they are concealed to ensure the correct materials have been used, they are correctly installed and they are in accordance with the design.

Figure 3.2 *Some areas need to be inspected before construction is complete*

One of the requirements from BS 7671 and GN3 is that the inspection should be carried out with the areas that are being inspected isolated from the supply. This is important when inspecting alterations and additions to an existing installation.

The alteration or addition should not be energized until the inspection and testing has been completed and the results verified as compliant. However some of the alteration and addition work may involve circuits or equipment which form part of the existing installation and these will be energized. When inspecting in these locations the relevant parts of the installation should be isolated. This process was covered in Chapter 1 of this studybook and so we shall not repeat it again here.

The requirements for initial verification are given in Chapter 61 of BS 7671 and this identifies the particular requirements for the inspection of the installation prior to it being placed into service.

The purpose of the inspection is to verify that the installed electrical equipment:

- Complies with appropriate British or equivalent Standards
- Has been correctly selected and erected
- Is not visibly damaged or defective so as to impair safety.

The results of the inspection are recorded on a Schedule of Inspections (for new installation work). There is a separate inspection schedule for the periodic inspection process. The information contained in the Schedule of Inspections is a summary of the items that are to be checked and BS 7671, Regulation 611.3 identifies items to be inspected. This list is the minimum that should be considered and where appropriate inspected for every installation.

IET Guidance Note 3, Inspection and Testing, contains details of the items to be inspected in Chapter 2. There is also an inspection checklist which identifies the items to be considered when inspecting an installation as part of the initial verification process. This list covers all aspects of the inspection and is categorized in headings related to the particular areas being inspected.

The list is quite comprehensive and covers several pages of information; the first section gives the inspection requirements and refers to the particular regulations within BS 7671 which relate to those specifically. The remainder identifies items related to the particular section of the installation and includes such areas as:

- General wiring accessories
- Lighting controls
- Lighting points
- Conduit systems; further broken down into rigid, steel, plastic and so on
- Trunking
- Insulated cables
- Protective conductors

and there are over 12 pages of information here on the inspection process.

Task

Familiarize yourself with the requirements of BS 7671 Regulation 611.3 before you continue with this chapter.

Inspection is one of the key requirements at initial verification and there are many problems which may only be identified by inspection. For example, the missing blanks from a new distribution board will not be identified by the testing process but the installation would not be safe to put into service.

We have already established that the inspection of an installation should be an ongoing process while the wiring and containment systems are being installed. For example, all conduit and trunking runs must be complete before any cables are installed and, to confirm they are complete and all connections are tight, an inspection must be carried out.

For steel enclosures the inspection should confirm that there are no sharp edges on which the insulation may be damaged during the installation process. Where metal trunking is installed the fitting of earthing links at joints and connections, where these are required, should be confirmed.

For plastic conduit and trunking there would not be a requirement for earthing links, but the installation of expansion joints and confirmation that the other connections are all securely glued, would form part of the inspection before cables are installed.

Task

Familiarize yourself with the requirements of Part 2 of Guidance Note 3 for the inspection requirements at initial inspection before you continue with this chapter.

Part 2 Carrying out the inspection

When carrying out the inspection we are going to be using our human senses and we need to consider the way in which the various senses are to be used. We shall consider the items that need to be inspected and the application of the senses as part of this process.

Let's consider the connection and identification of conductors as our first example.

The connection of conductors covers a number of items of inspections:

- **Correct sequence:** the conductors should be in the correct terminals for the equipment and in the correct sequence. The sequence in the distribution board line, neutral and earth terminals should be the same for all the circuits so each circuit conductor is in the same sequence in each set of terminals. The sense of sight would be used for this.
- **Correct termination:** the terminals should be correctly made and secure, for example not too much insulation removed (sight), correctly tightened (touch).

- **Correctly identified:** the terminations should be correctly identified. The identification of most terminals of equipment is identified by the manufacturer. The conductors should be in the correct terminals (sight).

The identification of conductors involves two main considerations. The first is that the conductors are correctly identified by colour or number and this relates to the correct connection of the conductors. The coloured or numbered conductors should be in the right terminals (sight).

On some occasions we use conductors for functions other than the one indicated by the colour. For example, it is common to use flat profile 3 core and circuit protective conductor (cpc) for the strappers in a two-way lighting circuit. These cable cores are coloured brown, black and grey, these being the three phase colours. When used as strappers in the lighting circuit they should all be coloured brown. The inspection would be to confirm that these have been correctly identified using either sleeving or tape to show they are line conductors in a single phase circuit.

Remember

All single phase line conductors are to be coloured brown.

During the initial verification inspection process the senses of touch and sight are most commonly used. The senses of touch may be used on existing equipment to determine whether equipment is running over temperature. The sense of hearing may be used to identify arcing at switches and chatter at contactors during a periodic inspection. However, these are only identifiable when the installation is in operation and during initial verification the installation is not in service so these senses are not usually appropriate.

Figure 3.3 *Some inspection can be done during the construction phase*

Some of the inspection items must be carried out during the construction stages of the installation, such as an inspection of the cables which will be concealed later. Others, such as the connection of conductors at accessories, may also be checked during construction. For this to be done the inspector must either be present during the construction or be actually responsible for the construction of the installation.

The inspection of the installation also requires examination of the environmental conditions in which it is to operate, the use any building is to be put to, and the type of wiring system and the load likely to be imposed on it.

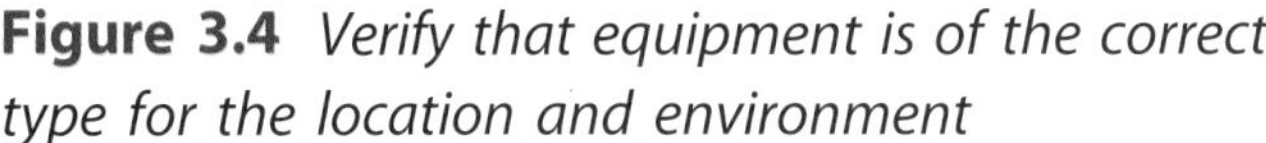

Figure 3.4 *Verify that equipment is of the correct type for the location and environment*

During the inspection we will be looking to make sure that the type of installation is suitable for its purpose. For example, a wiring system serving damp farm buildings should be suitable for the environment and fitted out of the reach of animals.

Figure 3.5 *Inspection is needed to verify that the installation is suitable for its purpose*

In situations such as the roof space of a dwelling the flat profile multicore thermoplastic cables should be neatly clipped to the side of a joist above the level of the loft insulation where possible. In new properties the level of insulation required sometimes makes this impractical and so the inspector would confirm the csa of conductors used is in accordance with the design.

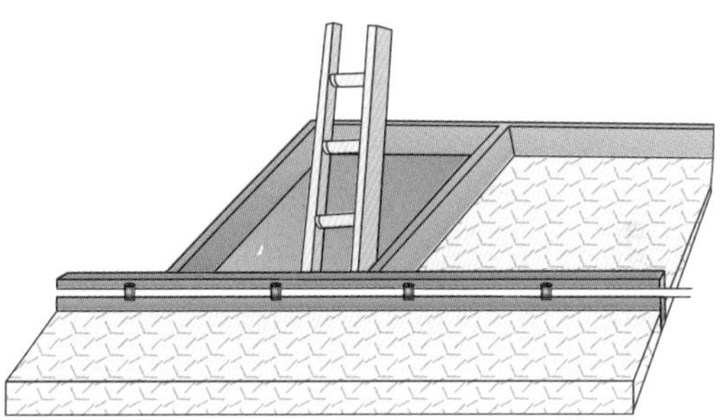

Figure 3.6 *Cables clear of the loft insulation*

In commercial and industrial installations it is likely that cable management systems such as compartmentalized dado trunking, skirting trunking or steel conduit and trunking would be used. During the inspection we should be on the lookout for anything which may reduce the integrity of the wiring system. For example, the proximity of thermoplastic cables to a heat source, condensation or dampness where black enamelled conduit has been used and unprotected cables installed.

Task

A new installation has been carried out and an inspection of the distribution board at the origin of the installation is to be performed. Using the information contained in GN3 compile a list of the items to be checked at the distribution board. There should be at least ten items in your list.

The items to be checked include:

1 ____________________

2 ____________________

3 ____________________

4 ____________________

5 ____________________

6 ____________________

7 ____________________

8 ____________________

9 ____________________

10 ____________________

11 ____________________

12 ____________________

Part 3 Specific inspection items

Having considered the requirements for the inspection and the areas and items which need to be inspected we will take a look at some specific examples of inspection, beginning with protective conductors.

Remember

This is an inspection and there will be tests applied after the inspection and so we are just using the human senses here and not test instruments.

Earthing conductor

The earthing conductor connects the installation MET to the earthing arrangement provided by the supplier or the installation earth electrode.

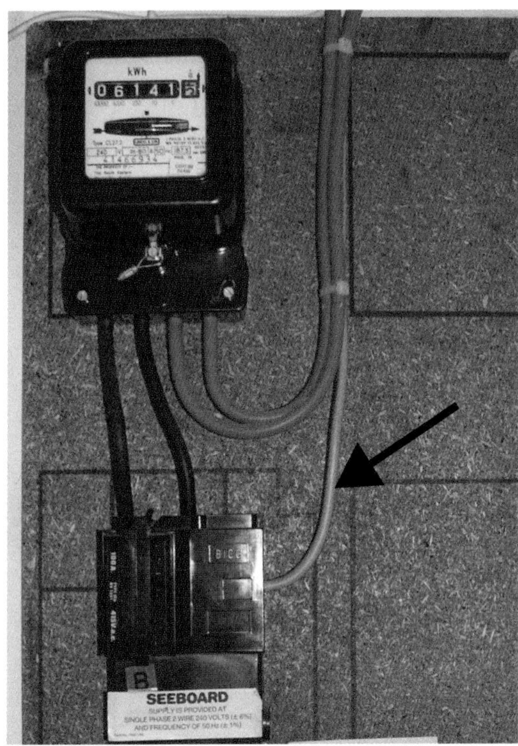

Figure 3.7 *The earthing conductor needs to be inspected*

The earthing conductor will be inspected to establish the following:

- i The material and csa of the conductor. The material of the conductor is to be recorded on the Electrical Installation Certificate and the type of material will affect the required csa which will depend on the type of system and the csa of the supply conductors.
- ii That the conductor is correctly connected at both ends (where possible). This includes: correctly terminated, secure and tight.
- iii That the conductor is undamaged and continuous throughout its entire length.
- iv Where the main earthing terminal (MET) is separate from the distribution equipment the MET should be labelled **Safety Electrical Connection Do Not Remove**.
- v That the conductor is suitably insulated or protected against corrosion.

The details regarding the earthing conductor should be made available to the inspector by the designer of the installation and the inspector's job is to confirm that what is required is actually installed.

Protective bonding conductors

Protective bonding conductors fall into two categories and the inspection requirements are similar for both.

Main protective bonding conductors

The main protective bonding conductors connect any extraneous conductive parts, such as structural steelwork and the metallic installation pipes of gas and water installations, to the MET.

The main protective bonding conductor will be inspected to establish the following:

- i The material and csa of the conductor. The material of the conductor is to be recorded on the Electrical Installation Certificate and the type of material will affect the required csa which will depend on the type of system:
  - a For TN-S and TT systems the csa is based on the csa of the earthing conductor
  - b For TN-C-S systems the csa is based on the csa of the supply neutral conductor.
- ii The conductor is correctly connected at both ends (where possible). This includes: correctly terminated, secure and tight.

iii The conductor is undamaged and continuous throughout its entire length.

iv Where the main protective bonding conductor connects to the extraneous conductive part there should be a **Safety Electrical Connection Do Not Remove** label.

v The conductor is suitably insulated and protected against corrosion or damage.

Figure 3.8 *Main protective bonding connections to water service and structural steelwork*

Where the main protective bonding conductor is visible throughout its entire length this inspection will be enough to confirm the continuity of the main protective bonding conductor. If the conductor is not visible throughout the entire length, no matter how small the hidden section may be, the conductor will also need to be tested.

Supplementary bonding conductors

The supplementary bonding conductors, where these are required, connect the exposed and extraneous conductive parts in a particular part of the installation. They do not connect to the MET.

The supplementary bonding conductors will be inspected to establish the following:

i The material and csa of the conductor.

ii That the conductor is correctly connected at both ends (where possible). This includes correctly terminated, secure and tight.

iii That the conductor is undamaged and continuous throughout its entire length.

iv Wherever the supplementary bonding conductor connects to extraneous conductive parts there should be a **Safety Electrical Connection Do Not Remove** label.

v That the conductor is suitably insulated and protected against corrosion or damage.

Remember

Supplementary protective bonding conductors are subject to a minimum csa which is:

- **Where provided with mechanical protection minimum csa 2.5 mm^2**
- **Where mechanical protection is not provided minimum csa 4.0 mm^2.**

Circuit protective conductors

The cpcs connect the exposed conductive parts of each circuit to the MET. BS 7671 states that a cpc must be present at each point on the circuit and this will be the subject of a continuity of protective conductor test. At the inspection the cpcs will be inspected to establish the following:

i The material and csa of the conductor are correct compared with the design details.
ii That the conductor is correctly terminated at every point, secure and tight.
iii That the conductor is undamaged at the terminations.
iv That the cpcs are sleeved with green and yellow sleeving at the terminations.
v Where a core of a cable has been used that the conductor has been identified with green and yellow marking.
vi That the conductor is correctly identified and terminated at the distribution board.

The inspections of these various types of protective conductor have a number of features in common and share many of the same inspection items. This is true of many of the conductors in the installation, and the inspection activities will also be similar.

It is worth considering some of the other aspects of inspection relating to isolation and the protective devices, beginning with isolation.

Isolation

When carrying out the inspection of the installation the devices for isolation must be included. The number of isolators will depend on the type and complexity of the installation but every installation will have a main isolator at the origin.

A quick review of the functions of an isolator is worthwhile before we consider the actual inspection.

The requirement of an isolator is that it can safely isolate all the live conductors from the supply. Where a three phase four wire installation is involved it is permissible to have an isolator which disconnects all the line conductors and has a mechanical link for the neutral. This link should only be accessible once the line conductors have been isolated. There are two types of isolator:

- **Off-load:** this type is able to isolate part of the installation or equipment from the live conductors but not whilst it is carrying a load. This type of isolator must have the load switched off before the isolator is opened, and the isolator closed before the load is connected. The isolators which are installed by the DNO at their meter position are typically off-load devices. Once the installation is isolated, using the installation main isolator, then the DNO isolator may be opened. This allows the electrician to work on the meter tails and distribution equipment safely. Before the installation is re-energized the DNO isolator must be closed and then the main isolator for the installation can be switched on. These off-line devices can only be used where the load can be switched off by some other means before they are opened to isolate from the supply.
- **On-load:** this type is able to open the supply under load conditions. This type of isolator must be used at the origin of the installation as the main isolator. It has to be able to isolate the installation under load conditions and each online device will have a current rating indicating the maximum load current it can safely isolate.

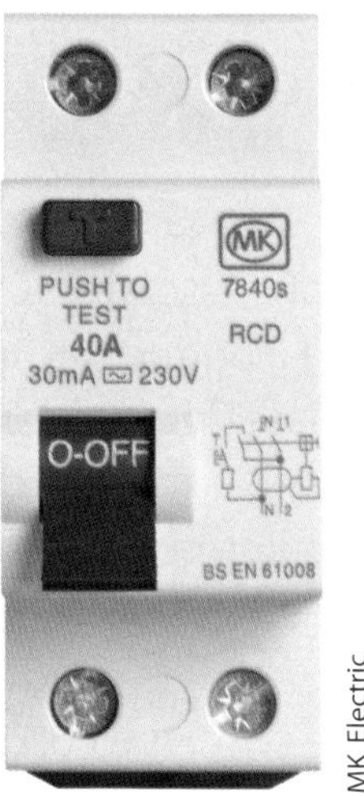

Figure 3.9 *Main isolator*

When carrying out the initial verification of the installation the requirements for the safe isolation and switching of the installation must be confirmed. This will require the inspector to establish the following facts:

- i The isolator is the correct type, i.e. online or off-line.
- ii The isolator switches the appropriate number of poles.
- iii The isolator complies with an appropriate British or equivalent Standard.
- iv The voltage rating is appropriate for the installation.
- v The current rating (if it is an online device).
- vi If the isolator is a fused switch or cb then the fuse rating or setting is correct.
- vii If the isolator is an residual current device (RCD) then the operating current $I_{\Delta n}$ is correctly selected for the location.
- viii The isolator is securely fixed.
- ix The conductors are undamaged at the terminations.
- x The conductors are correctly terminated at every point, secure and tight.
- xi The isolator and enclosure are not damaged.
- xii The enclosure complies with the ingress protection (IP) requirements for the location.

The information for items ii to vii has to be recorded on the Electrical Installation Certificate for the main isolator.

The inspector has to confirm that all installed isolators are in accordance with the design.

Finally, we shall consider the inspection requirements for overcurrent protective devices.

Overcurrent protective devices

Overcurrent protective devices include fuses, cbs and RCBOs and they all require inspection during the initial verification. There are some standard termination checks to be made regarding the cables connected to the devices and their connection to the busbar within the distribution board. Also ensuring they are correctly fixed within the distribution board would be carried out.

We need to consider other aspects for these devices. They are installed to provide protection against overload and short circuit currents in the installation and the inspector's job is to confirm that the correct type and rating of protective device has been installed and is correctly labelled. This involves confirming the device is compliant with the design of the installation and will include:

Current rating: the I_n value of the device is the current that the device will carry for an indefinite period without undue deterioration. Currents up to the rated I_n will have no discernible effect on the protective device. The current rating checks involve confirming the following:

- That the correct rating of protective device has been installed (I_n is in accordance with the design)
- That the I_n rating is suitable for the conductors connected to the device ($I_n \leq I_z$)

- That the correct type of device has been installed (e.g. for a cb is it Type B, C or D?) and that this complies with the design.

Remember

BS 88 type fuses also have different characteristics in the same way as the cb types. The correct type of fuse must be installed to comply with the design and this has to be confirmed by the inspector.

Fault current rating: the protective device must be able to disconnect the prospective fault current at the point at which it is installed within the installation. When the installation is tested the inspector will have to confirm that the measured prospective fault current does not exceed the rating of the device. However, at the inspection stage the inspector will have to confirm that the prospective fault current rating of the protective device meets the requirements of the design.

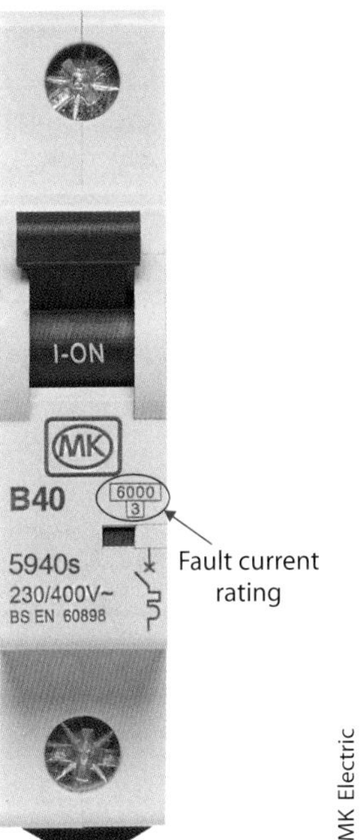

Figure 3.10 *Fault current rating*

You will have noticed that much of the inspector's responsibility at the inspection stage is to confirm that the equipment is correctly installed and complies with the appropriate standards. The inspector is also responsible for ensuring that the installed cables, conductors, protective devices and the like are in accordance with the designer's intentions. In Chapter 4 we shall look at the tests to be carried out. The inspector's job is to carry out the tests correctly and accurately and to record the results. The inspector is then responsible for confirming that the results show the installation meets the requirements of the design and BS 7671.

Note

More information on the design selection and coordination of protective devices and cable sizes is given in the *Planning and Selection for Electrical Systems* studybook in this series.

Task

Using manufacturers' information identify the additional details that need to be confirmed during the inspection of the following items:

a **A 100 A main isolator installed in a single phase consumer unit in a dwelling.**

____

____

____

b **A 16 A circuit breaker installed for a water heater circuit supplied from the consumer unit in (a).**

____

____

____

Part 4 General inspection items

The Electrical Installation Certificate must be accompanied by a Schedule of Inspections and this identifies the general headings for the inspection items. We have considered some of the specific areas of inspection but we should not lose sight of the general inspection areas which we considered when referring to BS 7671 and GN3 earlier in this chapter.

The standard form for the inspection schedule is contained in Appendix 6 of BS 7671 and it provides an aide memoire for the inspection process.

You will find it useful to refer to the Schedule of Inspections from BS 7671 as you work through the remainder of this chapter.

Note

The completion of the Schedule of Inspections uses checkboxes for the various items inspected. For Initial Verification the only two acceptable entries are ☑ where an item has been inspected and is acceptable, or N/A where an item is not applicable to the particular installation being inspected. Any items which are not acceptable must be corrected before the installation can be placed into service.

The way in which this Schedule of Inspections is laid out is relatively simple. Many of the specific items we have already considered are identified in the left-hand column of the schedule under the main heading **Methods of protection against electric shock**.

Note

The main headings in the standard form Schedule of Inspections are in bold and underlined. Subheadings are simply in bold and sub-subheadings are bold with a number prefix.

This column, 'Methods of protection against electric shock' is further divided into a number of subheadings and we have considered some items from Basic protection (Insulation and barriers and enclosures) and a number of the items under Fault protection (i) ADS (Presence of protective conductors, choice and setting of protective devices, etc).

ADS is the most common method of providing fault protection and items (ii), (iii) and (iv) are alternatives to this method. Installations using these

Task

Familiarize yourself with the Schedule of Inspections (for new installation work only) in Appendix 6 of BS 7671 before continuing with this chapter.

methods of fault protection have special requirements as identified by the notes at the foot of the standard form in BS 7671, Appendix 6.

In this left-hand column the presence of supplementary bonding conductors appears twice. First under ADS and then again under Additional protection and this requires some clarification.

The checkbox under the ADS heading is used where supplementary bonding is installed as a specific requirement of BS 7671 and this generally relates to special installations and locations identified in Part 7. This includes locations such as rooms containing a bath or shower, swimming pools and locations where livestock are housed.

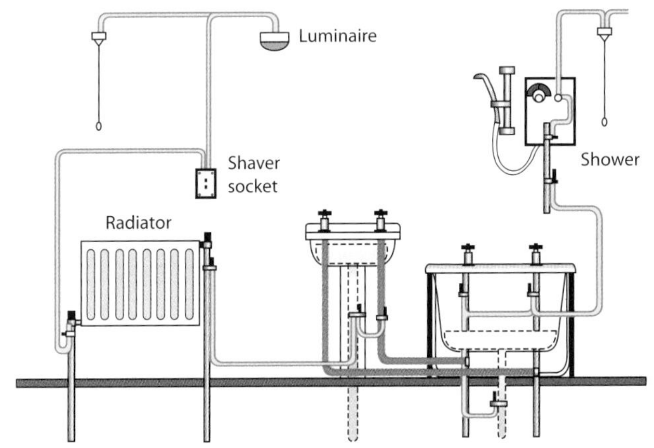

Figure 3.11 *Supplementary bonding conductors*

The checkbox under additional protection is used where supplementary bonding has been installed because the earth fault loop impedance for a circuit (or circuits) was above the acceptable value. BS 7671 offers the use of supplementary bonding as one option to overcome this situation. The other alternative is the use of RCDs but this is not always an acceptable option where the risk of nuisance tripping is unacceptable, such as data equipment and computer circuits.

When carrying out the initial verification it is important to establish whether supplementary bonding has been installed. The reason for its use should be detailed in the design information. As the inspector you will need to carry out the necessary inspection of any supplementary bonding and enter the results in the appropriate checkbox.

We now need to look at the right-hand side of the schedule which consists of a number of main headings and these relate to the general inspection of the installation. We will consider some of these areas starting with the prevention of mutual detrimental influence.

Prevention of mutual detrimental influence

This item relates to the detrimental effects between types of electrical services and between electrical and other services. Basically, as the inspector, you will be inspecting to confirm that the cables have been installed so that their performance is not affected by other services such as heating pipework, oil supply lines and chilled pipework. For example, by checking there are no cables installed above heating pipes or below oil supply pipes.

Segregation of services relates to Band I and Band II cables being installed separately, either spaced or installed in separate compartments of a containment system. Alternatively, the Band I circuits would need to be insulated to the same level as the highest rated Band II circuit.

All safety services (firefighting systems and alarms and emergency lighting systems) must be segregated from all other electrical services.

Band I circuits operate at < 50 V ac and include data, telephone and TV signal cables.

Identification

We have already looked at some of these issues such as the identification of conductors and labelling of protective devices, switches and terminals. Other warning labels such as the quarterly operation of RCDs and voltages in excess of 230 V, where these would not normally be expected, need to be inspected and confirmed. The diagrams and charts are necessary for you, the inspector, to carry out the inspection and testing of the installation.

Cables and conductors

Again we have covered some of these issues such as the correct selection and connection of conductors. There are a number of other inspection items in this section which we need to consider.

Erection methods: covers all aspects of the construction of the installation and will include checking that all the materials and equipment are:

- Suitable for the environment in which they are installed
- Adequately supported
- Securely fixed
- Compliant with the IP requirements.

Routing of cables within the prescribed zones: this item only applies where there are cables concealed within the walls of the premises. This is one of the areas of the installation which would need to be inspected during the construction of the installation.

The prescribed zones are:

- Vertically and horizontally through the accessories
- Within 150 mm from the ceiling
- Within 150 mm of any wall corner.

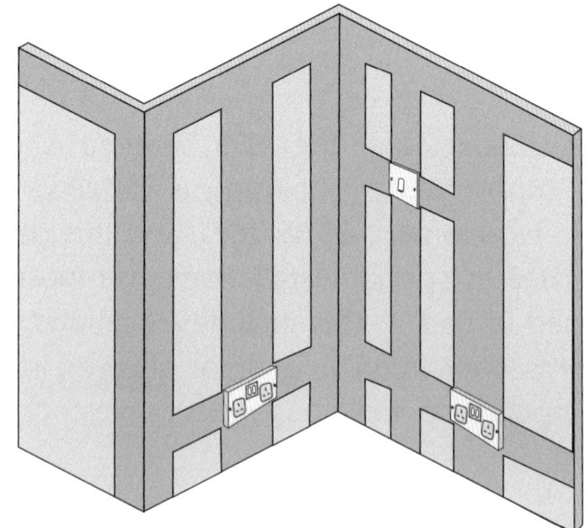

Figure 3.12 *Prescribed zones*

If cables are installed in this way they will also require some form of additional protection either from the type of cable or containment system or by the use of additional protection by use of an RCD. If the installation contains cables concealed within the walls these items need to be inspected and confirmed.

Presence of fire barriers, suitable seals and protection against thermal effects: wherever cables or containment systems pass through a fire barrier, the fire barrier must be reinstated around cables and containment systems. Where the internal area of the containment system exceeds 710 mm^2 the fire barrier needs to be reinstated within the containment system. The fire stopping must offer at least the same level of fire resistance and physical properties as the original material. You, the inspector, will need to confirm this has been carried out.

General

This section covers the general areas of the installation which are non-specific, some of which we have already considered.

Presence and correct location of appropriate devices for isolation and switching: these are the arrangements we use to control the installation, it does not refer to the functional switches the client uses to control the operation of equipment. The inspector needs to confirm that the appropriate isolation and switching has been installed and that the location of the equipment allows the installation to be suitably isolated and maintained safely.

Adequacy of access to switchgear and other equipment: the inspector needs to confirm that not only is the switchgear and equipment suitable, but also that it can be readily accessed. The location of switchgear and equipment should be such that the normal operation of the premises does not obstruct the access to the equipment.

Figure 3.13 *Not suitable access to equipment*

Particular protective measures for special installations and locations: this applies where an installation includes a special location or installation as identified in Part 7 of BS 7671. Part 7 contains information on additional requirements relating to the location or installation. The inspector needs to be familiar with the requirements of Part 7 relative to the special location or installation and confirm that these have been complied with.

Connection of single-pole devices for protection or switching in line conductors only: confirmation of the correct connection of single pole switches and protective devices will also be subject to a test. This is a visual check of the correct connection of these single pole devices before any testing is undertaken.

Correct connection of accessories and equipment: includes the correct termination of conductors and that they are mechanically and electrically secure. Each accessory and all items of electrical equipment should be inspected.

Presence of undervoltage protective devices: undervoltage devices are primarily used in motor control circuits where the supply needs to be disconnected if the voltage falls below an acceptable level. The means of providing this protection is generally by the use of a contactor and the appropriate current rating for the equipment needs to be confirmed. Like any other switching device there will be a load current that will need to be isolated.

Selection of equipment and protective measures appropriate to external influences: the inspector needs to confirm that the equipment is suitable for the environment in which it is installed and the appropriate IP requirements are complied with.

Selection of appropriate functional switching devices: this relates to the operation switches which will be used by the client to operate the installation. It includes light switches, timers, thermostats, photocells and movement sensors. The inspector should confirm that these functional controls are suitable both for the operation and that their location is appropriate.

The Schedule of Inspections may be used as an aide memoire for the inspection items but it is important to remember that there are a number of inspection items related to each of the items and that they apply to the whole installation.

For complex installations it is common practice to produce a Schedule of Inspections for each distribution board. This allows the particular items related to each section of the installation to be readily identified.

Note

There is a sample of a completed Schedule of Inspections in Part 5 of IET Guidance Note 3, Inspection and Testing.

Try this

An inspection is to be carried out on a newly installed circuit supplying a kiln in a small domestic workshop. The circuit is wired using 10 mm^2 flat profile twin and cpc themoplastic cable and is contained in surface mounted plastic mini-trunking in the workshop. It is run on the surface clipped direct to the building structure through to the garage where the consumer unit is located. The kiln is controlled by a metal-clad double pole isolator surface mounted adjacent to the kiln and is protected by a 40 A type C circuit breaker in the consumer unit.

List the items to be inspected for this circuit during initial verification before testing is undertaken.

Congratulations, you have now completed Chapter 3 of this studybook. Complete the self assessment questions before you go on to the next chapter.

SELF ASSESSMENT

Circle the correct answers.

1 Which of the following human senses is not used when carrying out the inspection of an installation?

a. Sight
b. Touch
c. Taste
d. Hearing

2 One of the functions of the initial inspection is to ensure that all the equipment has been correctly selected and:

a. Erected
b. Labelled
c. Invoiced
d. Listed on the schedules

3 Main protective bonding conductors are to be inspected and one item to be confirmed is that they are:

a. Labelled 'Safety Electrical Connection Do Not Remove'
b. Installed using bare copper conductors only
c. Terminated to all exposed conductive parts
d. Totally enclosed throughout their length

4 Circuit protective conductors must be:

a. Only installed where class II equipment is to be used
b. Only installed where class I equipment is to be used
c. Present at every point on the circuit
d. Covered with green sleeving

5 Band I and Band II circuits are installed in a new installation. The inspector will need to confirm that these circuits are:

a. Separated
b. Segregated
c. In the same enclosure
d. Run parallel to each other

Progress check

Tick the correct answer

1. When carrying out the initial verification of a new circuit the supply to the installation has to be isolated. The first action to be taken by the inspector is to:

- ☐ a. Safely isolate the installation
- ☐ b. Securely lock off the main isolator
- ☐ c. Obtain permission to isolate from the client
- ☐ d. Identify the circuit to be inspected and tested

2. The user of an electrical installation should be advised that once safe isolation of a circuit has been carried out that part of the installation will:

- ☐ a. Not be affected
- ☐ b. Function normally
- ☐ c. Operate in an emergency
- ☐ d. Will not function normally

3. An inspector is carrying out an inspection of an electrical installation and has failed to isolate a distribution board from which the cover has been removed. One effect of this could be:

- ☐ a. Inconvenience to the user
- ☐ b. A shock risk to the inspector
- ☐ c. Less time to complete the inspection
- ☐ d. The use of the installation will be restricted

4. The safety requirements for the test equipment by an inspector can be found in:

- ☐ a. BS 88
- ☐ b. GS 83
- ☐ c. BS 67
- ☐ d. GS 38

5. During the safe isolation of a circuit, tests have been carried out between all live conductors. To confirm isolation has been achieved, tests must also be carried out between:

- ☐ a. Line and neutral conductors
- ☐ b. Live and neutral conductors
- ☐ c. All live conductors and earth
- ☐ d. Neutral conductors and the MET only

6. The preferred length of exposed metal tip on a test probe when confirming safe isolation is:

- ☐ a. 2 mm
- ☐ b. 3 mm
- ☐ c. 4 mm
- ☐ d. 5 mm

7. The type of inspection and test carried out on a newly installed circuit is:

☐ a. Initial Verification

☐ b. Periodic Inspection

☐ c. Initial Certification

☐ d. Periodic Certification

8. Inspection of a new installation begins when:

☐ a. The installation is commissioned

☐ b. Construction is complete

☐ c. Testing is complete

☐ d. Construction starts

9. Information on the requirements for testing installations can be found in BS 7671, Part:

☐ a. 3

☐ b. 4

☐ c. 5

☐ d. 6

10. The document issued on the completion of a new installation is a:

☐ a. Periodic Inspection Report

☐ b. Electrical Installation Certificate

☐ c. Electrical Installation Condition Report

☐ d. Minor Electrical Installation Works Certificate

11. Which of the following documents is NOT required by the inspector before initial verification can be carried out?

☐ a. Bill of quantities

☐ b. Specification

☐ c. Design data

☐ d. Drawings

12. The system shown in Figure 1 is:

☐ a. TN-S

☐ b. TN-C-S

☐ c. TT

☐ d. TN-C

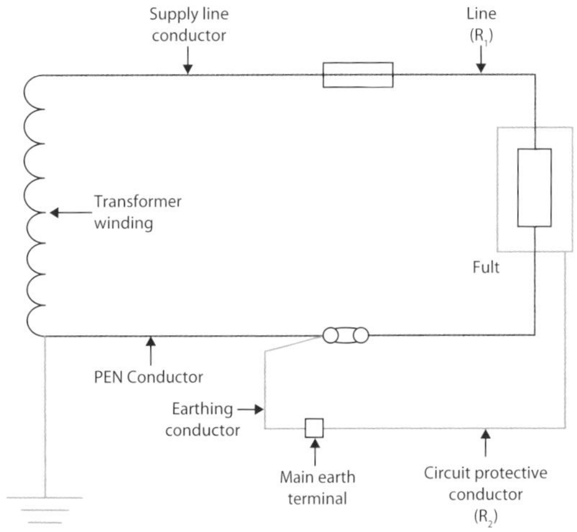

Figure 1

13. Which of the following human senses would be best used to check whether a conductor is securely terminated at a circuit breaker:

☐ a. Sight

☐ b. Touch

☐ c. Taste

☐ d. Hearing

14. BS 7671 identifies the requirement for the initial verification inspection in:

☐ a. Chapter 61

☐ b. Chapter 62

☐ c. Chapter 63

☐ d. Chapter 64

15. A detailed list of inspection items can be found in:

- ☐ a. IET Guidance Note 1
- ☐ b. IET Guidance Note 3
- ☐ c. BS 7671
- ☐ d. BS 1361

16. When inspecting a steel trunking system prior to the installation of any cables, which of the following would NOT be included in the inspector's checklist?

- ☐ a. Earthing links are in place
- ☐ b. Trunking securely fixed
- ☐ c. Lid is correctly fitted
- ☐ d. No sharp edges

17. The check of identification of conductors will include making sure that the live conductors are correctly:

- ☐ a. Secured
- ☐ b. Terminated
- ☐ c. Coloured or numbered
- ☐ d. Sequenced in the terminals

18. Supplementary protective bonding conductors should be inspected to ensure they connect:

- ☐ a. Exposed and extraneous conductive parts
- ☐ b. Extraneous conductive parts to the MET
- ☐ c. Between exposed conductive parts only
- ☐ d. Exposed conductive parts to the MET

19. The maximum distance from any corner of a wall for the prescribed zones is:

- ☐ a. 100 mm
- ☐ b. 125 mm
- ☐ c. 150 mm
- ☐ d. 175 mm

20. The inspection of appropriate functional switching devices would include a:

- ☐ a. Circuit breaker
- ☐ b. Main isolator
- ☐ c. Light switch
- ☐ d. RCD

4

Testing and commissioning an installation (Part 1)

RECAP

Before you start work on this chapter, complete the exercise below to ensure that you remember what you learned earlier.

- During the initial verification inspection of a new installation all the items ________________ to that particular installation must be ________________.
- The human senses of ________________, hearing, touch and ________________ may be used when inspecting electrical ________________.
- The results of the initial verification inspection are recorded on a ________________ of ________________.
- Inspection is one of the ________________ requirements at initial verification because there are many ________________ which will not be identified by ________________.
- During the initial verification inspection process the most commonly used senses are those of ________________ and ________________.
- The inspection of the cables which will be concealed ________________ the ________________ must be carried out during the ________________ stage.
- Where a main protective bonding conductor connects to an ________________ conductive part, inspection should confirm the presence of a ________________ warning ________________.
- The correct connection of a conductor includes confirming it is correctly terminated, ________________ and ________________.

- The inspection process includes confirming that the ____________ ratings of protective devices are suitable for the ___________ carrying ___________ of the conductors connected to the device and that the device is the correct ___________.
- On the Schedule of Inspections for initial verification the only two ______ entries are _____ where an item has been inspected and is acceptable, or N/A where an item is not __________ to the particular __________ being inspected.
- At initial verification any inspection items which are not ____________ must be ____________ before the installation can be ____________ into service.

LEARNING OBJECTIVES

On completion of this chapter you should be able to:

- Specify the requirements for the safe and correct use of instruments to be used for testing and commissioning, including:
  - Checks required to prove that test instruments and leads are safe and functioning correctly
  - The need for instruments to be regularly checked and calibrated.
- State the tests to be carried out on an electrical installation prior to energizing in accordance with BS 7671 and IET Guidance Note 3.
- Identify the correct instrument for each test to be carried out in terms of:
  - The instrument is fit for purpose
  - Identifying the right scale/settings of the instrument appropriate to the test to be carried out.
- Explain why it is necessary for test results to comply with standard values and state the actions to take in the event of unsatisfactory results being obtained.
- Explain why testing is carried out in the order specified in BS 7671 and IET Guidance Note 3.
- State the reasons why it is necessary to verify the continuity of circuit protective conductors and ring final circuit conductors.
- State the methods for verifying the continuity of circuit protective conductors and ring final circuit conductors and interpreting the obtained results.
- State the effects that cables connected in parallel and variations in cable length can have on insulation resistance values.

- Specify the procedures for completing insulation resistance testing.
- Explain why it is necessary to verify polarity.
- State the procedures for testing to identify correct polarity.
- State the method of testing earth electrode resistance prior to energizing the installation.

Part 1 General requirements for testing

This chapter considers the requirements for the testing of electrical systems at initial verification prior to the connection of the supply. This includes the requirements for the test instruments to be used, the sequence of testing and the recording and verification of results.

Whilst working through this chapter you will need to refer to BS 7671, Requirements for electrical installations, IET Guidance Note 3 (GN3) Inspection and Testing, and Health and Safety Executive Guidance, HSE GS 38; Electrical Test Equipment used by Electricians. You will also need to refer to manufacturers' information from catalogues or online.

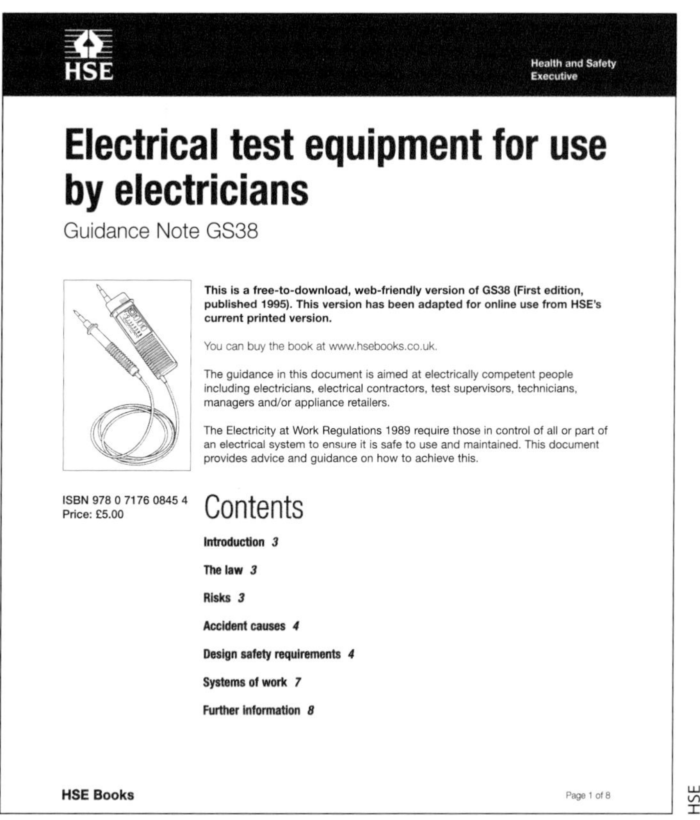

HSE

Health and Safety Executive

Electrical test equipment for use by electricians

Guidance Note GS38

This is a free-to-download, web-friendly version of GS38 (First edition, published 1995). This version has been adapted for online use from HSE's current printed version.

You can buy the book at www.hsebooks.co.uk.

The guidance in this document is aimed at electrically competent people including electricians, electrical contractors, test supervisors, technicians, managers and/or appliance retailers.

The Electricity at Work Regulations 1989 require those in control of all or part of an electrical system to ensure it is safe to use and maintained. This document provides advice and guidance on how to achieve this.

ISBN 978 0 7176 0845 4
Price: £5.00

Contents

HSE Books

Page 1 of 8

HSE

Figure 4.1 *HSE Guidance GS 38*

Having completed the inspection of the new installation the next stage is to test to confirm that it complies with the design and the requirements of BS 7671. The testing process can be generally divided into two stages. Tests carried out:

- Before the installation can be energized
- Once the installation is energized and before it can be placed in service.

The tests to be carried out before the installation is energized are often referred to as the 'dead tests'. The tests where the installation is energized in order for the tests to be carried out, often referred to as the 'live tests', are covered in Chapter 5.

Before we go into detail on the actual testing we should first appreciate the tests which need to be carried out. For initial verification BS 7671 and GN3 detail the sequence in which these 'dead tests' are to be carried out 'where relevant and practical'.

a Continuity of protective conductors, main and supplementary bonding conductors
b Continuity of ring final circuit conductors
c Insulation resistance
d Protection by SELV, PELV or by electrical separation
e Protection by barriers or enclosures provided during erection
f Insulation of non-conducting floors and walls
g Polarity
h Earth electrode resistance

Once the electrical supply has been connected, recheck the polarity before conducting further tests:

h Earth electrode resistance
i Protection by automatic disconnection of supply
j Earth fault loop impedance
k Additional protection
l Prospective fault current
m Phase sequence
n Functional tests
o Other tests such as confirmation of voltage drop may also be undertaken where appropriate.

You will notice that the earth electrode resistance test appears in both lists, being the last dead test and the first live test. This is because there are two methods of carrying out this test and both will be considered in the testing procedures.

We must also consider the requirements for the use and suitability of the instruments to be used. Test instruments are available in a number of formats from the basic individual instruments for each test to the multifunctional test instrument which combines a number of test functions in a single instrument.

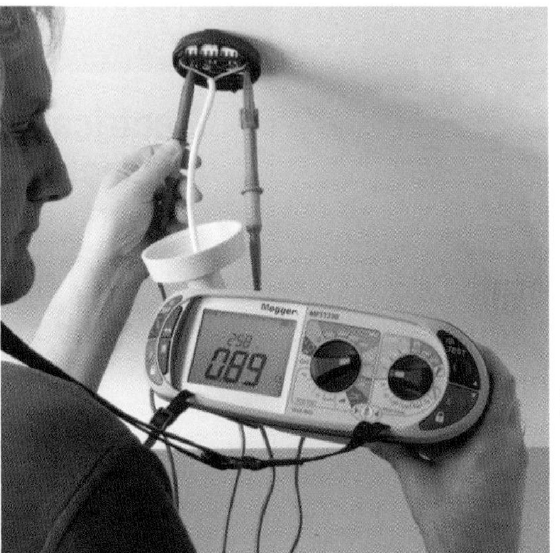

Image courtesy of Megger

Figure 4.2 *Multifunction test instrument*

When using a multifunction test instrument the inspector will need to set the instrument to the particular function for the test to be undertaken.

In this studybook we shall refer to the particular instrument required for the test and the specified performance requirements for each.

There is an element of risk involved when undertaking testing. The inspector must take appropriate action to minimize the dangers which may be encountered both for the inspector and those in the vicinity whilst inspection and testing is undertaken.

In addition the inspector should:

- Comply with the requirements of the Electricity at Work Regulations
- Understand the test equipment being used, including its rating
- Understand the characteristics of the installation being tested
- Confirm the instruments comply with the appropriate British Standards; this is generally BS EN 61010, however older instruments would have been manufactured to BS 5458 which has been withdrawn
- Confirm the test leads, probes and clips are in good condition and not damaged
- Comply with the requirements of HSE Guidance GS 38.

Note

GS 38 is available as a free download or online version on the HSE website.

Particular care is required wherever voltages associated with the tests being performed exceed 50 V ac and this includes some of the 'dead tests' as well as all the 'live tests'. Shock hazards may also occur from capacitive loads such as conductors charged during insulation resistance testing. In addition electric shock may occur as the result of voltages appearing on earthed metalwork whilst carrying out some of the live tests.

Confirming it is safe to proceed with testing, in addition to the considerations above, will include confirming the instrument accuracy as the verification process requires accurate test values. The accuracy of the instrument is generally considered in two parts.

Calibration: this should be carried out on a new test instrument before it is used and is generally done by the manufacturer of the test instrument. This calibration relates the instrument accuracy to a national standard and confirms that, within the manufacturer's tolerances, the instrument is giving accurate readings.

This national standard is verified by the United Kingdom Accreditation Service (UKAS) which is the only body recognized by the government to assess and provide calibration services. The calibration equipment used throughout the country is also regularly calibrated to this UKAS standard.

The instrument should be regularly calibrated in accordance with the manufacturer's instructions which, in most cases, is annually.

Task

Familiarize yourself with the guidance in GS 38 before continuing with this chapter.

CALIBRATION

COMMENTS ____________________

____

BY __________ DATE __________

NEXT CALIBRATION __________

Figure 4.3 *Typical calibration label*

Courtesy of Kewtech

Figure 4.4 *Typical checkbox*

Ongoing accuracy: due to the nature of the electrical installation work and the use of the test instruments, we need to confirm that during the period between calibrations the instrument is continuing to give accurate results. The test instruments are carried from site to site in a vehicle, subjected to all sorts of environmental conditions, vibration and possible impact. All of these can affect the accuracy of the instrument and so a regular check is required to confirm the instrument is still accurate. This is done with a regular, say monthly, check and the results are recorded.

To set up the record system the instrument would be checked immediately after calibration using either self-made or proprietary equipment. At the regular ongoing check, the results would be recorded and this will highlight any change in accuracy to the instrument. This process allows the inspector to be confident that the instrument is accurate and provides an early warning if this situation changes. The number of installations which may have to be retested if a problem is discovered is likely to be only those tested in the interval since the last check.

Ongoing Accuracy Test Record

Instrument Details		
Serial No. :	Type :	Tolerance :
Model :	Manufacturer :	Quick Check No. :

		Insulation Resistance MΩ									Continuity Ω			RCD ms			EFLI Ω		
Reference Values																			
Checked By	Date	0.5 250V	2.0 500V	200 1000V	0.5 250V	2.0 500V	200 1000V	0.5 250V	2.0 500V	200 1000V	0.5	1.0	2.0	$I_{\Delta n}$	5x $I_{\Delta n}$	1/2x $I_{\Delta n}$	Socket loop	Local loop	Local +1.0 Ω

Figure 4.5 *Typical ongoing accuracy record sheet*

The majority of test instruments rely on internal batteries for their power source and there are two further checks that need to be carried out on the instrument before it is put to use.

Battery condition: the internal battery is important for all the instrument functions in both dead and live testing. Before the instrument is used the inspector should confirm that the battery has a suitable output voltage level. How this is done and what output voltage is acceptable will vary from one manufacturer to another. The accuracy of the instrument is dependent upon this battery voltage and so it should always be checked before testing begins.

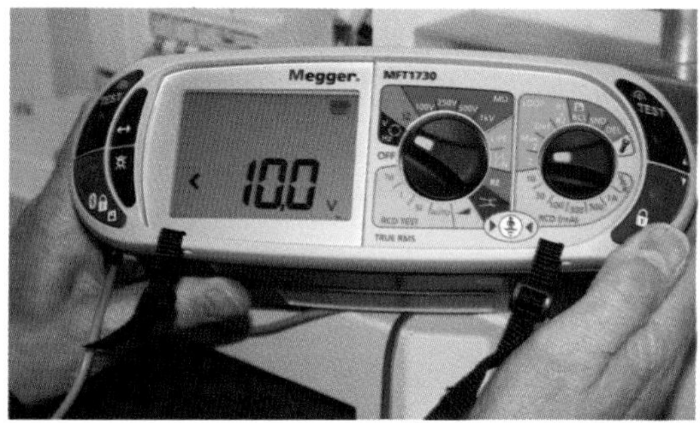

Figure 4.6 *Checking the battery voltage*

Instrument function: the inspector should also confirm that the instrument is functioning correctly before carrying out the dead tests. This may be done by simply operating the test instrument with the test leads connected together (a low resistance) and with the test leads apart (a high resistance). The instrument function cannot be confirmed before carrying out the live tests.

a) 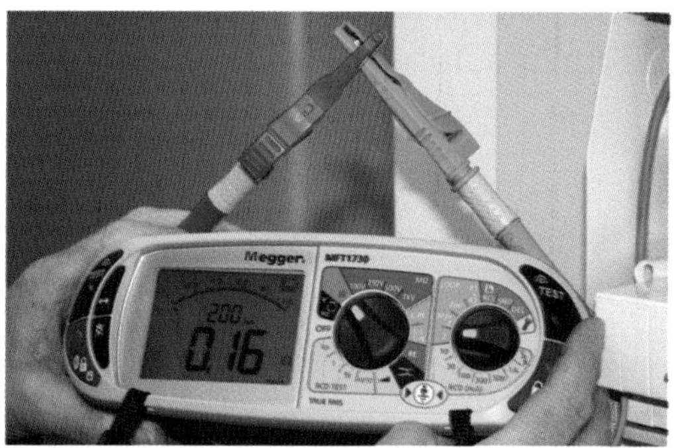

b) 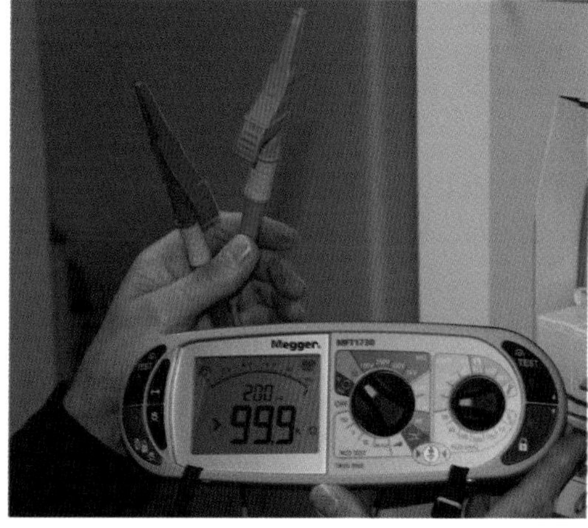

Figure 4.7 *Checking the instrument function*

Task

Produce a list of all the standard checks that need to made on a test instrument and leads before it is used for testing during initial verification.

Part 2 Testing the continuity of protective conductors

Remember

These tests are to be carried out in the order given in BS 7671 and GN3 during the initial verification of an electrical installation.

Just to remind ourselves, the sequence of the 'dead tests' is:

- **a** Continuity of protective conductors, main and supplementary bonding conductors
- **b** Continuity of ring final circuit conductors
- **c** Insulation resistance
- **d** Protection by SELV, PELV or by electrical separation
- **e** Protection by barriers or enclosures provided during erection
- **f** Insulation of non-conducting floors and walls
- **g** Polarity
- **h** Earth electrode resistance.

The first test we are going to carry out is for the continuity of protective conductors.

Remember

Before any of the dead tests are carried out the inspector must confirm that the circuit(s) being tested are safely isolated from the supply. This is particularly significant where alterations and/or additions to existing installations are undertaken. New installations should be tested with the installation completely isolated from the supply.

Continuity of protective conductors

Protective conductors include:

- Circuit protective conductors (cpc)
- Main protective bonding conductors
- Supplementary bonding conductors.

There are two methods of testing to confirm the continuity of these conductors and we shall consider the use and advantages of both these methods.

Method 1

This is often referred to as the $R_1 + R_2$ test and is used to confirm the continuity of the circuit protective conductors. During initial verification this test is best carried out once the accessories have been terminated but before they are fixed back so that the terminals are accessible.

Purpose

The purpose of the test is to confirm that:

- There is a circuit protective conductor present at every point on the circuit/installation
- The cpc at each point is connected to the installation main earthing terminal.

The term '$R_1 + R_2$ test' comes from the fact that the test involves linking the line and cpc together at the distribution board and measuring between the line and cpc at every point on the circuit.

The highest value obtained on each circuit is the $R_1 + R_2$ value for the circuit, which is the resistance of the line conductor (R_1) and the cpc (R_2) to the furthest point (electrically, not necessarily in actual distance) on the circuit. This resistance forms part of the earth fault loop impedance for the circuit and so this test confirms continuity of the cpc and determines the $R_1 + R_2$ of the circuit for later use.

In practice, because we are testing between the line and cpc conductors at each point, the test method can also be used to confirm that the polarity of the line and cpc is correct for our radial circuits.

Note

The $R_1 + R_2$ test will not confirm the polarity of radial socket outlet circuits where the test is carried out from the socket fronts and a visual confirmation of polarity is required.

Test instrument

We are going to be measuring conductor resistance and this will be a low value of resistance as that is the main feature of a conductor. The test instrument to be used for this test is a Low Resistance Ohmmeter which has specific characteristics including:

- An output voltage between 4 V and 24 V
- A short circuit current of 200 mA
- A resolution of 0.01 Ω.

Note

The characteristics of the instruments used to carry out tests on electrical installations are given in IET Guidance Note 3, Section 4.

Because the values of resistance are expected to be low the effect of the resistance of the connections and leads can be significant and so the inspector must compensate for this resistance. This may be done by either:

- Measuring the resistance of the test leads and subtracting this resistance from the measured values

  or
- Using the null facility on the test instrument, where this is provided, to subtract the test lead resistance and so give true values direct from the instrument.

Most digital test instruments have the null facility and the precise method will vary from one manufacturer to another.

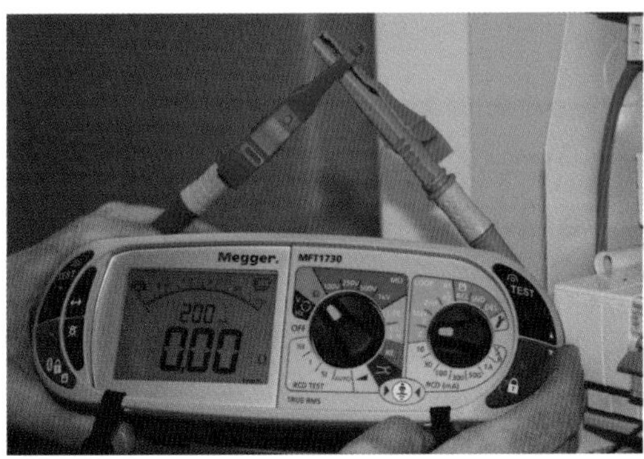

Figure 4.8 *Low resistance ohmmeter with test leads nulled*

The most important things to remember when measuring or nulling the test leads is to ensure that:

- The test leads are fitted with the crocodile clips
- The clips are joined together with the fixed jaws together **NOT** the sprung jaws.

The sprung jaws are only connected to the leads by the spring within the crocodile clip and this will add resistance which is not present when the solid jaw is clamped against the conductor. If the leads are incorrectly nulled then too much resistance will be automatically removed from the reading and the test results will not be accurate.

Having checked the instrument and nulled the test leads we need to prepare the circuit for the test. Before the test can be carried out we must ensure that the circuit is isolated from the supply.

A link is then placed between the line and cpc at the distribution board. With smaller distribution boards, such as a domestic consumer unit, it is often possible to place the two conductors together in a terminal of the earth bar.

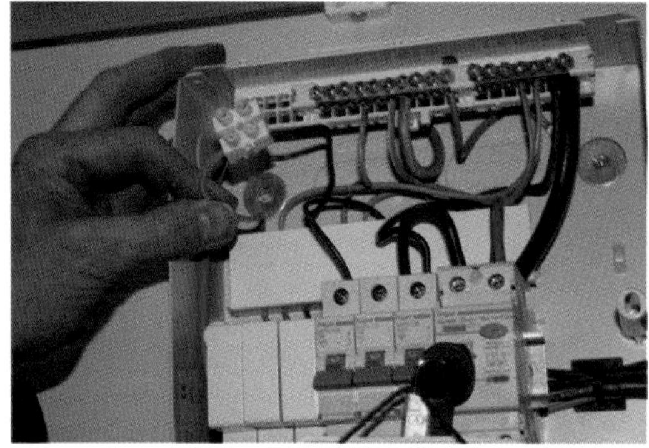

Figure 4.9 *Linked line and cpc at distribution board*

Remember

On larger boards it may be necessary to use a link and if this is the case the resistance of the link wire should be included in the null process.

We can now carry out the test by measuring between the line and cpc conductors at every point on the circuit, noting the value and recording the highest value as the $R_1 + R_2$ for the circuit.

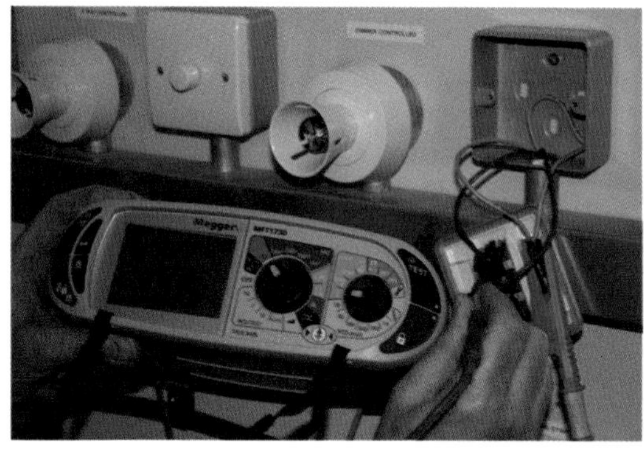

Figure 4.10 *Measure between line and cpc at every point on the circuit*

Once the testing is completed the link is removed and the circuit accessories are fixed in position.

Test results												
Ring final circuit continuity (Ω)			Continuity (Ω) $(R_1 + R_2)$ or R_2		Insulation resistance (MΩ)		Polarity	Z_s (Ω)	RCD (ms)			Remarks (continue on a separate sheet if necessary)
r_1 (line)	r_n (neutral)	r_2 (cpc)	$(R_1 + R_2)$*	R_2	Live – Live	Live – E	✓	Ω	$@I_{\Delta}n$	$@5I_{\Delta}n$	Test button operation	
J	K	L	M	N	O	P	Q	R	S	T	U	V
			1.3									

Courtesy of the ECA

Figure 4.11 *The highest test result is recorded as $R_1 + R_2$*

Try this

Produce a bullet point summary of the full process for carrying out a test to confirm continuity of a cpc using the $R_1 + R_2$ method.

Summary of the $R_1 + R_2$ test process:

- ____
- ____
- ____
- ____
- ____
- ____
- ____
- ____
- ____

Before we look at the verification of the test results we will consider the second method of carrying out a continuity of protective conductor test.

Method 2

This is often referred to as the R_2 or the long or wander lead test as it involves the use of a long lead to measure between the protective conductor at the origin of the installation or circuit and each point on the circuit.

Note

This method must be used to confirm the continuity of protective bonding conductors as there is no associate line conductor and so the $R_1 + R_2$ method is not appropriate.

We used the example of a circuit for Method 1 and so we will consider confirming continuity of a main protective bonding conductor for this method.

The selection, check and preparation of the instrument is going to be exactly the same for this test as it was for Method 1.

We will be using the Low Resistance Ohmmeter and must confirm that it is not damaged, the battery is OK and the leads are not damaged. The test leads will need to be nulled out but for this test we will be using a long lead and this must be included in the null process. A proprietary long lead for this purpose can be purchased from most of the instrument manufacturers.

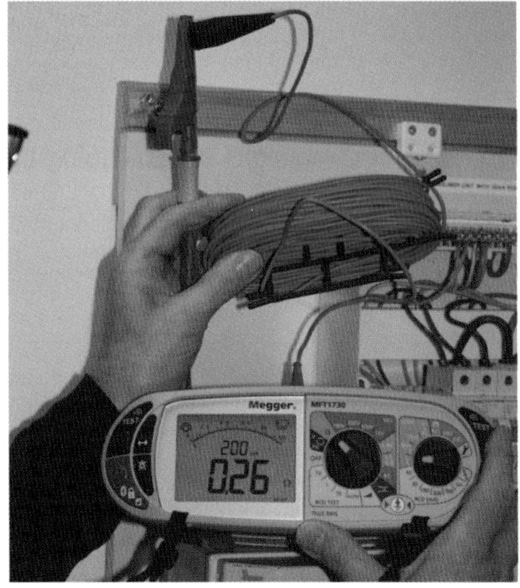

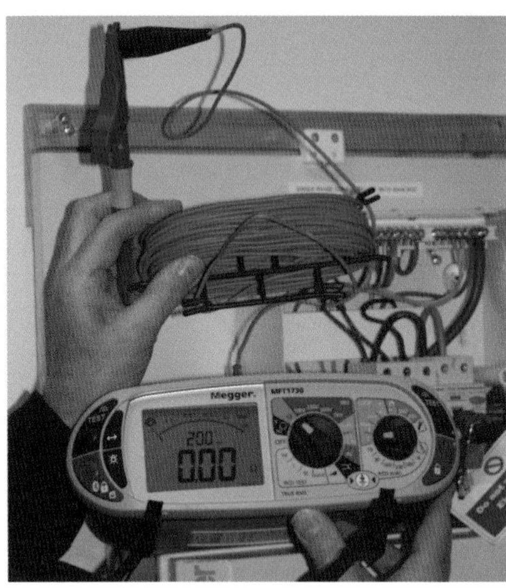

Figure 4.12 *Long lead nulled out*

The main protective bonding conductor must be disconnected from the main earthing terminal or the extraneous conductive part for this test to remove parallel paths. It does not matter which end is disconnected so whichever is easiest to access.

Remember

One end of the protective bonding conductor must be disconnected to remove any parallel paths.

As the protective bonding conductor is to be disconnected the whole of the installation must be safely isolated from the supply as an essential part of the fault protection is being removed.

The first step would be to obtain permission to isolate the installation. For a brand new installation this should not be a problem as the installation will not be energized. Where this test is carried out on an existing installation as part of an alteration or addition, then it is essential to obtain this permission first. This permission must be obtained from the person responsible for the electrical installation (the duty holder) not just anyone.

Remember

The installation must be isolated from the supply for this test and the permission of the responsible person must be obtained before isolation takes place.

Having obtained permission and safely isolated and locked off the supply we can disconnect the main protective bonding conductor from the main earthing terminal. The long lead is run out from the point of connection to the exposed conductive part back to the MET. One end of the long lead is connected to the main protective bonding conductor at the point of connection to the extraneous conductive part. The long lead is run back to the MET where it is connected to the test instrument; the other test lead is connected to the disconnected main protective bonding conductor. The test is then carried out and the value recorded.

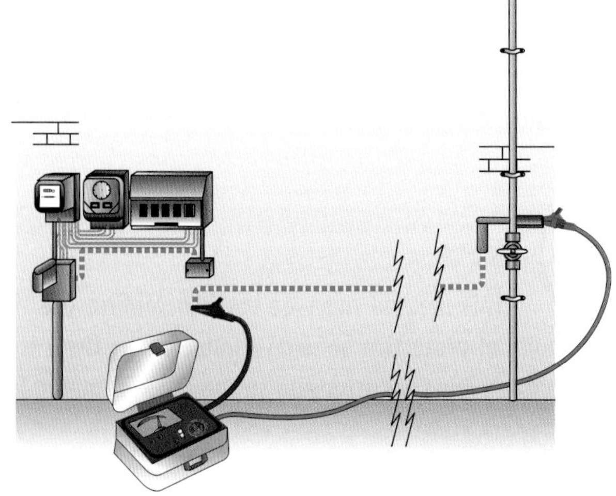

Figure 4.13 *Long lead (R_2) test on a main protective bonding conductor*

The test leads are then disconnected and the main protective bonding conductor reconnected before the supply to the installation is reinstated. The result of this test is recorded on the Electrical Installation Certificate and there is no facility to record the actual value, although once measured it should be noted on the certificate for reference.

Note

Where the main protective bonding conductor is completely visible throughout its entire length, continuity may be confirmed by a visual inspection of the conductor. If the conductor is lost from sight, no matter how short the distance, a test to confirm continuity must be carried out.

This method may also be used to confirm the continuity of cpcs and the result would be recorded on the Schedule of Test Results. The continuity of cpc may be confirmed by either method and the $R_1 + R_2$ or the R_2 value is to be recorded. The unused column is the only one on the schedule which may be left blank.

However, if the R_2 test is used a further test will need to be carried out to confirm correct polarity and the value of $R_1 + R_2$ will not be established.

Try this

Produce a bullet point summary of the full process for carrying out a test to confirm continuity of a main protective bonding conductor using the long lead (R_2) method.

Summary of the R_2 test:

- ____________________
- ____________________
- ____________________
- ____________________
- ____________________
- ____________________
- ____________________
- ____________________
- ____________________
- ____________________
- ____________________
- ____________________
- ____________________

Verification of the results

Confirming the continuity of protective conductor involves verifying the test results are acceptable. The main method of doing this is to compare the measured value with the value expected for the conductors measured. Guidance Note 3 contains information on conductor resistance in mΩ/m for conductors in Appendix 1, Table B1.

The information contained in Table B1 will allow the inspector to confirm the results are acceptable. The table contains generic details on the conductor resistance and this may be used in one of two ways when carrying out initial verification.

If we know the length of the circuit being tested the expected resistance can be calculated and the measured resistance compared with this expected value.

Example: A radial circuit has been installed using 2.5 mm^2 flat profile twin and cpc cable and is 30 m long to the furthest point. To determine the expected $R_1 + R_2$ we need to use the information from Table B1 and the conductor length. As the cable is 2.5 mm^2 flat profile cable the cpc will be 1.5 mm^2 and so the $R_1 + R_2$ resistance per metre will be 19.51 mΩ/m.

To determine the expected $R_1 + R_2$ resistance for the circuit:

$$R_1 + R_2 = \frac{\text{m}\Omega/\text{m} \times \text{L}}{1000} = \frac{19.51 \times 30}{1000} = 0.5853\,\Omega$$

As the instrument has a resolution of 0.01 the measured value should be in the range 0.58 Ω to 0.59 Ω depending on the manufacturer's settings (how values are rounded up or down).

$R_1 + R_2$ resistance in mΩ/m at 20 °C		
csa in mm^2		Resistance in mΩ/m
Line	cpc	Copper
2.5	-	7.41
2.5	1.0	25.51
2.5	1.5	19.51
2.5	2.5	14.82

Figure 4.14 *$R_1 + R_2$ values for 2.5 mm^2 cables*

Alternatively we may not know the actual length of the cable and so we can check the measured resistance value with the tabulated value to determine the length and then compare that with the distance on site.

Example: A 10 mm^2 main protective bonding conductor is installed to gas installation pipework and when testing to confirm the continuity of this conductor the measured resistance is 0.07 Ω. The approximate length of the conductor should be:

$$L = \frac{\text{measured R1 + R2}}{\text{Tabulated resistance}} = \frac{0.07}{\left(\frac{1.83}{1000}\right)}$$

$$= \frac{0.07}{0.00183} = 38.25\,\text{m}$$

So the length of the conductor would be approximately 38 m.

Task

Familiarize yourself with Table B1 in IET Guidance Note 3, Inspection and Testing before continuing with this chapter.

$R_1 + R_2$ resistance in mΩ/m at 20 °C		
csa in mm^2		Resistance in mΩ/m
Line	cpc	Copper
10	-	1.83
10	4.0	6.44
10	6.0	4.91
10	10	3.66

Figure 4.15 *$R_1 + R_2$ values for 10.0 mm^2 cables*

The resistance values obtained from the continuity of protective conductor testing are used in this way to determine the compliance. The factors which could affect the values obtained are:

- *Loose connections*: where terminations are not correctly tightened then a loose connection will introduce additional resistance and so a higher measured resistance will be the result.
- *Incorrect csa of conductor*: if the conductor is of a smaller csa the resistance will be lower than the expected value for the circuit. Conversely, if the csa of the conductor is larger the resistance will be lower and so the measured resistance will be lower than the expected value.

Note

Where short lengths of conductor are involved, say 3 m of 10 mm^2 copper conductor, then the resistance will be very low ($3 \times 0.00183 = 0.0055\ \Omega$). The test instrument resolution is 0.01 Ω and so this low resistance may be displayed as 0.00 Ω. Continuity has been confirmed and the result to be recorded is < 0.01 Ω as it is less than the instrument can accurately measure.

Where installations include steel containment systems (conduit and trunking) this must be earthed. There is no reason why a suitably constructed steel containment system cannot be used as a protective conductor for circuits installed using single core cables. This practice has however gone out of fashion and a cpc is normally installed when carrying out this type of installation. This results in the containment system forming a parallel path and so the measured values will be lower than the expected values.

The continuity of the earthing for containment system also needs to be confirmed and this may be done using the long lead method. This is preferably done during the installation process and before any cables are installed. Steel has a resistivity approximately ten times that of copper; however the csa of a steel containment system is generally much larger.

Remember

Where circuits are installed in steel containment systems the steel containment must be earthed. This will create parallel paths which will result in the measured values being lower than expected.

The verification process can therefore identify problems with the installation and for initial verification the possibility of poor terminations is the most likely problem.

This completes the first of the tests to be carried out during initial verification and the recording and verification of the test results.

Try this

A test to confirm continuity of cpc for a radial circuit with a 2.5 mm^2 line conductor and 1.5 mm^2 cpc, produced a $R_1 + R_2$ value at the furthest point of 1.3 Ω. Using the information in Figure 4.14 determine the approximate length of the radial circuit.

Part 3 Testing continuity of ring final circuit conductors

Continuity of ring final circuit tests are to be carried out on all ring final circuits at initial verification. This is the first test to be applied to a ring final circuit as once the test is completed the continuity of the protective conductor will have been confirmed.

The purpose of the continuity of ring final circuits is to confirm that:

- The circuit is a ring
- There are no cross or interconnections in the ring.

The design of the ring circuit is unique insomuch as the circuit conductors are effectively connected in parallel. When the load is distributed around the ring the load current will be shared by the conductors. This enables a unique design where the current carrying capacity of the individual conductors is lower than the rating of the protective device.

For example: the standard ring final circuit in a dwelling is normally installed with 2.5 mm^2 live conductors which have a maximum current carrying capacity, when clipped direct, of 27 A. This circuit will normally be protected by a BS EN 60898 type B circuit breaker rated at 32 A which is higher than the cable rating. This is only acceptable because the circuit is wired as a ring and the load current is shared between the two parallel conductors. If the circuit is not actually a ring final circuit the cable will not be protected against overload. Cross or interconnection in a ring final circuit will also affect the current distribution around the ring.

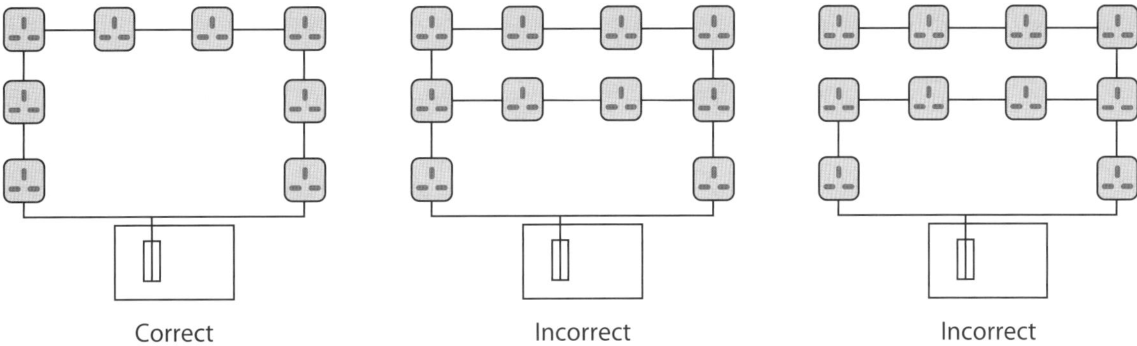

Figure 4.16 *Line diagrams showing correct and incorrect connections of a ring circuit*

Unfortunately it is relatively easy to make a mistake when installing ring circuits, particularly when using single core cables in conduit or trunking, so the inspector needs to determine that the ring is actually a ring with no cross or interconnections at initial verification.

The test instrument used for this test will again be the low resistance ohmmeter, this is used for all our continuity tests, and we shall need to carry out the same checks for calibration: no damage, battery OK, the instrument functions and the test leads must be nulled before testing.

The test is carried out in three steps and can be carried out from any point on the ring. As this test requires tests to be made at each socket outlet on the ring it requires careful consideration where the distribution board is energized, for example where a ring final circuit is added to an existing installation.

The test is best carried out from a suitable socket outlet on the circuit. To do this the ring final circuit is terminated at the distribution board and the circuit breaker locked off. The distribution board can be reinstated and left safe with the circuit under the control of the inspector.

A proprietary plug-in unit is a useful accessory when carrying out this test as it allows the test to be carried out from the socket fronts which means the sockets can be fixed during this test.

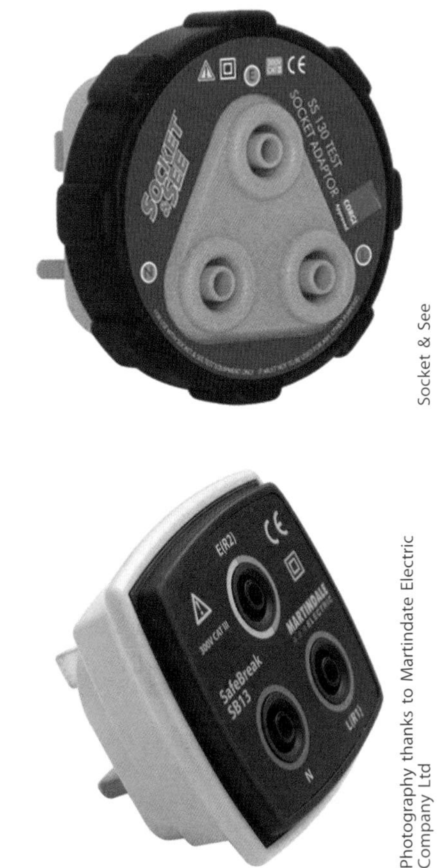

Figure 4.17 *Typical proprietary plug-in unit*

We shall consider undertaking the test from the distribution board or socket outlet.

Step 1

The first step of the test is to confirm the conductors are connected in a ring and to establish the resistance of each conductor from end to end. As the ring circuit begins and ends at the same protective device, we simply connect the instrument between the two line conductors and test to obtain a reading. This is recorded on the Schedule of Test Results as r_1.

For a standard ring circuit, the line conductor will be a 2.5 mm^2 copper conductor which has a resistance of approximately 0.007 Ω/m (actual 7.41 mΩ). The measured line to line resistance, divided by 0.007, will give an approximate total end to end cable length for the ring.

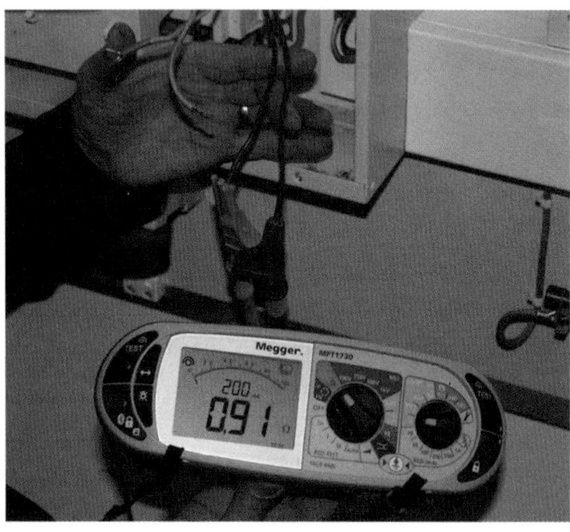

Figure 4.18 *Conductors disconnected from the distribution board and a low resistance ohmmeter connected across the two line conductors*

If our test result line to line on the ring circuit is say, 0.53 Ω, then we can estimate the total length of the conductor by using the formula length = total resistance ÷ resistance per metre, in this case:

$$\text{length} = \frac{r_1}{\text{Resistance per metre}} = \frac{0.53\,\Omega}{0.007\,\Omega} = 75.7\text{ m.}$$

This is an approximate value which gives us some idea of the total length of conductor involved.

We now repeat the test with the two neutral conductors and the results should be substantially the same, as the cables should follow the same routes, so within 0.05 Ω. This is recorded on the Schedule of Test Results as r_n.

The final part of this first step is to repeat the test with the cpc and where the installation is carried out using conventional flat twin and cpc cables the cpc is one size smaller than the live conductors. If we assume this to be the case the total resistance will be proportionally higher and as a rough guide it would be somewhere in the order of 1.67 times higher.

This value is arrived at by using the proportion of the csa and as resistance is directly proportional to csa we can establish the ratio by:

$$\frac{2.5\text{ mm}^2}{1.5\text{ mm}^2} = 1.67.$$

For our example we would expect the end to end resistance of the cpc to be approximately 0.53 × 1.67 = 0.885 Ω. Once measured this is recorded on the Schedule of Test Results as r_2.

If the values are not within an acceptable tolerance then the circuit requires some additional investigation to establish the reason, remember that the conductors should follow the same routes and be of approximately equal lengths. If a high resistance is found or an open circuit is established on any of the conductors then further investigation is needed.

Poor connections and loose terminals will all increase the resistance and this in turn can produce higher than expected values as a result.

Remember

Where more than one ring circuit is installed, the first check in the event of an open circuit is to ensure that the two conductors are for the same circuit. A test of continuity to the other ring circuit conductors will generally confirm whether this is indeed the case.

Where a steel containment system is installed this will be earthed. As a result the steel will be in parallel with the cpc and so we are unable to carry out the ring circuit test on the cpc in the same way. The continuity of the cpc would need to be confirmed using Method 2, as discussed earlier, in such cases. The confirmation of ring circuit continuity for the live conductors must still be carried out and this is done in the same way irrespective of the nature of the cpc.

Remember

We need to record the values we obtain when carrying out this step of the test:

r_1 = line to line resistance
r_2 = cpc to cpc resistance
r_n = neutral to neutral resistance

Providing the tests have confirmed that the conductors have been correctly identified and form a ring we can proceed with the next step.

Step 2

The next step is to 'cross connect' the line and neutral conductors, that is, connect the line of one end of the ring circuit to the neutral of the other end and vice versa. This is relatively easy when the installation is in sheathed cables but may be a little more difficult when using singles in trunking and conduit.

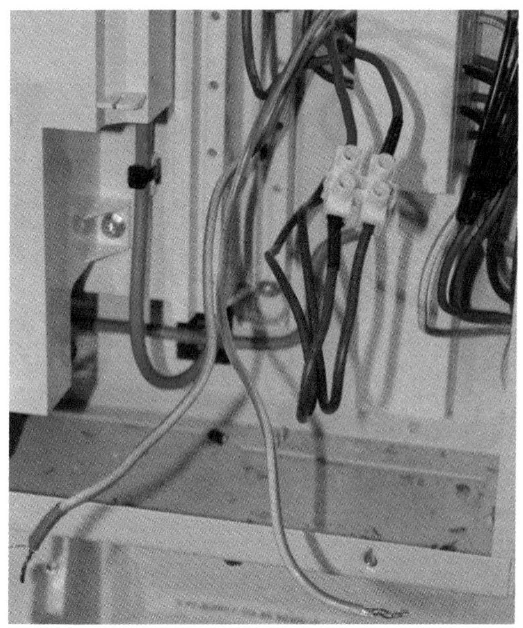

Figure 4.19 *The cross connection of the line and neutral conductors*

Note

Using a long lead a test may be carried out on each of the conductors to the socket on the ring closest to the point of test. This will result in one of the line conductors having a low resistance and the other a high resistance. Repeated on each of the ring conductors will give one of each with a high resistance (one end of the ring) and one of each with low resistance (the other end of the ring). The value of the resistance is not important or recorded as we are just identifying the two ends of the ring.

The resistance of the conductors is then measured across the connected pairs and the values obtained are noted. These values should be approximately a quarter of the value of the line and neutral resistances added together:

$$\left(\frac{r_1 + r_n}{4}\right).$$

Using a plug in adapter, we can test at each socket outlet between the line and neutral conductors, with the cross connections in place.

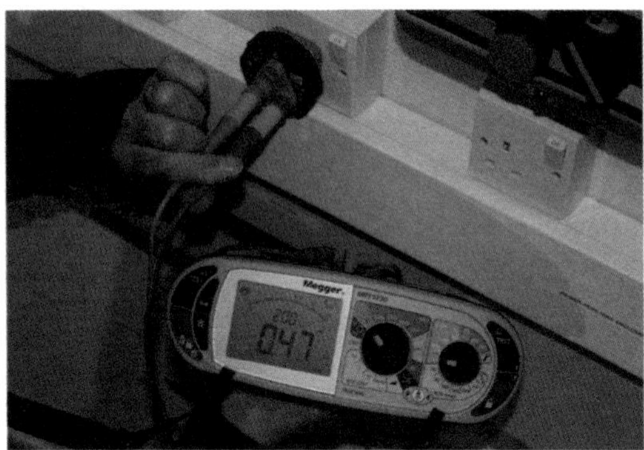

Figure 4.20 *Testing between L and N at the socket outlets*

The test readings obtained at each socket should be substantially the same as the reading taken from the test at the point where the cross connections were made. Socket outlets connected via a spur from the ring circuit will give higher values of resistance, and the actual increase will be proportional to the length of the branch cable.

If the resistance value is lower at the first socket and increases significantly as we move further away from the cross connections, this indicates that we have not cross connected the ring circuit correctly and have connected the line and neutral conductors of the same ends together. This is often the case with single core cables in a containment system if a check to determine the ends of the ring has not been carried out. Only one of the conductors has to have the connections swapped over to correctly cross connect and the test carried out to confirm ring circuit continuity and the readings should now be substantially the same at each point.

Remember

Socket outlets connected to the ring via a non-fused spur will generally have a higher resistance. This is because we have the resistance of the conductors forming the ring with the conductors for the spur in series with the ring giving a higher resistance.

Step 3

We now repeat the process from Step 2 only this time we cross connect the line and cpc of the ring circuit. The value of resistance will be higher than in the previous test where the cpc is a smaller csa than the live conductors. Again we carry out the test at each outlet, between line and cpc this time, and we may find some small variance in the values. As before, the values obtained at sockets connected via a spur will produce higher values, proportional to the length of the branch cable.

a)

b)

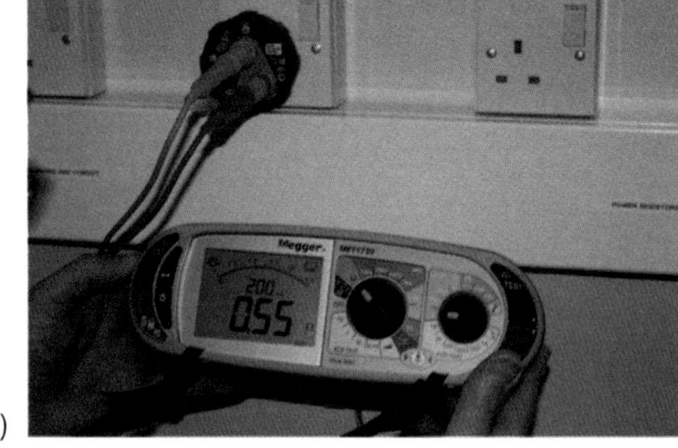

Figure 4.21 *Test between L and CPC at every socket*

The highest value obtained during this step of the test represents the $R_1 + R_2$ value for the ring circuit and should be recorded on the Schedule of Test Results in the $R_1 + R_2$ column.

The value obtained should be in the order of:

$$\left(\frac{r_1 + r_2}{4}\right)$$

using the $r_1 + r_2$ values obtained in Step 1.

Note

This quarter value expected at Steps 2 and 3 is due to the circuit comprising the two conductors connected in parallel and, because they are connected as a ring circuit, the effective length of the conductor is also halved to any point on the circuit, compared to the end to end length. The total resistance value is therefore halved (as the effective csa is doubled) and halved again (as the effective length is halved), hence a quarter of the original $r_1 + r_n$ or $r_1 + r_2$ value. This is shown in Figures 4.22 and 4.23.

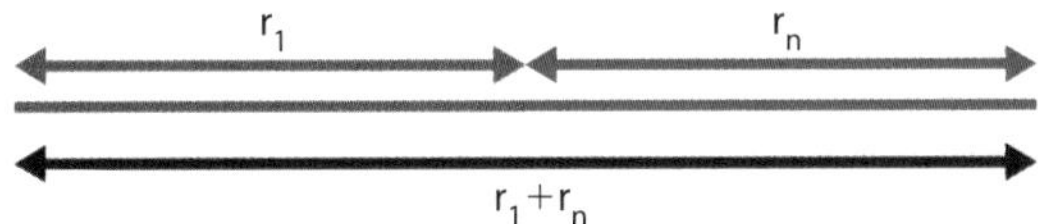

Figure 4.22 *$r_1 + r_n$ shown pictorially*

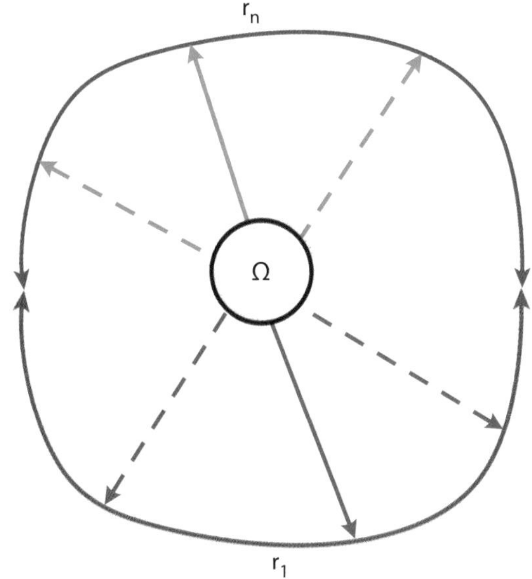

Figure 4.23 *Wherever we test L-N or L-CPC we have 2 × csa and ½ length of conductor*

Once we have completed all three steps we can remove the final cross connection and terminate the conductors and complete the circuit installation ready for the next test.

If we have carried out Steps 2 and 3 from the socket fronts using a socket adapter the polarity of the circuit will also have been confirmed. If the tests have been carried out from the socket terminals then a visual inspection of the connections is required to confirm the polarity is correct.

In practice, on successful completion of the ring final circuit continuity test we can record:

- r_1, r_2 and r_n
- $R_1 + R_2$
- Polarity correct.

Test results								
Ring final circuit continuity (Ω)			Continuity (Ω) $(R_1 + R_2)$ or R_2		Insulation resistance (MΩ)		Polarity	Z_s (Ω)
r_1 (line)	r_n (neutral)	r_2 (cpc)	$(R_1 + R_2)$*	R_2	Live – Live	Live – E	✓	Ω
J	K	L	M	N	O	P	Q	R
0.53	0.52	0.89	0.36				✓	

Courtesy of the ECA

Figure 4.24 *Results recorded for the example ring final circuit*

Try this

The continuity of a ring final circuit is being tested and at Step 1 the results are $r_1 = 0.37\ \Omega$, $r_n = 0.36\ \Omega$ and $r_2 = 0.62\ \Omega$. All the socket outlets are connected into the ring.

Determine:

a The expected value at each socket when the line and neutral are correctly interconnected.

____

____

b The expected value at each socket when the line and cpc are correctly interconnected.

____

____

Part 4 Testing insulation resistance

Having carried out the tests for continuity of conductors the next test in the sequence is to confirm the insulation resistance for the installation.

In the previous tests we were concerned with establishing that a good electrical connection was made by particular conductors and that the resistance of these conductors was sufficiently low:

- For high current to flow in the event of a fault to earth occurring
- To maintain an equal potential between exposed and extraneous conductive parts within the installation.

Insulation resistance testing

When we carry out insulation resistance testing, we are testing the resistance of the insulation separating live parts, conductors in particular, from each other and from earth. So this time we shall be looking for high values of resistance and the instrument used must be capable of measuring high values of resistance, in the range of MΩ.

We are also testing to establish that the insulation is going to be able to withstand the rigours of everyday operation and the voltages likely to be encountered. To test this we use a voltage which is generally higher than that to which the insulation will normally be subjected. The applied test voltage is dependent upon the normal operating voltage of the circuit to be tested.

Nominal Circuit Voltage	Test Voltage (dc)	Minimum Insulation Resistance
SELV and PELV only	250 V	0.5 MΩ
Up to and including 500 V (excluding SELV and PELV)	500 V	1.0 MΩ
Over 500 V	1000 V	1.0 MΩ

Figure 4.25 *Insulation resistance applied test voltages and minimum acceptable values*

Note

Information on the required test voltage and minimum acceptable values is given in BS 7671, Part 6, Table 61 and in IET GN3 Table 2.2.

These tabulated values are for the installation and not for individual circuits and the factors affecting insulation resistance need to be appreciated to understand why this is the case.

Factors affecting insulation resistance

It is important to remember that insulation resistance is different to conductor resistance and there are two factors which affect the insulation resistance of installed cables.

The resistance of conductor insulation is directly proportional to its thickness and inversely proportional to its length (resistance gets higher as the insulation thickness increases and lower as its length increases). When carrying out the insulation resistance tests the thickness of the insulation is generally fixed and so the only variable is the length.

When several cables are connected in parallel, such as at a distribution board, then the overall effect is to connect a number of resistances in parallel, so the overall effect is a reduction in resistance and the total resistance will be less than that of the lowest individual resistance.

Insulation resistance reduces:

- As the length of conductor increases
- With the number of conductors connected in parallel.

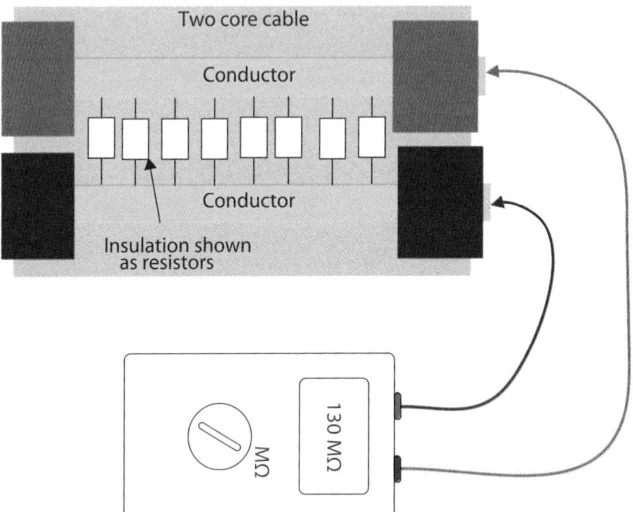

Figure 4.26 *As length increases more resistors are connected in parallel*

Example: An insulation resistance test carried out between live conductors of a number of individual circuits produces the following results: 10 MΩ, 20 MΩ, 50 MΩ, 100 MΩ and 50 MΩ. If these circuits are then all connected to the same distribution board and the insulation resistance of the whole installation is measured between live conductors with all the circuits connected the resulting insulation resistance will be:

$$\frac{1}{R_T} = \frac{1}{R_1} + \frac{1}{R_2} + \frac{1}{R_3} + \frac{1}{R_4} + \frac{1}{R_4}$$

$$= \frac{1}{10} + \frac{1}{20} + \frac{1}{50} + \frac{1}{100} + \frac{1}{50}$$

$$\frac{1}{R_T} = 0.1 + 0.05 + 0.02 + 0.01 + 0.02 = 0.2$$

$$R_T = \frac{1}{0.2} = 5\,\text{M}\Omega$$

The insulation resistance for the whole installation is 5 MΩ.

We can see that the insulation resistance for the whole installation is lower than the lowest individual circuit insulation resistance.

Insulation resistance test instrument (insulation resistance ohmmeter)

An insulation resistance ohmmeter is used to carry out the insulation resistance test and this must meet the requirements of BS 7671 for the insulation being tested. For most general installations the nominal operating voltages are 230/400 V, so the test instrument must be capable of producing a test voltage of 500 V dc. As we established earlier there are separate criteria for circuits operating at other voltages and instruments used for testing these circuits must meet the appropriate requirements.

The reason for using a higher voltage level is because they are sufficiently high to reveal any breakdown or weakness in the insulation, which is voltage sensitive. This is generally achieved by the use of an instrument with a battery power source and electronic circuitry to produce the required output. Most instruments have a digital display which may also include a virtual analogue display together with the digital readout.

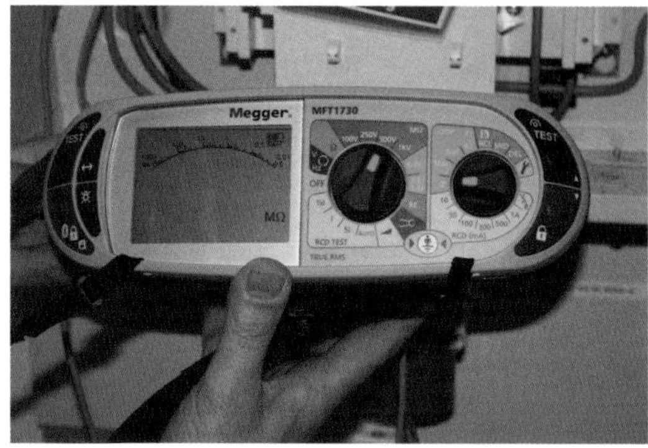

Figure 4.27 *Insulation resistance ohmmeter*

Safety whilst carrying out the insulation resistance tests

There are two main aspects to the safe implementation of the insulation resistance test.

The **FIRST** is that the test should be carried out on circuits disconnected from the supply. To assist the test engineer some instrument manufacturers have built voltage indicators into the equipment. If this indicator is activated then no tests should be carried out until the supply has been isolated. Where test equipment does not have this facility, the circuits being tested should be checked to confirm there are no supplies before the insulation resistance tests are carried out. Where circuits contain capacitors the test equipment may charge up the capacitor and care will need to be taken to avoid discharging the capacitor through your body on completion of the test.

The **SECOND** safety consideration that should always be given serious thought is that the test voltages being injected into the installation are high and could cause serious accidents. Whilst the instrument output is unlikely to result in a fatal electric shock the involuntary reaction to the shock can result in falls from height and other physical injuries. Precautions should be taken to ensure nobody can become part of the circuit when the test is being carried out.

Preparing the installation for testing

Before we can carry out our insulation resistance tests there are a number of procedures that must be carried out.

These include:

- Ensuring the supply is securely isolated and locked off and that there is no supply to the installation or circuits to be tested
- Removing all loads including incandescent lamps
- Disconnecting all equipment that would normally be in use
- Disconnecting and bypassing (linking out) any electronic equipment that would be damaged by the high voltage test (this includes dimmer switches, photocells, PIRs, electronic controllers and control gear and certain RCDs)
- Ensuring there are no connections between any line or neutral conductor and earth
- All circuit breakers switched on and all fuses in place
- Putting all control switches in the ON position (unless they protect equipment that cannot otherwise be disconnected)
- Testing two way or two way and intermediate switched circuits with the switches in each position unless they are bridged across during the testing.

In addition BS 7671 requires that the insulation resistance is measured between all live conductors and all live conductors and earth with the protective conductors connected to the earthing arrangement. This means that where the insulation resistance testing of cables during construction, such as testing underground cables before the backfill, either:

- The protective conductor and armour is connected to the earthing arrangement, using a fly lead for example

  or

- The cable must be tested again once the protective conductor is finally connected to the earthing arrangement.

Once the preparations have been completed, testing for insulation resistance can begin.

Insulation resistance test on a new installation

For a new electrical installation in a dwelling, for example, the tests may be carried out to the meter tails before they are connected to the energy meter or DNO's isolator. Where this is not possible the tests may be carried out at the consumer unit.

The main switch or switches must be on, all fuses complete and in place and all circuit breakers switched on.

The first test is between line and neutral.

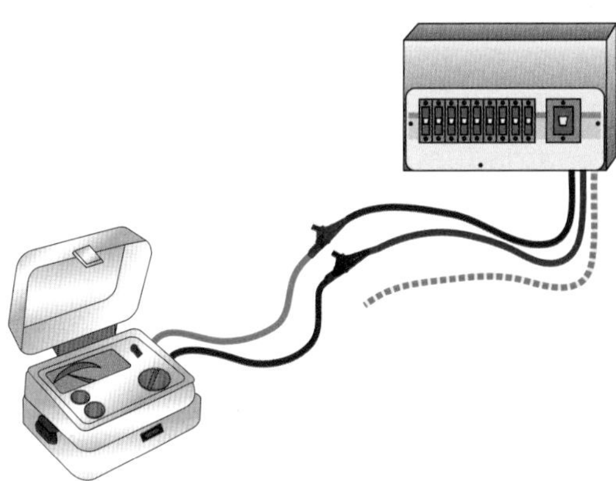

Figure 4.28 *An insulation test instrument connected to the tails of a domestic consumer unit. All switches in the unit are in the ON position*

The resistance for this should be greater than 1.0 MΩ. However, if we are testing a new installation the resistance should be much higher. For a standard dwelling we would expect the reading to be over the maximum the instrument can measure. So if the maximum range on the instrument is say 999 MΩ then the recorded figure in such cases would be > 999 MΩ.

If a load has been left connected the result is going to be 0.00 MΩ L-N, whilst a neon indicator left in circuit will give a value of around 0.24 MΩ. A number of neon indicators left in circuit will act as resistors in parallel and bring the value down even further.

A lower than expected result will require investigation as it will need to be corrected before the installation can be placed into service. Repeating the test on each circuit in turn will generally allow any faulty circuit to be identified. The circuit breakers should be in the off position for these tests so isolate the circuits from one another. Once the faulty circuit(s) has been identified, a further breakdown of this circuit can be carried out to locate the fault.

Note

Further information on fault location can be found in the *Fault Finding and Diagnosis* studybook in this series.

Once a satisfactory result has been obtained for the Line to Neutral test, the test between live conductors and earth can be carried out. This can be carried out either individually L-E and N-E or by linking line and neutral together and testing between them and earth, with all the circuit breakers on and fuses in place. Providing a satisfactory result is obtained, the live conductors do not need to be tested to earth individually. If an unsatisfactory result is obtained then test between each live conductor and earth and any faulty circuit is identified as before.

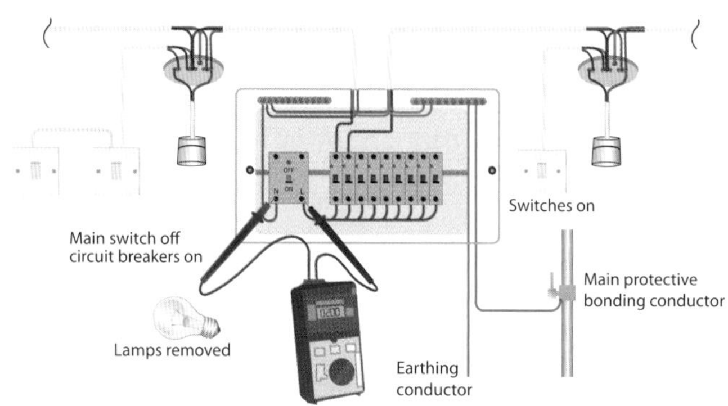

Insulation resistance test between the installation live conductors at the consumer unit

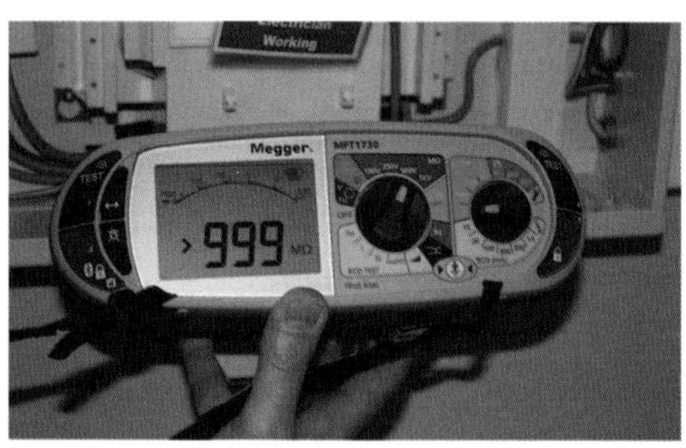

Figure 4.29 *Insulation resistance testing at the consumer unit*

Try this

List five factors that must be considered before carrying out an insulation resistance test.

1 ____________________

2 ____________________

3 ____________________

4 ____________________

5 ____________________

Insulation resistance testing on larger installations

In theory there is very little difference between carrying out an insulation resistance test on a small or a complex installation. In practice however, there are a number of extra considerations that must be made.

On poly-phase installations (typically three phase and neutral supplies) the test must be carried out between all live conductors and all live conductors and earth, just as we did for the single phase installation. In these types of installations the tests between live conductors is more involved as we have to test between each line and every other line and between each line and neutral. Tests are also required between each live conductor and earth. There is a total of ten test stages but these can be linked so all the line conductors can be connected together and tested to neutral in one test and providing the result is satisfactory then individual Line to Neutral tests would not be required.

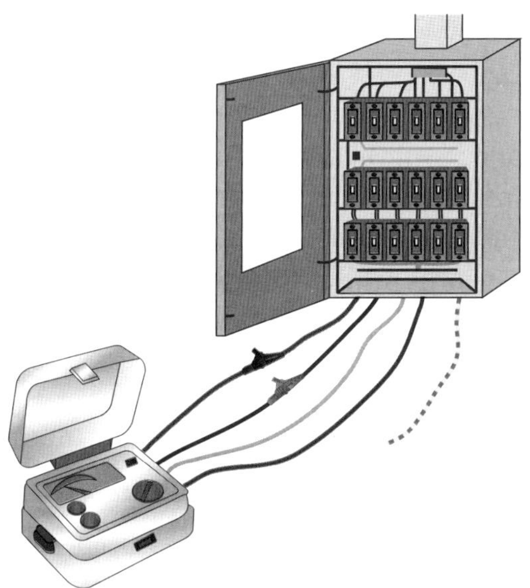

Figure 4.30 *Insulation resistance test being carried out on a three phase distribution board*

Remember

We are testing insulation resistance which is measured in MΩ and so no allowance has to be made for any linking cables used during insulation resistance testing.

A large new installation is prepared for insulation resistance testing with all the loads removed and all switches on. An insulation resistance ohmmeter connected to the whole installation will quite possibly give an unacceptable test result. This would most likely be due to the considerable number of circuits connected in parallel and the combined length of all the circuits in the installation.

Remember

We are measuring insulation resistance and the longer the total length of the cables and the more circuits there are in parallel the lower the overall insulation resistance will be.

BS 7671 offers a solution to this problem for complex installations by allowing them to be subdivided. This sub-division can be defined as:

> Each distribution circuit including the distribution cable, the distribution board and all the final circuits supplied from the distribution board with all the circuits connected is to be tested as a single item.

This is the only sub-division that is allowed and the installation cannot be further sub-divided.

This approach is only permissible for complex installations and so, for example, a dwelling with a circuit supplying a remote garage could not be sub-divided.

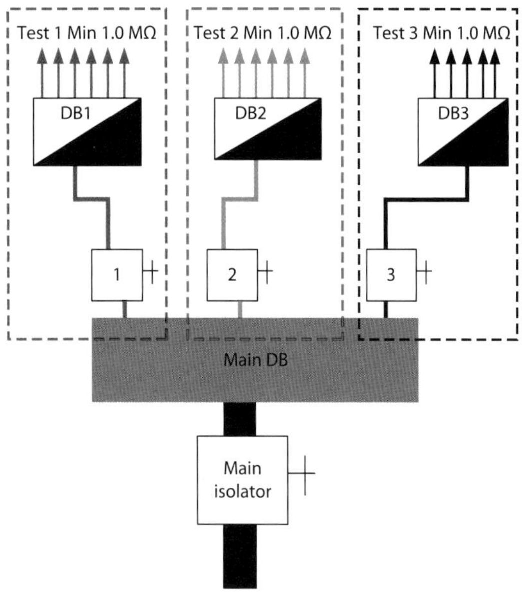

Figure 4.31 *Insulation resistance tests carried out on a complex installation*

- Test 1: includes Isolator 1, the distribution cable indicated red, DB1 with all circuit breakers on and all the final circuits indicated in red. Minimum value 1.0 MΩ.
- Test 2: includes Isolator 2, the distribution cable indicated green, DB2 with all circuit breakers on and all the final circuits indicated in green. Minimum value 1.0 MΩ.
- Test 3: includes Isolator 3, the distribution cable indicated black, DB3 with all circuit breakers on and all the final circuits indicated in black. Minimum value 1.0 MΩ.

Insulation resistance (MΩ)	
Live-Live	Live-E
O	P
>299	>299

Courtesy of the ECA

Figure 4.32 *Recorded results for the insulation resistance tests*

Where the resistance exceeds the maximum range of the instrument the display will have an indication of this. This indication will vary from manufacturer to manufacturer with some manufacturers using a > symbol, others a ↑ symbol and so on. In such an event the result should be recorded on the Schedule of Test Results as greater than the instrument maximum for example > 299 MΩ as in Figure 4.32.

Try this

Produce a bullet point summary of the full process for carrying out an insulation resistance test on a new 230 V single phase installation.

Summary of the insulation resistance test.

- ______________________________
- ______________________________
- ______________________________
- ______________________________

- ____________________
- ____________________
- ____________________
- ____________________
- ____________________
- ____________________
- ____________________
- ____________________
- ____________________
- ____________________
- ____________________

Part 5 Electrical separation, barriers and enclosures

Electrical separation is a recognized method of providing shock protection as an alternative to ADS. BS 7671 identifies that electrical separation for circuits supplying more than one item of equipment are to be under the control of skilled or instructed persons. This means they are not generally used and are not suitable for installations in dwellings. As these are considered as installations used in exceptional circumstances we will not consider these in depth in this studybook.

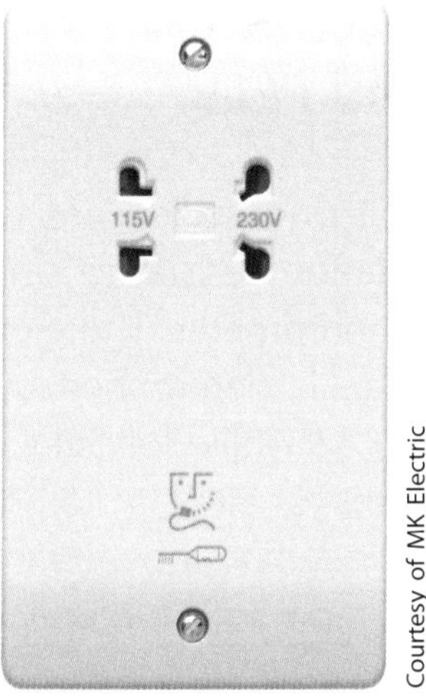

Figure 4.33 *Typical bathroom shaver socket*

Electrical separation may be used in an installation to supply one item of equipment and the most common example of this is the use of the shaver socket in domestic bathrooms. The shaver socket includes an isolating transformer to BS EN 61558-2-6 and supplies the one item of equipment, the shaver.

There are a number of supply options which may be used for electrical separation but the basis of the shaver socket is the use of an isolating transformer which electrically separates the primary supply from the secondary output.

SELV and PELV, whilst alternative sources of supply are acceptable, generally incorporate the use of an isolating transformer manufactured to BS EN 61558-2-6. A test to confirm isolation is required to confirm the separation of the secondary circuit from the primary circuit and all other circuits not supplied through the transformer. As electrical separation is used only in special circumstances we will consider the tests to be applied where SELV or PELV are used.

BS 7671 requires the separated secondary side to be either:

- Installed separated from all other circuits either by distance or within separate enclosure

  or
- Insulated to the highest voltage present.

Tests for electrical separation for SELV and PELV

The tests to be undertaken are very similar to those for insulation resistance using an insulation resistance ohmmeter. The electrical separation test voltage is determined by the primary LV voltage and so whilst for SELV and PELV the circuit voltage is ≤ 50 V ac or 120 V dc, the test voltage is based on the primary voltage, typically 230 V ac, and so the test is carried out at 500 V dc.

For SELV, the test is carried out between:

- All the SELV live conductors linked together and all the primary circuit live conductors linked together

  and
- All the SELV live conductors linked together and the primary circuit cpc.

Test voltage is generally 500 V dc.

Minimum acceptable value is 1.0 MΩ.

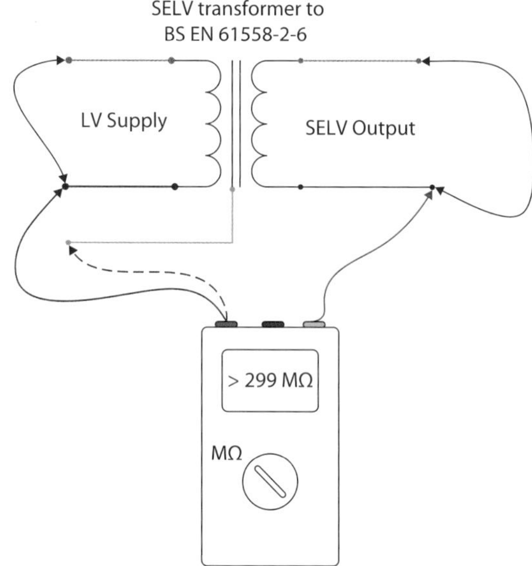

Figure 4.34 *Test for SELV separation*

The same process is followed for PELV but without the test to earth as the cpc continues to the PELV equipment.

Protection by barriers or enclosures

So far all of the tests have involved the use of instruments to electrically test the soundness of the installation. It is however possible to have the situation where equipment can pass the electrical tests but still leave live parts exposed to touch.

In order to ensure this is not the case tests are carried out to ensure that there is no possibility of contact with live parts. Such risks may arise as a result of modifications made to items of equipment, such as making entry holes into consumer units and accessories, in order to take cables into them.

There are two principal tests which may be undertaken and both refer to the requirements identified within the IP code.

The first requirement is that all barriers and enclosures must meet the requirements of IP XXB, and this involves the use of the 'standard finger' test probe.

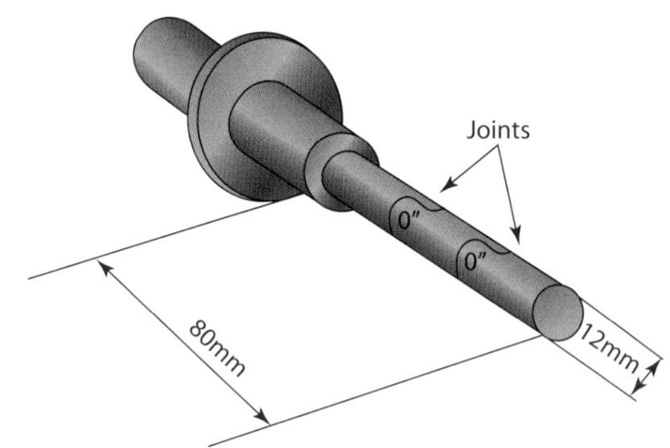

Figure 4.35 *The BS finger test probe*

The 'standard test finger' is capable of bending through 90° twice, as a normal finger does, and is intended to establish whether there is any possibility of contact with live parts through the insertion of a finger, without the risk of electric shock to the person carrying out the test.

The test finger forms part of a SELV circuit with an indicator lamp or buzzer. All the live parts within the enclosure are connected together to one side of the SELV output and the probe connected to the other output. When the probe is entered into the hole and rotated through the possible combinations, should it come into contact with a live part an indication is given by the lamp or buzzer.

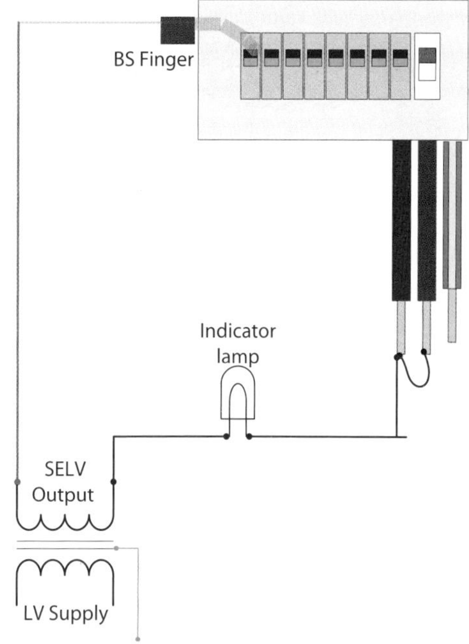

Figure 4.36 *BS Finger test circuit*

However, the general practice is to ensure that any holes are sealed and so meet the requirements of the IP code and therefore testing is not generally required.

The second test is applied to the top surfaces of enclosures and is more onerous than that required for IP 2X or IP XXB. For this test any opening on the top surface of the enclosure must offer protection against the entry of a wire or solid object larger than 1 mm in diameter (IP4X). Again a specific 1 mm diameter probe would be used for this test.

Should any of the openings fail to meet the requirements then the opening must be reduced to meet the requirements.

Remember

Providing the openings are of suitable size, and any unused openings are closed, a visual inspection will generally be sufficient to ensure the installation meets the requirements.

Note

The requirements of the IP code are covered in more detail in the *Termination and connection of conductors* studybook in this series.

Try this

Draw the circuit diagram for the test to confirm electrical separation of a SELV circuit from the LV supply.

Part 6 Polarity

Polarity testing

When we were carrying out the $R_1 + R_2$ testing earlier in this studybook it was stated that we could use this method to confirm the polarity of circuits being tested. The long lead test can also be used, only on this occasion the lead is connected to the line conductor and the test is to each line connection on the circuit. We have to ensure that:

- All single pole protective and control devices are connected in the line conductors only
- The centre pin of ES lampholders are connected to the line conductor only
- All equipment and socket outlets are correctly connected.

This must be done before the installation is connected to the supply.

All single pole switches, overcurrent protection devices and control contacts must be in the line conductor.

If we consider a circuit where this is not the case then the circuit and equipment will not be isolated when the switch or circuit breaker is off or the fuse removed and so the circuit cannot be made safe. A further implication is that if the protective device is used for fault protection and is connected in the neutral conductor, then a fault to earth will not be detected and the protective device will not operate. The fault path in Figure 4.37 demonstrates this.

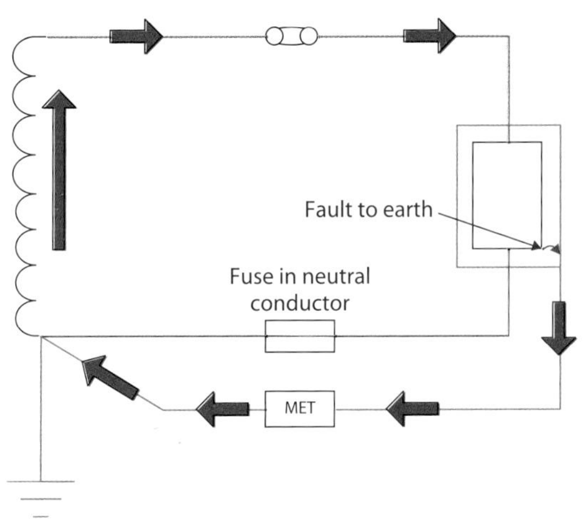

Figure 4.37 *The fault path with the fuse in the neutral conductor*

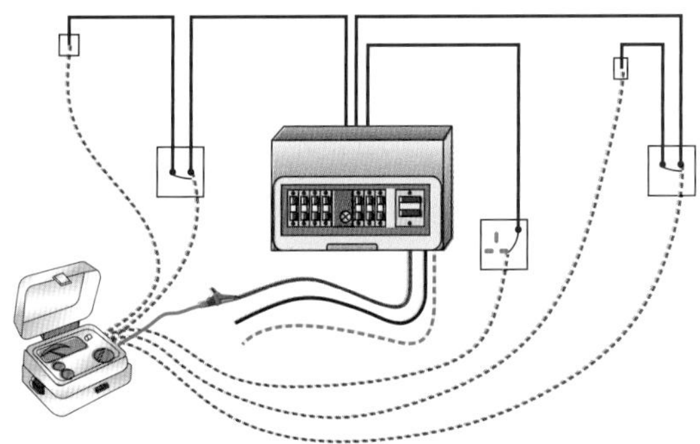

Figure 4.38 *Polarity testing*

Polarity tests are normally carried out using a low resistance ohmmeter. There is no requirement to record readings as this is a check to ensure that the conductors are correctly connected. However the successful result is recorded on the Schedule of Test Results as a ✓.

Insulation resistance (MΩ)		Polarity	$Z_s(\Omega)$
Live-Live	Live-E	✓	Ω
O	P	Q	R
		✓	

Courtesy of the ECA

Figure 4.39 *Correct polarity recorded on the Schedule of Test Results*

Many commercial and industrial installations are connected to a three phase supply and many include some three phase loads. Control devices and isolators used in these circuits must switch the three phases simultaneously so that a single phase cannot be left connected.

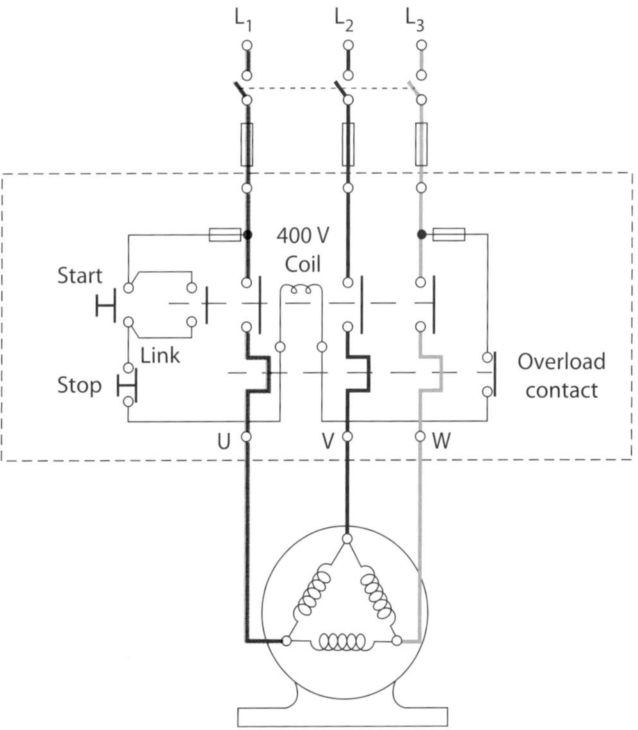

Figure 4.40 *Three phase direct-on-line starter with a triple pole switch fuse*

Try this

State the three conditions which are to be checked when carrying out a test to confirm polarity.

1 ____

____

2 ____

____

3 ____

____

Part 7 Earth electrode resistance

This particular test is carried out to confirm the resistance of earth electrodes (R_A) and there are two methods of doing this. One method involves a dead test which we shall consider here and the other a live test which is covered in the next chapter of this studybook.

The dead test method using an earth electrode resistance tester:

- **Must** be used for earth electrodes for generators and transformers
- May be used for installation earth electrodes.

The live test method can only be used where:

- The installation and the installation earth electrode form part of a TT system

  and
- The installation is protected by an RCD.

Earth electrode test instrument method

This method involves the use of a test instrument specifically designed for the purpose. There are two main types of instrument for this, one having three terminals, the other having four terminals. The four terminal instrument requires two of the terminals to be connected to the electrode being tested. A three lead instrument does this internally and requires only the one connection to the electrode. You should refer to the individual manufacturer's instructions to ensure the correct connection of the test instrument.

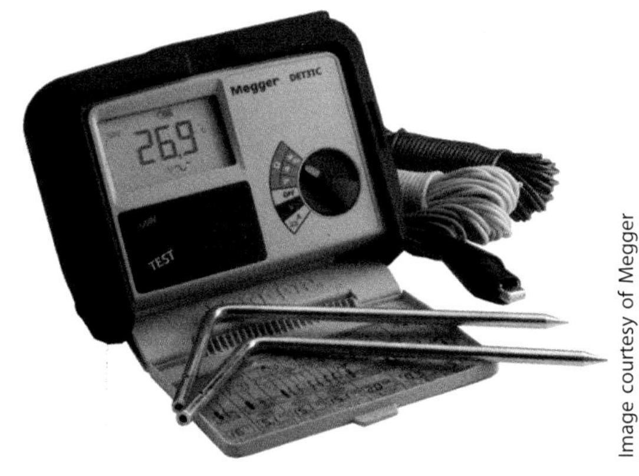

Image courtesy of Megger

Figure 4.41 *Earth electrode test instrument*

The remainder of the requirements are the same for both tests and so we shall consider the test instrument with three terminals for ease of reference.

Remember

The connection of the instrument may vary from one manufacturer to another so always check the instructions to ensure the connections are correctly made before testing begins.

This test is carried out with the earth electrode disconnected from the installation so it is important to obtain permission and safely isolate and lock off the main isolator for the installation before disconnecting the earthing conductor.

Remember

Even when the installation is completely new the supply may still be available at the main isolator and it is important to ensure that the installation cannot be energized during this test. The inspector will not have control over the main isolator as the test is undertaken outside.

For this test it is often helpful to make the required connection directly to the earth electrode and with the earthing conductor disconnected from the main earthing terminal. The test is then carried out at the earth electrode. The test may be made from the earthing conductor but due to the nature of the test this often proves difficult to achieve.

Two additional test electrodes are used for the test:

- The first, the current electrode, installed 10 × the length of the installation earth electrode away from the electrode being tested
- The second, the voltage electrode, is installed halfway between the installation earth electrode and the current electrode.

During the test there are three measurements to be taken and these are performed as described above and then with the voltage electrode 10 per cent further away from, and then 10 per cent closer to, the installation electrode as shown in Figure 4.42.

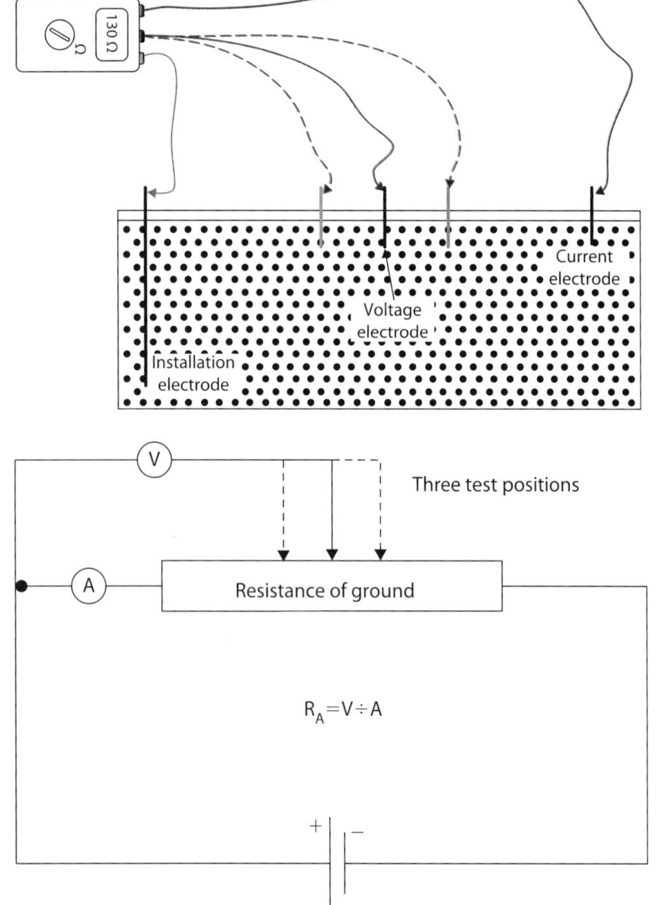

Figure 4.42 *Earth electrode resistance test*

If the installation electrode is 3 m long then the arrangement would be:

- Current electrode at 30 m
- Voltage electrode at 15 m, 18 m and 12 m from the installation electrode.

The principal of the test is that the instrument passes current between the two outside electrodes and measures the voltage drop across the connection to earth of the installation electrode and the centre electrode.

This provides enough information for the instrument to calculate and display the resistance of the electrode, in ohms, on the instrument scale.

This test is repeated with the centre electrode approximately 3 m closer to and 3 m further away from the installation electrode.

If these three tests produce results that are substantially the same, within 5 per cent, then an average of the results should be calculated and recorded as the electrode resistance for the installation.

When a potential is applied to an earth electrode, either during a test or under fault conditions, there is a voltage gradient produced around the earth electrode. The resistance of the ground rises in a similar pattern and the effect of this is shown in Figure 4.43. The test measurements need to be outside the area of the voltage and resistance gradients to ensure an accurate result.

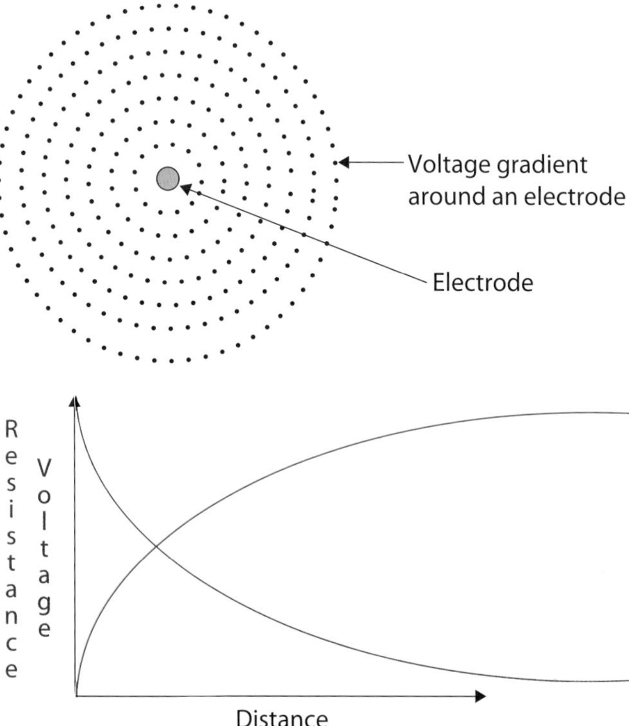

Figure 4.43 *Voltage gradient around an earth electrode*

If the results are not substantially in agreement, within 5 per cent (this is covered in the example calculation opposite), it indicates that the resistance areas of the electrodes are overlapping. The current electrode must be moved further away from the installation earth electrode and the series of tests repeated.

The main drawback to this method of testing is that it requires a considerable amount of open space adjacent to the installation. This space needs to be suitable for the installation of the test electrodes at the three locations, so metalled car parks, footpaths and the like are not suitable.

As a result, whilst this method has to be used for generator and transformer electrodes the occasions where this is used for installation earth electrodes are relatively few. Installation earth electrodes are generally tested using an earth fault loop impedance test instrument.

For TT systems the term R_A is used for the resistance of the earth electrode and the protective conductor connecting it to the exposed conductive parts (the earthing conductor). As the resistance of the earthing conductor is usually very low we will consider the term as the resistance of the earth electrode.

Example: An earth electrode resistance test on an installation earth electrode, where the installation is protected by a 100 mA RCD, produced the following results: 130 Ω, 135 Ω and 126 Ω. The value to be recorded as R_A will be the average value of the resistances:

$$\frac{R1 + R2 + R3}{3} = \frac{130 + 135 + 126}{3} = \frac{391}{3} = 130.33\,\Omega$$

Five per cent of the average value is 6.5 Ω and as all the measured values are within 6.5 Ω the test result is considered within the accuracy tolerance and so no further action is required. The result is recorded on the Electrical Installation Certificate and the information to be entered is shown in Figure 4.44.

Having completed the earth electrode resistance test the test result needs to be verified to confirm it meets the requirements of BS 7671. BS 7671 states that $R_A \times I_{\Delta n} \leq 50$ V, with the 50 V being the maximum touch voltage, and we can see from this that the maximum acceptable earth electrode resistance depends on the $I_{\Delta n}$ rating of the RCD.

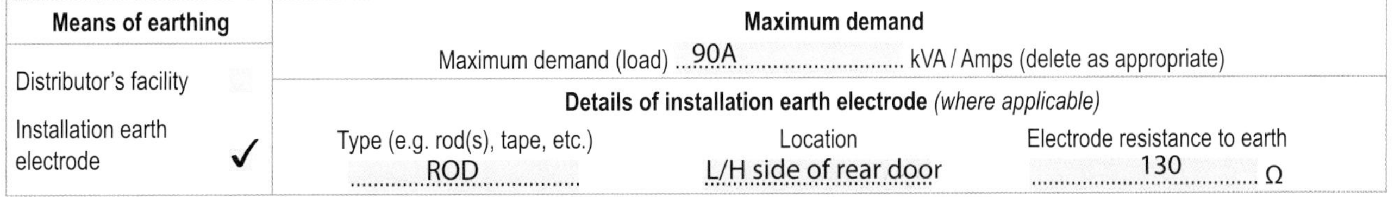
PARTICULARS OF INSTALLATION REFERRED TO IN THE CERTIFICATE — Tick boxes and enter details as appropriate

Means of earthing		Maximum demand		
Distributor's facility		Maximum demand (load) ...90A... kVA / Amps (delete as appropriate)		
		Details of installation earth electrode *(where applicable)*		
Installation earth electrode	✓	Type (e.g. rod(s), tape, etc.) ROD	Location L/H side of rear door	Electrode resistance to earth 130 Ω

Courtesy of the ECA

Figure 4.44 *Details recorded following the earth electrode resistance test*

The maximum acceptable R_A can be determined from:

$$R_A(\text{max}) = \frac{50\,\text{V}}{I_{\Delta n}}.$$

So for our example the maximum R_A would be:

$$\frac{50\,\text{V}}{100\,\text{mA}} = \frac{50}{0.1} = 500\,\Omega.$$

As the actual R_A is 130 Ω this is acceptable.

The maximum R_A values for an installation earth electrode for the most common RCD ratings are given in Figure 4.45.

Maximum earth electrode resistance values	
RCD $I_{\Delta n}$	Maximum R_A in Ω
30 mA	1667 Ω*
100 mA	500 Ω*
300 mA	167 Ω
500 mA	100 Ω

* See Note

Figure 4.45 *Maximum R_A values for the common RCD ratings*

In some circumstances it may be necessary to have an RCD rated differently and the $R_A(\text{max}) = \frac{50\,\text{V}}{I_{\Delta n}}$ formula may be used to determine the requirements. By transposing the formula we are able to determine the maximum RCD rating for a given earth electrode resistance using $I_{\Delta n}\,(\text{max}) = \frac{50\,\text{V}}{R_A}$.

Note

BS 7671 gives the following information: ***'The resistance of the installation earth electrode should be as low as practicable. A value exceeding 200 Ω may not be stable.'***

The test should be carried out in the normal environmental conditions for the location and allowance must be made for changes in soil conditions such as drying and freezing. BS 7671 also advises that values exceeding 200 Ω may not be stable and so for the 30 mA and 100 mA RCDs in Figure 4.45 we should be aiming to achieve a value of less than 200 Ω.

Part 6 of BS 7671 identifies in a note to the regulation for earth electrode resistance that: *'Where a measurement of R_A is not practicable the measured value of the external earth fault loop impedance may be used'*. For most installations protected by an RCD and forming part of a TT system the resistance of the earth electrode is carried out using an earth fault loop impedance tester and this requires the supply to be available for the test. The earth electrode resistance test method may be appropriate for such installations where there is no supply available. The live test is covered in the next chapter of this studybook.

Try this

A test to determine the resistance of an installation earth electrode produced the following results: 141 Ω, 146 Ω and 137Ω. The installation is protected by a 300 mA RCD.

Determine:

a **The value of earth electrode resistance to be recorded on the certificate.**

____

____

b **If the results are suitably accurate.**

____

____

c **Whether the recorded value meets the requirements for the RCD installed.**

____

____

Congratulations, you have finished this chapter of the studybook. Complete the self assessment questions before continuing to Chapter 5.

SELF ASSESSMENT

Circle the correct answers.

1 The instrument to be used when carrying out a test to confirm continuity of protective conductors is a:

a. Continuity tester
b. Multifunction tester
c. Low resistance ohmmeter
d. High resistance ohmmeter

2 A ring final circuit wired in 2.5 mm^2 cable has a conductor length of 50 m. When measuring the continuity of the line conductor the resistance will be approximately:

a. 0.03 Ω
b. 0.37 Ω
c. 3.7 Ω
d. 37 Ω

3 When carrying out continuity tests it is essential that the:

a. Test leads are nulled
b. Building is unoccupied
c. Installation is energized
d. Earthing conductor is disconnected

4 The insulation resistance test on a circuit operating at 240 V should be at a test voltage of:

a. 250 V dc
b. 500 V dc
c. 750 V dc
d. 1000 V dc

5 When an insulation resistance test is carried out on a complete installation a lower than acceptable reading may be due to:

a. The resistance of the conductors
b. An RCD being used in the installation
c. An open circuit in a continuity bonding
d. The total length of the cables being tested

6 When a polarity test is carried out one of the items to be confirmed is that all single pole switches are connected in:

a. The line conductor
b. The neutral conductor
c. Series to ensure safe operation
d. Either the line or neutral conductor

7 When measuring the resistance of an earth electrode where there is no supply available the minimum number of test readings to be taken is:

a. 2
b. 3
c. 4
d. 5

8 The value to be recorded on the certificate following an earth electrode resistance test is the:

a. highest resistance
b. lowest resistance
c. average resistance
d. sum of the resistances

Testing and commissioning an installation (Part 2)

RECAP

Before you start work on this chapter, complete the exercise below to ensure that you remember what you learned earlier.

- Test instruments should be regularly ___________ and checked for ___________ accuracy.
- Tests for continuity are carried out using a _____________ resistance _____________ and the test leads should be ____________________ to ensure accurate results.
- The two methods for confirming continuity of protective conductors are the ___________ method and the _____________ lead or _____________ method.
- The test voltage for an insulation resistance test on a circuit which operates at 230 V is ____________ and the minimum acceptable value is ____________.
- Insulation resistance _____________ as the length of cable _____________ and insulation resistance _____________ as the _____________ of cables connected in _____________ increases.
- When testing insulation resistance all loads must be _____________ or _____________ and electronic controls _______________.
- Insulation resistance tests are to be carried out between all _______________ conductors and all ________________ conductors and _______________.

- One of the purposes of a polarity test is to confirm that all ____________________ pole ______________ and ______________ devices are in the ______________ conductor only.
- An earth electrode resistance test instrument ______________ be used to determine the resistance of an earth electrode for a ____________________.
- The earth electrode resistance tester method of measurement requires an additional ______________ electrodes and a ______________ of ______________ test measurements.

LEARNING OBJECTIVES

On completion of this chapter you should be able to:

- Specify the methods for measuring earth electrode resistance and correctly interpreting the results.
- Identify the earth fault loop paths for the following systems:
  - TN-S
  - TN-C-S
  - TT.
- State the methods for verifying protection by automatic disconnection of the supply, including:
  - The measurement of the earth fault loop impedance (Z_s) and external impedance (Z_e)
  - Establish Z_e from enquiry
  - Calculate the value of Z_s from given information
  - Compare Z_s and the maximum tabulated figures as specified in the Requirements for Electrical Installations.
- Specify the methods for:
  - Determining prospective fault current
  - Testing the correct operation of residual current devices (RCDs).
- State the methods used to check for the correct phase sequence and explain why having the correct phase sequence is important.

- State the need for functional testing and identify items which need to be checked.
- Specify the methods used for verification of voltage drop and state the cause of volt drop in an electrical installation.
- State the appropriate procedures for dealing with customers and clients during the commissioning and certification process, including:
  - Ensuring the safety of customers and clients during the completion of work activities
  - Keeping customers and clients informed during the process
  - Labelling electrical circuits, systems and equipment that is yet to be commissioned
  - Providing customers and clients with all appropriate documentation upon work completion.

Part 1 Supply polarity and earth electrode testing

This chapter considers the requirements for the testing of electrical systems at initial verification once the supply is connected. This includes the requirements for the test instruments to be used, the sequence of testing and the recording and verification of results.

Whilst working through this chapter you will need to refer to BS 7671, Requirements for electrical installations, IET Guidance Note 3 (GN3) Inspection and Testing and Health and Safety Executive Guidance, HSE GS 38; Electrical Test Equipment used by Electricians. You will also need to refer to manufacturers' information from catalogues or online.

In this chapter we will consider the initial verification process to be carried out once the supply is connected. It is important to remember that at this stage the supply is only used to allow the inspector to carry out the necessary live tests and it is not until these tests are complete and the results verified that the installation can be placed into service.

Incoming supply polarity

Before any live testing is undertaken the inspector should first confirm that the incoming supply to the installation is correct polarity. Having carried out confirmation of polarity throughout the installation we need to confirm the supply polarity is correct, otherwise the whole installation will be incorrect polarity despite all previous tests.

Figure 5.1 *Approved Voltage Indicator*

The polarity is confirmed using an Approved Voltage Indicator which meets all the requirements of HSE Guidance GS 38. The check for polarity is carried out at the incoming terminals of the main isolator and is carried out between:

- All live conductors
- All live conductors and earth.

For a single phase installation this is between line and neutral, line and earth, and neutral and earth. On a three phase installation the check is carried out between L_1 and L_2, L_1 and L_3, L_2 and L_3, L_1 and N, L_2 and N, L_3 and N, L_1 and E, L_2 and E, L_3 and E, and N and E.

For a three phase 400/230 V supply the result should be approximately, allowing for the DNO's permitted tolerances:

- L_1 and L_2, L_1 and L_3, L_2 and L_3 = 400 V
- L_1 and N, L_2 and N, L_3 and N = 230 V
- L_1 and E, L_2 and E, L_3 and E = 230 V
- N and E = 0 V.

For a single phase 230 V supply the result should be between:

- L and N = 230 V
- L and E = 230 V
- N and E = 0 V.

The result of this check is recorded as a tick on the Electrical Installation Certificate.

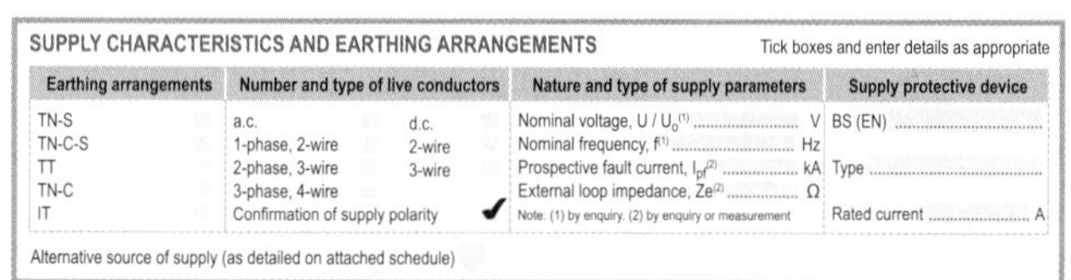

SUPPLY CHARACTERISTICS AND EARTHING ARRANGEMENTS — Tick boxes and enter details as appropriate

Earthing arrangements	Number and type of live conductors		Nature and type of supply parameters	Supply protective device
TN-S	a.c.	d.c.	Nominal voltage, $U / U_0^{(1)}$ V	BS (EN) ....
TN-C-S	1-phase, 2-wire	2-wire	Nominal frequency, $f^{(1)}$ .... Hz	
TT	2-phase, 3-wire	3-wire	Prospective fault current, $I_{pf}^{(2)}$ .... kA	Type ....
TN-C	3-phase, 4-wire		External loop impedance, $Ze^{(2)}$ .... Ω	
IT	Confirmation of supply polarity ✔		Note: (1) by enquiry. (2) by enquiry or measurement	Rated current .... A

Alternative source of supply (as detailed on attached schedule)

Courtesy of the ECA

Figure 5.2 *Supply polarity confirmed*

Having confirmed that the incoming supply polarity is correct we can continue with the live tests.

Earth electrode resistance test

In Chapter 4 we covered the process of testing the earth electrode resistance using an earth electrode resistance tester. For electrical installations protected by an RCD and forming part of a TT system we may measure R_A using an earth fault loop impedance tester.

Whilst this method is not as accurate as the earth electrode resistance tester method BS 7671 does acknowledge this as an acceptable method in these circumstances and it is considerably easier to carry out in most cases.

We need to consider just what it is we are testing using this method and this is shown in Figure 5.3.

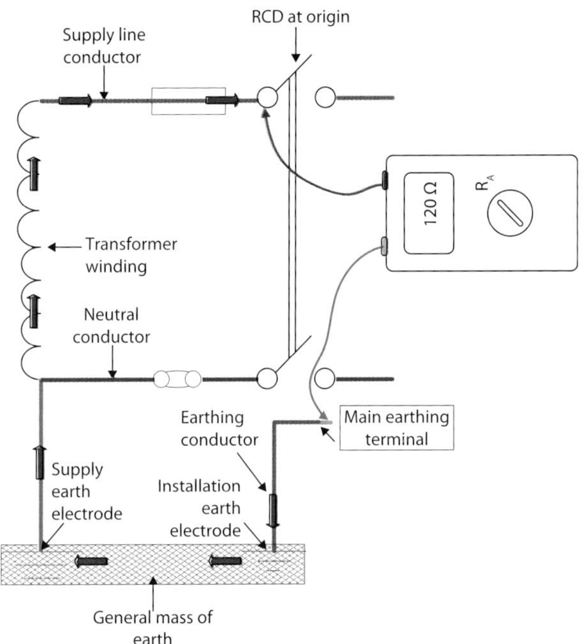

Figure 5.3 *An earth electrode resistance test using an earth fault loop impedance tester*

The greatest resistance in the earth fault path is that of the electrode and the general mass of earth, with the supply conductor and transformer adding little resistance. Many instruments carry out this test using two leads only but some require the neutral connection for the instrument to function.

To carry out this test the earthing conductor must be disconnected from the main earthing terminal and so it is essential the installation is isolated from the supply before the earthing conductor is disconnected.

Remember

A test for insulation resistance is carried out with the exposed conductive parts connected to earth so all the protective conductors should be connected. The earthing conductor must now be disconnected from the MET for the external fault path to be measured.

The instrument that is used for this test is an earth fault loop impedance tester and as this is a live test it is essential that the test leads comply with the requirements of HSE Guidance GS 38. Once the installation has been safely isolated and locked off and the earthing conductor has been disconnected, the test instrument is connected to the disconnected earthing conductor and then to the incoming line terminal of the RCD main switch. The test is carried out and the instrument is disconnected in the reverse order. The earthing conductor must then be reconnected to the main earthing terminal.

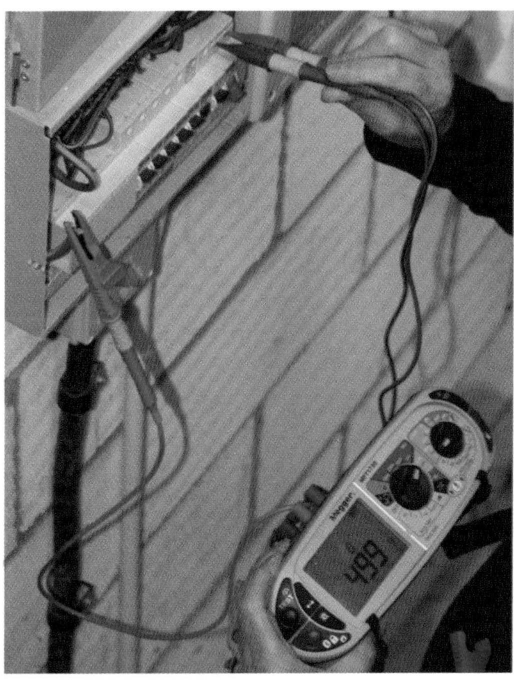

Figure 5.4 *Testing R_A using an earth fault loop impedance tester method*

Remember

Some test instruments will require a connection to the incoming neutral of the RCD in addition to the connections to the incoming line and disconnected earthing conductor.

The test result is recorded on the Electrical Installation Certificate.

PARTICULARS OF INSTALLATION REFERRED TO IN THE CERTIFICATE Tick boxes and enter details as appropriate

Means of earthing	Maximum demand		
Distributor's facility	Maximum demand (load) 90A kVA / Amps (delete as appropriate)		
	Details of installation earth electrode (*where applicable*)		
Installation earth electrode ✓	Type (e.g. rod(s), tape, etc.) ROD	Location L/H side of rear door	Electrode resistance to earth 130 Ω

Courtesy of the ECA

Figure 5.5 *Details recorded following the earth electrode resistance test*

Having completed the earth electrode resistance test the test result needs to be verified to confirm it meets the requirements of BS 7671. BS 7671 states that $R_A \times I_{\Delta n} \leq 50$ V, with the 50 V being the maximum touch voltage, and we can see from this that the maximum acceptable earth electrode resistance depends on the $I_{\Delta n}$ rating of the RCD.

The maximum acceptable R_A can be determined from $R_A(\text{max}) = \frac{50\text{ V}}{I_{\Delta n}}$.

So, for example, the maximum R_A for a 300 mA RCD would be $\frac{50\text{ V}}{300\text{ mA}} = \frac{50}{0.3} = 167\ \Omega$.

The maximum R_A values for an installation earth electrode for the most common RCD ratings are given in Figure 5.6.

Maximum earth electrode resistance values	
RCD $I_{\Delta n}$	Maximum R_A in Ω
30 mA	1667 Ω★
100 mA	500 Ω★
300 mA	167 Ω
500 mA	100 Ω

Figure 5.6 *Maximum R_A values*

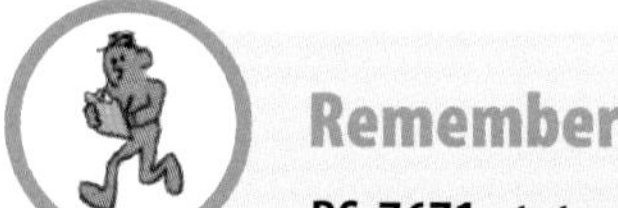

Remember

BS 7671 states that values above 200 Ω (★) may prove to be unreliable.

We have effectively carried out an external earth fault loop impedance (Z_e) test at the origin of a TT installation.

Try this

Produce a bullet point summary of the full process for carrying out an earth electrode resistance test using the earth fault loop impedance tester method.

Summary of the earth electrode resistance test:

- ____________________
- ____________________
- ____________________
- ____________________
- ____________________
- ____________________

- ____________________
- ____________________
- ____________________
- ____________________
- ____________________
- ____________________

Part 2 Earth fault loop impedance testing

The live tests are listed in a particular sequence in BS 7671 but the standard does not require these tests to be carried out in the exact sequence in which they are listed. However, there are some basic principles which need to be applied to the test sequence which we shall discuss as we work through the tests.

Earth fault loop impedance testing

The earth fault loop impedance test is the first in the sequence of live tests and can be considered in two separate stages:

- External earth fault loop impedance (Z_e)
- System earth fault loop impedance (Z_s).

External earth fault loop impedance (Z_e)

The test to confirm Z_e is the first to be carried out and the purpose of this test is to confirm that the earth path provided by the distribution network is present and that the value is within the defined limits.

This particular test is vital to confirm that there is a suitable return path from the electrical installation to the source earth of the system. Other tests which are subsequently carried out will involve introducing a potential on the exposed and extraneous conductive parts of the electrical installation. If there is no return path to Earth then there is a considerable risk of electric shock to the inspector and anyone else within the premises. For this reason it is essential that this is the first in the sequence of live tests carried out.

The DNO provides details of the maximum earth fault loop values for the public distribution network as:

- TN-S = 0.8 Ω
- TN-C-S = 0.35 Ω.

When testing Z_e the expected result should be ≤ the stated values.

Note

A value of 21 Ω is sometimes given by the DNO for a TT system. This is NOT the external earth fault loop impedance for the system, it is the maximum earth electrode resistance for the supply electrode at the DNO transformer. In the majority of cases the actual supply earth electrode resistance is considerably lower than this.

Remember

The DNO is not obliged to provide an earth connection and if they are unable to provide a connection within the declared parameters they can decline to provide an earth connection. The consumer then has to provide the earth for the installation and the supply will become TT.

The test instrument used is the earth fault loop impedance tester and the test procedure is exactly the same as that used for the earth electrode test carried out at the beginning of this chapter.

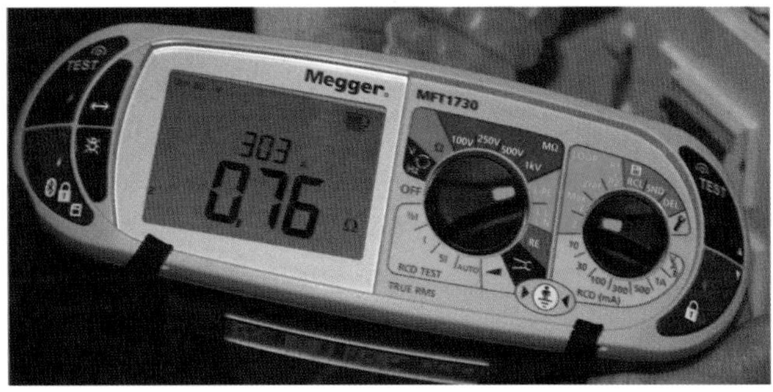

Figure 5.7 *Set to measure Z_e*

As the earthing conductor is to be disconnected for this test, permission will be required from the responsible person before the installation is isolated. When adding to an existing installation the measurement of Z_e will require the existing installation to be isolated at a convenient time, hence agreement and permission from the responsible person is required. With a completely new installation it will not generally be a consideration as the installation has still to be energized and placed in service.

Once the permission has been given the installation is safely isolated and locked off. The earthing conductor is then disconnected from the MET. The earth fault loop impedance tester is checked for calibration and to ensure it is not damaged. The test leads and probes are checked to ensure they comply with the requirements of GS 38. The test instrument is connected to the disconnected earthing conductor and the incoming line terminal of the main switch. The test is undertaken and the result recorded on the Electrical Installation Certificate. The earthing conductor is then reconnected before the installation is energized for the other live tests.

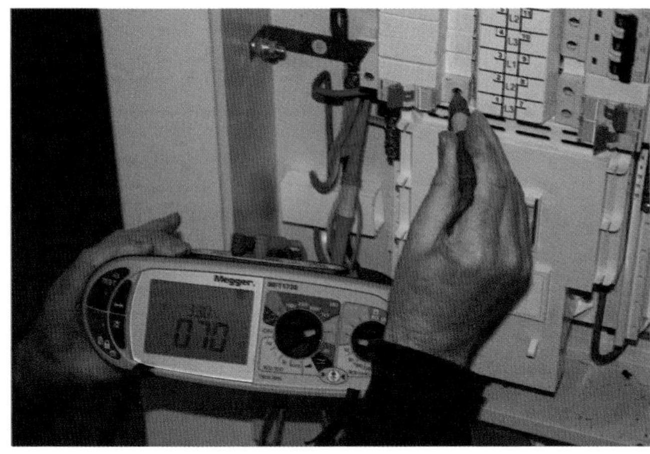

Figure 5.8 *Test between the incoming supply terminals and the earthing conductor*

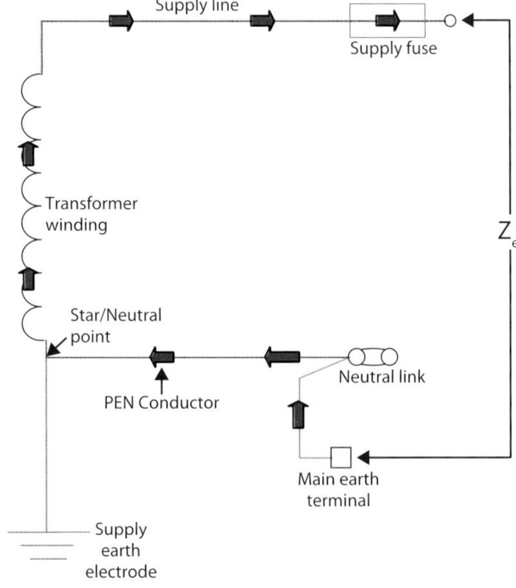

Figure 5.9 *Z_e circuit for a TN-C-S system*

The result is compared to the DNO maximum value to ensure that the external earth fault loop path is acceptable.

The result of the test is then recorded on the Electrical Installation Certificate.

SUPPLY CHARACTERISTICS AND EARTHING ARRANGEMENTS — Tick boxes and enter details as appropriate

Earthing arrangements	Number and type of live conductors		Nature and type of supply parameters	Supply protective device
TN-S	a.c.	d.c.	Nominal voltage, U / U_0[1] V	BS (EN) ....
TN-C-S	1-phase, 2-wire	2-wire	Nominal frequency, f[1] .... Hz	
TT	2-phase, 3-wire	3-wire	Prospective fault current, I_{pf}[2] .... kA	Type ....
TN-C	3-phase, 4-wire		External loop impedance, Ze[2] ...0.25... Ω	
IT	Confirmation of supply polarity		Note: (1) by enquiry. (2) by enquiry or measurement	Rated current .... A

Alternative source of supply (as detailed on attached schedule)

Courtesy of the ECA

Figure 5.10 *Z_e recorded on the Electrical Installation Certificate*

Remember

Z_e is the first test to be carried out with the supply energized as it is essential to confirm that the earth return path is present and acceptable before any other tests are carried out.

System earth fault loop impedance (Z_S)

We will consider the testing of Z_S at this point but in practice this may not be the most appropriate time to undertake this test.

The reasons for this are that when testing Z_e we had to remove covers at the origin to access the main switch incoming terminals. When testing Z_S we have to test at the furthest point on every radial circuit and every accessible socket outlet on ring final circuits. To do this safely we will need to reassemble the switchgear at the origin of the installation. We will then need to dismantle the switchgear again to carry out the test for prospective fault current (PFC) at the origin. In practice it is generally accepted that the PFC tests are carried out before Z_S to save this assembling and dismantling process.

The earth fault loop impedance Z_S is carried out for each circuit to confirm that the impedance is low enough to allow the protective device to disconnect within the required time. In the event of a fault to earth the fault path consists of the circuit line conductor and cpc ($R_1 + R_2$) and the external earth fault loop path (Z_e) and so we can determine the expected Z_S value for a circuit using the formula $Z_S = Z_e + (R_1 + R_2)$. The test is carried out with the conductors at a temperature considerably lower than their normal operating temperature as they are not in service or carrying the full load current.

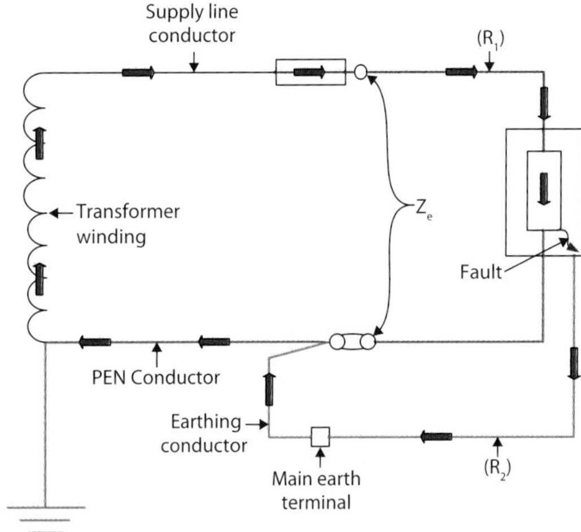

Figure 5.11 *TN-C-S earth fault loop path [$Z_S = Z_e + (R_1 + R_2)$]*

BS 7671 provides maximum earth fault loop impedance values for the different types of protective device and disconnection times. These values are given at the normal operating temperature of the conductors and as the test will be at a lower temperature we must compensate for the temperature difference.

Remember

The resistance of conductors used in electrical installations increase as temperature increases. It may take several hours on load for a conductor to reach its normal operating temperature at which the conductor resistance will be at its highest.

One method of compensating for the difference between the conductor temperature at the time of testing and the normal operating temperature of the conductor is to apply a multiplier of 0.8 to the BS 7671 tabulated values.

Task

Familiarize yourself with Tables 41.2 to 41.4 in BS 7671 before continuing with this chapter.

Example: A circuit installed using thermoplastic insulated conductors is protected by a 32 A BS EN 60898, Type B circuit breaker. From the table in BS 7671 the maximum earth fault loop impedance is 1.44 Ω. This is at the operating temperature of the conductor which in this case is 70 °C. To compensate for the difference between the normal operating temperature and the conductor temperature when the test was carried out we must use the multiplier (referred to as the rule of thumb). So the maximum measured Z_s = 1.44 × 0.8 = 1.152 Ω.

This process would need to be applied for each test undertaken to determine whether the measured Z_s is acceptable and so provide disconnection within the required time.

Alternatively, we can use temperature corrected values for the maximum measured Z_s which can be found in IET Guidance Note 3, Inspection and Testing and the IET On-Site Guide. Many instrument manufacturers and industry bodies, such as the Electrical Contractors Association and the NICEIC, publish temperature corrected earth fault loop impedance tables which may be used with their forms of certification.

The values given in Guidance Note 3 have been adjusted to compensate for the conductor temperature difference and so a direct comparison can be made between the measured value and the GN3 tabulated values. We can see that the figure for the circuit in our example is 1.16 Ω which is slightly higher than our calculated figure. This is because the GN3 tables are determined for testing at an ambient temperature of 10 °C and a divisor of 1.24 is used for the compensation so $\frac{1.44\ \Omega}{1.24} = 1.1613\ \Omega$ or 1.16 Ω when rounded to 2 decimal places.

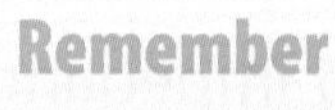

Remember

BS 7671 classifies types of circuits for disconnection times and these are:

- **Final circuits rated ≤ 32 A require disconnection within 0.4 seconds for TN systems and 0.2 seconds for TT systems**
- **Distribution circuits and final circuits rated > 32 A require disconnection within 5 seconds for TN systems and 2 seconds for TT systems.**

Task

Familiarize yourself with Table B4 in Appendix B of the IET Guidance Note 3 before continuing with this chapter.

Task

Using BS 7671 note the maximum tabulated earth fault loop impedances for the following:

1 For final circuits up to 32 A protected by BS EN 60898 Type B circuit breakers.

a 5 A

____

____

b 15 A

____

____

c 32 A

____

____

2 For distribution circuits protected by BS88-3 Fuses.

a 20 A

____

____

b 32 A

____

____

In order to carry out this test the circuit has to be energized and the inspector will have to access live terminals at the furthest point on radial circuits. Most instrument manufacturers produce an additional test lead with a 13 A plug fitted to carry out this test on ring and radial socket outlet circuits. Where this is not available the use of a plug-in adapter will be of considerable benefit when testing socket outlets.

The instrument used to carry out the test is the earth fault loop impedance tester and there are often two options for completing the test. The first is a test carried out at approximately 25 A and is often referred to as the high current test. The second option is a low current or 'no trip' test which uses a much lower current (mA) and is used where the circuit is protected by an RCD for example. This second option provides a less accurate result as interference from harmonics on the system and the use of very low current using repeated sampling does not produce the same effect on the system.

A problem can be encountered with some circuit breakers, such as BS EN 60898 6 A type B's, due to the level of current used for the high current test which may be over four times the rating of the device. Where such problems occur the value of Z_S should be determined by calculation as described later in this chapter.

Where testing is to be carried out on circuits which do not have socket outlets, access will be required to the live terminals at the furthest point on the radial circuit. Care will need to be taken and the inspector should ensure that the area around the test point is secured to prevent danger to the inspector and others during the process. It may be that the circuit will need to be isolated in order to safely access the live terminals and then be energized for the test. If this is the case then the area around the test point must be clearly identified and secured to prevent access by other people.

Remember

The furthest point on the circuit refers to the furthest point electrically and not necessarily the point furthest away from the origin. It will be the point where the highest $R_1 + R_2$ value was obtained.

The test procedure to carry out this test will require us to first identify the furthest point on the radial circuit and secure the area. Obtain access to the line and earth connection at this point and select an earth fault loop impedance tester. The usual checks will be carried out such as calibration, in date and not damaged, and the leads are compliant with GS 38. The test instrument is then connected to the earthing terminal and the line conductor, and the test carried out. The result is noted and the instrument connected and the circuit reinstated. The result is compared with the appropriate table to confirm the value is acceptable and then recorded on the Schedule of Test Results.

Test results							
Insulation resistance (MΩ)		Polarity	Z_s (Ω)	RCD (ms)			Remarks (continue on a separate sheet if necessary)
Live – Live	Live – E	✓	Ω	$@I_{\Delta n}$	$@5I_{\Delta n}$	Test button operation	
O	P	Q	R	S	T	U	V
			1.02				

Courtesy of the ECA

Figure 5.12 *Z_S recorded on the Schedule of Test Results*

Sometimes it is not practical or possible to measure the Z_S for a circuit. Under these circumstances it is acceptable to use the measured values of Z_e and $R_1 + R_2$ to calculate the Z_S for the circuit. This is possible because when carrying out both these tests there were no parallel paths connected. When Z_S is tested all the parallel paths are in place so the actual value may be slightly lower. If the calculation method is used to determine Z_S then this must be recorded on the Schedule of Test Results.

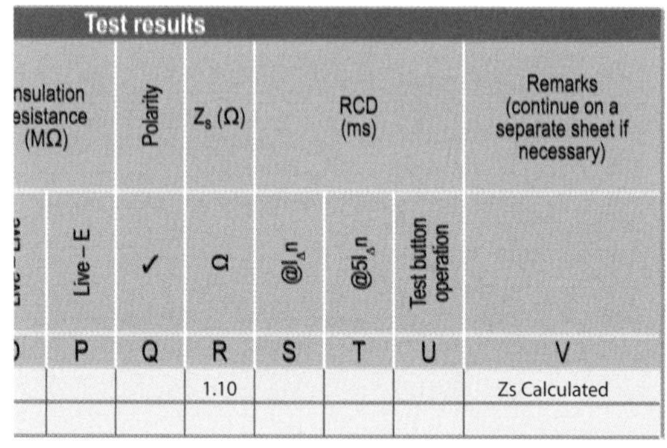

Test results							
nsulation esistance (MΩ)		Polarity	Z_s (Ω)	RCD (ms)			Remarks (continue on a separate sheet if necessary)
	Live – E	✓	Ω	$@I_{\Delta n}$	$@5I_{\Delta n}$	Test button operation	
)	P	Q	R	S	T	U	V
			1.10				Zs Calculated

Courtesy of the ECA

Figure 5.13 *Record showing Z_S calculated for this circuit*

Remember

Z_S can only be determined by calculation when both Z_e and $R_1 + R_2$ are actual measured values.

Task

Using the maximum tabulated earth fault loop impedances from BS 7671 determine the maximum measured Z_s values for the following.

1 For final circuits up to 32 A protected by BS EN 60898 Type B circuit breakers:

a 5 A

b 15 A

c 32 A

2 For distribution circuits protected by BS88-3 Fuses:

a 20 A

b 32 A

Try this

Produce a bullet point summary of the full process for carrying out an earth fault loop impedance test for a radial 13 A socket outlet circuit.

Summary of the earth fault loop impedance test:

- ________________________
- ________________________
- ________________________
- ________________________
- ________________________
- ________________________
- ________________________
- ________________________
- ________________________
- ________________________

Part 3 Prospective fault current testing

Prospective fault current

As mentioned earlier, once we have measured Z_e and reconnected the earthing and bonding conductors, we can also carry out the test to establish the prospective fault current (PFC) at the origin of the installation. We need to establish the PFC in order to ensure that the protective devices can safely disconnect the prospective fault current which is likely to occur at the point at which they are installed. This will require tests to be carried out at the origin of the installation and at any remote distribution boards.

PFC is the maximum fault current that will flow at any point on the installation if a fault having zero impedance occurs between live conductors or between live conductors and Earth. The maximum value for the installation will be at the supply intake position. Between which points this maximum fault current occurs will depend upon the type of system involved.

The PFC is generally determined by direct measurement but BS 7671 does allow the value to be determined by enquiry from the DNO or private supplier. The value provided by the DNO is going to be the maximum fault current that may occur at any consumer's connection to the system. This means that it could be considerably higher than the actual measured value.

The highest PFC will occur at the main intake position and we shall need to determine this value and record it on the certificate. In general terms the maximum values will be found between live conductors.

Single phase supply: TN or TT system line to neutral

Three phase supply: TN or TT system line to line.

However, on single phase systems the PFC should be tested between line and Earth with all the protective conductors of the installation connected.

Direct measurement of PFC is carried out using a PFC tester. This is often a function option on the earth fault loop impedance setting of a multifunction instrument. Some instruments display a loop impedance measurement and a PFC value simultaneously.

Remember

It is important that this is carried out with all the earthing and bonding conductors connected to the MET.

Some test instruments require three lead connections for this test function and the connection of the leads is important. The instrument manufacturer's instructions should always be followed when undertaking this test.

Single phase installation

The test is undertaken as close to the origin as is practical and so this is generally at the main isolator and MET. Using a PFC tester the instrument is checked to confirm that calibration is in date and it is not damaged. The test leads must be checked to confirm they comply with GS 38 and the instrument is then connected between the incoming line and neutral terminals of the main isolator and the value of the prospective short circuit current (PSCC) is measured. The instrument is then connected to the incoming line and the MET and the value of prospective earth fault current (PEFC) is measured. The highest of these fault currents is recorded as the PFC for the installation.

Note

With some three lead test instruments it may be necessary to test PSCC with both the neutral and earth connections for the test instrument connected to the neutral terminal. The instrument requires the neutral to function but tests between the line and earth terminals of the instrument. To test PSCC these two connections must be on the neutral terminal or the instrument will repeat the PEFC test.

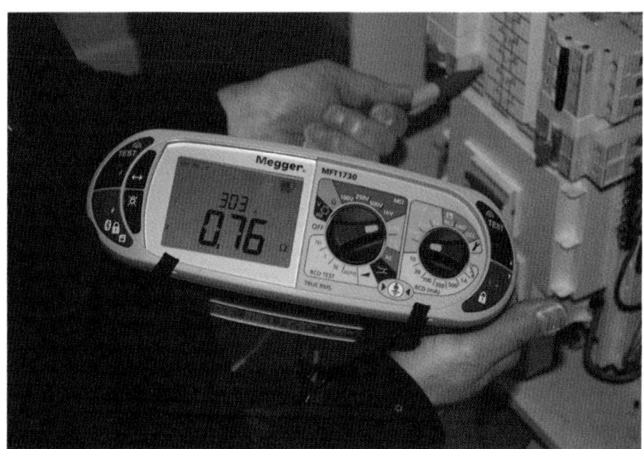

Figure 5.14a *Connections between line and Earth*

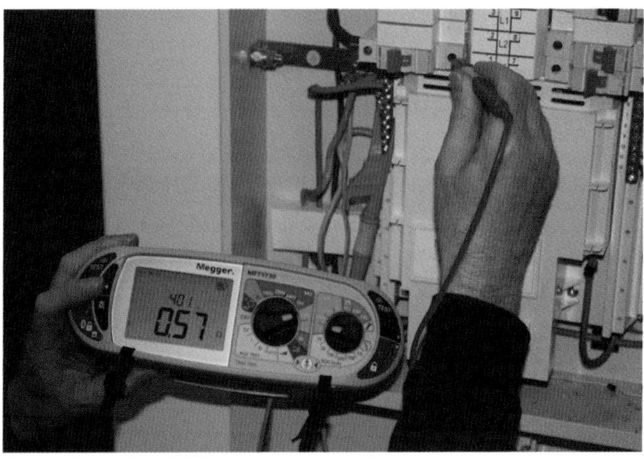

Figure 5.14b *Connections between line and neutral*

Calculation

Where a PFC test function is not available the PFC may be determined by measurement of the line to neutral and line to earth loop impedances and then calculated using Ohms law. The impedance values are measured using the same connections as the direct current readings, only the test result will be in Ohms. Once we have established the impedance values we can then determine the PFC by dividing the voltage, L-N and L-E by the respective impedance value. So if the L-N impedance was 0.04 Ω and the L-N voltage was 230 V then:

$$\text{PSCC} = \frac{230}{0.04} = 5750 \text{ A} = 5.75 \text{ kA}.$$

If the L-E impedance is 0.06 Ω and the L-E voltage 230 V then:

$$\text{PEFC} = \frac{230}{0.06} = 3830\text{A} = 3.83 \text{ kA}.$$

So the recorded PFC would be 5.75 kA.

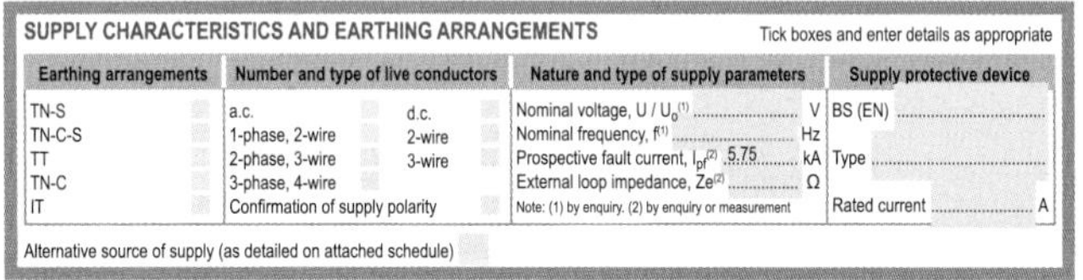

SUPPLY CHARACTERISTICS AND EARTHING ARRANGEMENTS — Tick boxes and enter details as appropriate

Earthing arrangements	Number and type of live conductors		Nature and type of supply parameters	Supply protective device
TN-S	a.c.	d.c.	Nominal voltage, U / U_0 (1) V	BS (EN) ....
TN-C-S	1-phase, 2-wire	2-wire	Nominal frequency, f (1) .... Hz	
TT	2-phase, 3-wire	3-wire	Prospective fault current, I_{pf} (2) 5.75 kA	Type ....
TN-C	3-phase, 4-wire		External loop impedance, Ze (2) .... Ω	
IT	Confirmation of supply polarity		Note: (1) by enquiry. (2) by enquiry or measurement	Rated current .... A

Alternative source of supply (as detailed on attached schedule)

Courtesy of the ECA

Figure 5.15 *PFC recorded on the certificate*

Three phase supplies

Where a three phase supply is provided the highest PFC will be the PSCC between phases at the origin of the installation.

Note

Unless the test instrument is specifically designed to be connected to and test at 400 V NEVER connect between phases to measure impedance or current. Only if the instrument is designed for the purpose should actual measurements be taken and the manufacturer's instructions should be followed at all times.

The calculation of the PFC between phases can be determined by calculation using the line to neutral PSCC values. Most supply cables have equally sized line and neutral conductors so the impedance value line to line should be the same as the line to neutral value. We could determine the PFC by the using the formula:

$$\text{PFC} = \sqrt{3} \times I_{\text{Line}}.$$

However, as a 'rule of thumb' we can determine PFC by:

$$\text{PFC} = 2 \times I_{\text{Line}}.$$

From our example the PSCC (which will be the PFC in this case) will be:

$$\text{PFC} = 2 \times 5.75 \text{ kA} = 11.5 \text{ kA}.$$

(Using the √3 value the answer would be in the order of l0 kA.)

The simple rule of thumb calculation can be readily carried out and always provides a margin of safety, being slightly higher.

If a problem with compliance is encountered using this figure, then a more detailed calculation would need to be undertaken.

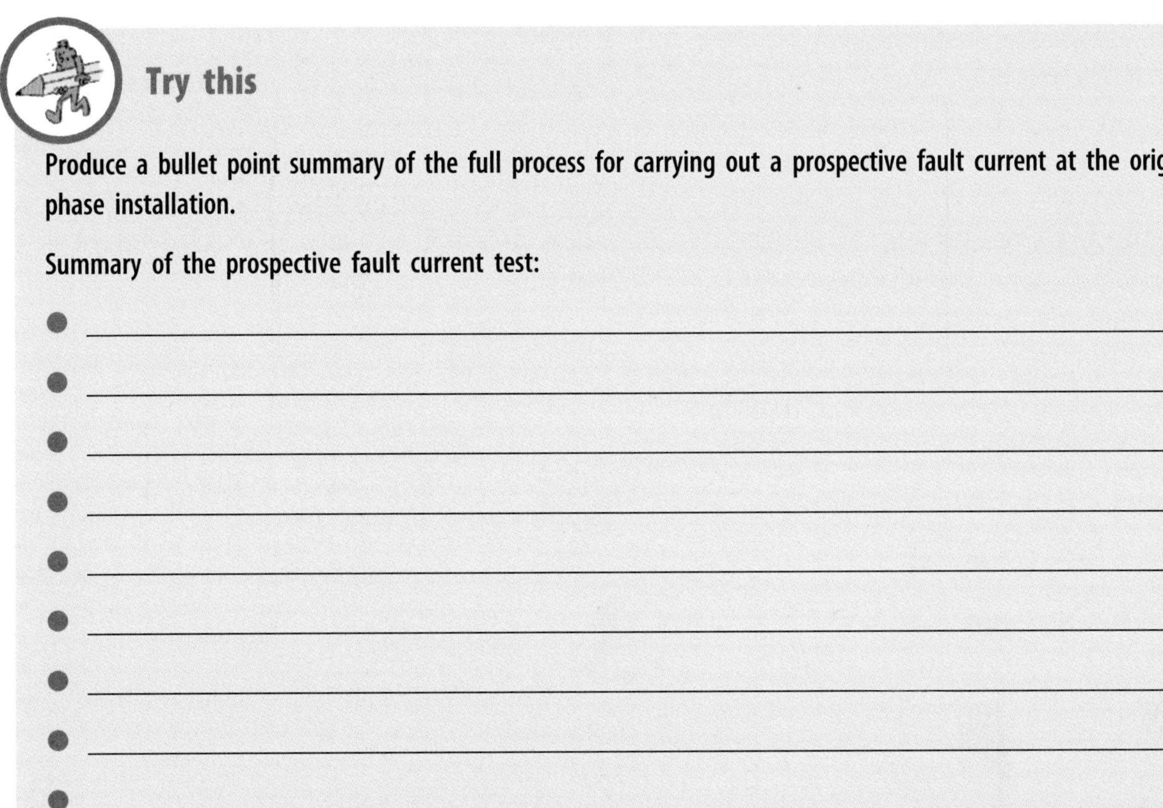

Try this

Produce a bullet point summary of the full process for carrying out a prospective fault current at the origin of a single phase installation.

Summary of the prospective fault current test:

- ____________________
- ____________________
- ____________________
- ____________________
- ____________________
- ____________________
- ____________________
- ____________________
- ____________________
- ____________________
- ____________________

Part 4 Testing RCDs

Testing residual current devices

Tests have to be carried out to confirm the operation of RCDs, which are a test of the functionality of the RCD and not the electrical installation itself. This is another of the tests that could be carried out at the distribution board before the Z_S tests are undertaken. There is a popular misconception that RCDs have to be tested either at a number of/all points on a circuit or at the furthest point. The RCD can be tested at the output terminals of the RCD and this is often the easiest place to test, particularly where RCDs protect any circuit other than a socket outlet circuit.

There are many occasions where RCDs are used to provide additional protection against electric shock. Wherever such a device is installed we must test to ensure that disconnection is achieved within the time required to provide protection from electric shock.

BS 7671 identifies specific installations and requirements for RCDs and these are in two main categories:

- Additional protection: provided by RCDs ≤ 30 mA and are used in installations or locations where there is an increased risk of electric shock
- Fault or fire protection: protection against electric shock where suitable earth fault loop impedance cannot be achieved (most TT installations) or where there is an increased risk of fire.

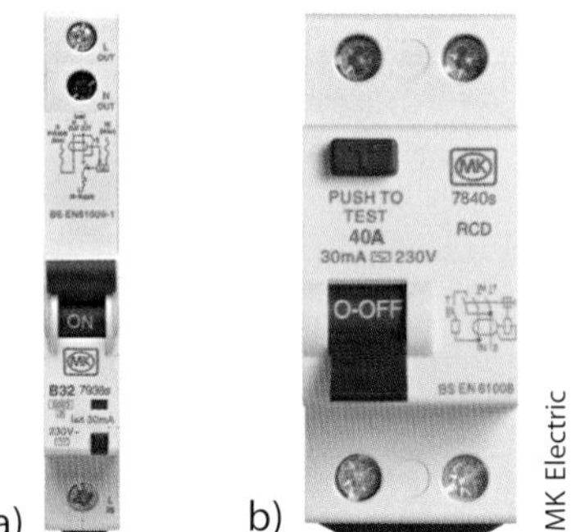

Figure 5.16 *Typical RCBO and RCD*

The two most common ratings for RCDs are 100 mA and 30 mA, and both types require testing to ensure correct operation. There are two different tests which need to be carried out on each device:

- Simulation of a fault by using an RCD test instrument
- Operation when the integral test button is operated.

It is important that the electrical fault simulation tests are carried out before the test button is checked as this may affect the performance of the device.

An RCD test instrument is used for the test and needs to supply a range of test currents appropriate to the device being tested and display the time taken for the device to operate.

One of the principal requirements is that the duration of each test does not exceed 2 seconds.

This makes it possible to test most time delay or 'S' type RCD devices which have been installed to ensure discrimination between RCDs of different operating currents. This is covered later in this chapter.

In addition, most RCD test instruments have the facility to carry out the test in both the positive and negative half cycles of the supply. Each of the tests should be carried out in both half cycles and the highest value obtained should be recorded.

Remember

The RCD test instrument will need to have leads suitable to carry out the tests on circuits supplying both socket outlets and fixed equipment. We shall need leads with both a moulded plug and split leads, similar to those used for the earth fault loop impedance tester.

Additional protection

We shall start by considering the tests to be carried out on a 30 mA RCD installed to provide additional protection.

There are three tests to be carried out in this instance and each test is carried out on both the positive and negative half cycles of the supply, making six tests in all.

Note

It is important to refer to the instrument manufacturer's instructions to ensure that the functions and operation of the instrument are fully understood before beginning the tests.

There is no given sequence for the tests and, theoretically they can be carried out in any order. As this RCD is installed for additional protection, the sequence of tests given here is the most appropriate and we shall consider why this is so once the test procedure has been detailed.

Each test is based upon an applied test current and the device should operate within the prescribed time in each case. The test current is determined by the operating current known as the $I_{\Delta n}$ of the RCD.

The RCD tester is checked to confirm that calibration is in date and it is not damaged and the leads are compliant with GS 38. The test instrument is then set to the operating current of the RCD, in this case 30 mA. We then have to select the test current which is to be applied using a second selector.

Five times $I_{\Delta n}$

Note

This test is only carried out on RCDs rated no more than 30 mA which are used for additional protection.

BS 7671 states that an RCD used for additional protection shall:

- Not exceed 30 mA
- Operate within 40 ms when tested at $5 \times I_{\Delta n}$ for the device.

This test for our 30 mA example will be carried out at 150 mA.

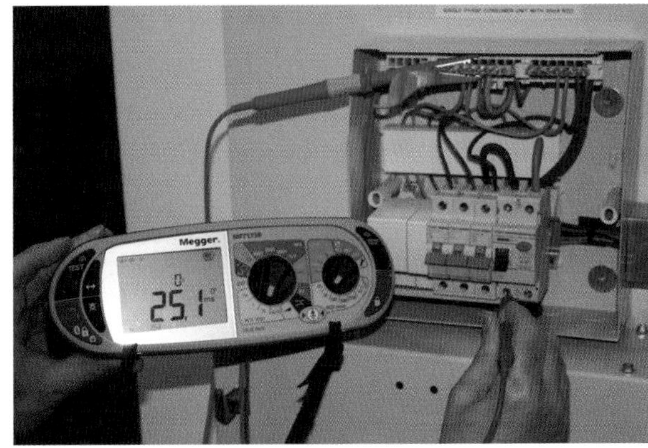

Figure 5.17 *RCD test instrument set to 30 mA and a test current of $5 \times I_{\Delta n}$*

Using a two lead test instrument and testing at the outgoing terminals of the RCD, the test instrument is connected to the earth bar and the outgoing line of the RCD. Most RCD test instruments begin the process with the 0° setting shown on the display, and this will be the condition for the first test. With the RCD switched on the test is carried out and the RCD should trip, with the time displayed on the screen of the instrument. Note the time shown.

The test instrument is then changed to the 180° setting, the RCD is reset and the test is then repeated. The time is noted and the highest of the two times (0° and 180°) is recorded on the Schedule of Test Results as the $5 \times I_{\Delta n}$ value.

One times $I_{\Delta n}$

The test instrument is now set to the $1 \times I_{\Delta n}$ setting and the instrument generally reverts to the 0° setting at the same time. The RCD is switched on and the test carried out, the RCD should trip and the time taken is noted.

The instrument is then set to the 180° setting, the RCD switched on and the test repeated. The highest of the two operating times is recorded on the Schedule of Test Results as the $1\times I_{\Delta n}$ value.

Remember

40 ms = 0.04 seconds and 200 ms = 0.2 seconds and 300 ms = 0.3 seconds.

Half times $I_{\Delta n}$

The test instrument is now set to the $\frac{1}{2} \times I_{\Delta n}$ setting and the instrument generally reverts to the 0° setting at the same time. The RCD is switched on and the test carried out and the RCD should not trip when the test instrument applies the test for 2 seconds. Some test instruments do not have the facility to carry out this test on both half cycles of the supply. Where possible the instrument is then set to the 180° setting, the RCD switched on and the test repeated. The result of this test is not recorded.

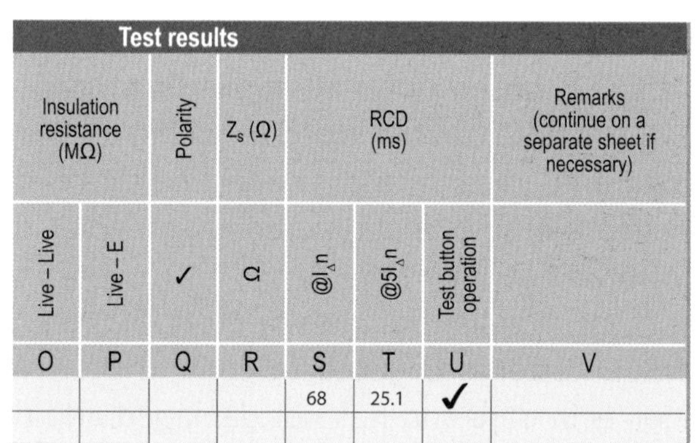

Test results							
Insulation resistance (MΩ)		Polarity	Z_s (Ω)	RCD (ms)			Remarks (continue on a separate sheet if necessary)
Live – Live	Live – E	✓	Ω	@$I_{\Delta n}$	@$5I_{\Delta n}$	Test button operation	
O	P	Q	R	S	T	U	V
				68	25.1	✓	

Courtesy of the ECA

Figure 5.20 *RCD test results recorded on the Schedule of Test Results*

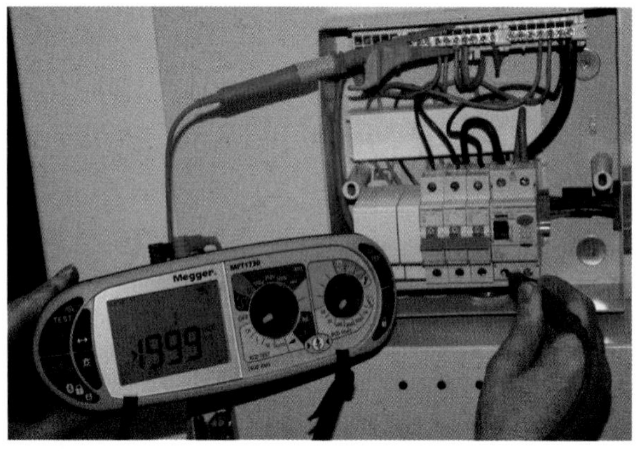

Figure 5.18 *RCD test instrument set to 30 mA and a test current of $\frac{1}{2} \times I_{\Delta n}$*

The results of the test need to be verified as meeting the requirements.

Note

These tests and the required operating times are appropriate for all RCDs installed to provide additional protection (≤ 30 mA) irrespective of their rated operating current.

Test sequence

As stated earlier there is no set sequence for these tests. Some test instruments have an auto test which, once selected and started, carries out the required tests automatically, allowing the inspector to be free to reset the RCD at each stage.

RCD Operating times		
Test current	Operating time	Time delay or S type
$5 \times I_{\Delta n}$	40 ms	
$1 \times I_{\Delta n}$ (BS 4293)	200 ms	200ms + 50 to 100% of delay
$1 \times I_{\Delta n}$ (BS EN 61008 & 9)	300 ms	130–500 ms (S type)
$\frac{1}{2} \times I_{\Delta n}$	No trip	

Figure 5.19 *Operating times for RCDs*

This may be useful when testing from a socket outlet on a circuit but not necessary when the test is performed from the output terminals of the RCD. The automatic test sequence is generally ½ × $I_{\Delta n}$, 1 × $I_{\Delta n}$ and 5 × $I_{\Delta n}$.

The reasons for the sequence suggested here (5 × $I_{\Delta n}$, 1 × $I_{\Delta n}$, ½ × $I_{\Delta n}$) are as follows:

The 5 × $I_{\Delta n}$ is carried out to confirm the RCD will operate in the required time to prevent a fatal electric shock. This is the condition in which we really want to confirm the device works first time as it is the primary function of an RCD installed to provide additional protection.

The ½ × $I_{\Delta n}$ test is to establish whether the device is likely to suffer from nuisance tripping under normal operation. If the test is carried out as the first test there is no assurance that the device has not tripped simply because the mechanism is sticking. If the ½ × $I_{\Delta n}$ test is carried out as the final test the RCD will have operated at least four times so if it is going to nuisance trip it will do so then.

RCDs installed for fault or fire protection

As we discussed earlier, RCDs with an operating current ($I_{\Delta n}$) > 30 mA are often installed to provide fault protection where suitable earth fault loop impedance cannot be achieved (most TT installations) or where there is an increased risk of fire. These devices will also need to be tested to ensure they are performing to the required standard.

The test process for RCDs with an operating current ($I_{\Delta n}$) greater than 30 mA is exactly the same **EXCEPT** the 5 × $I_{\Delta n}$ test is not carried out. In which case only the 1 × $I_{\Delta n}$ test and the ½ × $I_{\Delta n}$ test are required.

Functional test

The final test to be carried out on every RCD is the functional test which simply involves operating the integral test button to confirm the mechanism is operating. This is also the regular quarterly test to be carried out on the RCD by the user of the installation. The initial verification test not only confirms the operation of the mechanical trip mechanism but also ensures that any residual magnetism in the core of the RCD is discharged and leaves the RCD ready for operation.

This functional test does not confirm the correct operating time of the RCD, simply that the mechanism is working correctly. The electrical test is required to confirm the correct operating times.

RCDs connected in series

In some circumstances it is necessary to install RCDs in series with one another, for example where a distribution cable and final circuits are connected to a TT system.

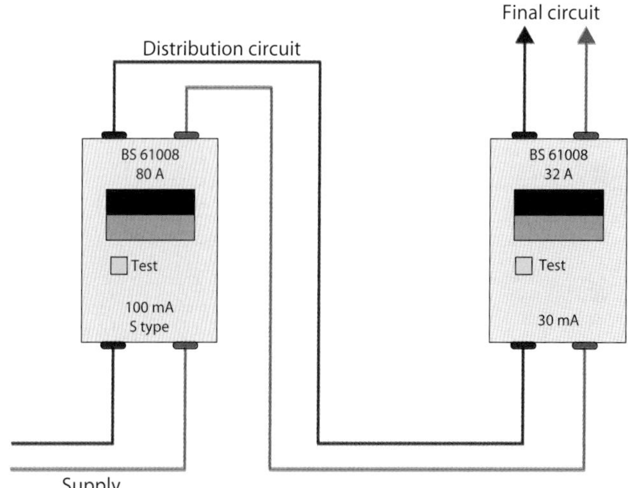

Figure 5.21 *RCDs connected in series*

The correct operation of these RCDs must be achieved, as a fault on the final circuit should not cause the RCD upstream to operate first. Whilst from Figure 5.21 this looks as though it will not happen let's consider our test procedure for the 30 mA RCD.

Remember

An RCD should not operate at a current of 50 per cent $I_{\Delta n}$ and should always operate at a current of 100 per cent $I_{\Delta n}$.

When the 5 × $I_{\Delta n}$ test is undertaken the fault current applied is 150 mA which is greater than the $I_{\Delta n}$ of the 100 mA RCD. As the 100 mA RCD is upstream from the 30 mA RCD and will see a current greater than its $I_{\Delta n}$, it will operate before the 30 mA RCD.

When the 1 × $I_{\Delta n}$ test is undertaken the applied current is 30 mA and this is less than 50 per cent of the $I_{\Delta n}$ of the 100 mA so the 100 mA RCD will not trip and the 30 mA should disconnect within the required time.

Should a fault occur on the 30 mA final circuit it is therefore possible, depending on the fault current which flows, for the 100 mA RCD to operate first.

To prevent this and ensure correct operation of the devices to minimize disruption, a time delay or S type RCD is used. These S type RCDs are manufactured to BS EN 61008 and 61009 and can be adjusted between 130 ms and 500 ms which allows the operation of the upstream RCD to be delayed and the downstream RCD to operate first. If the downstream RCD fails to operate then the upstream RCD will still disconnect the supply after the delay period.

Earlier RCDs to BS 4293 are time delay RCDs and the operating time of these devices can also be adjusted to allow the correct operation of the RCDs.

Try this

Produce a bullet point summary of the full process for carrying out a test to confirm the correct operation of a 30 mA RCD at the output terminals of the RCD. You should include the actual test current applied at each stage of the test.

Summary of the RCD test:

- ____________________
- ____________________
- ____________________
- ____________________
- ____________________
- ____________________
- ____________________
- ____________________
- ____________________
- ____________________

Part 5 Phase sequence, functional testing and voltage drop

Phase sequencing

For three phase installations there is a further test to be carried out to confirm the phase sequencing is correct throughout the installation. This test is carried out at the origin of the installation and then at every three phase distribution board, isolator and, where applicable, items of equipment. It is not carried out at three phase motor terminals as changing the phase sequence is used to regulate the direction in which the motor will turn.

There are two recognized types of test instrument used for this test:

- Rotating disc type
- Indicator lamp type.

The installation needs to be energized to carry out this test and so care is needed when accessing the terminals and making the connections. The instrument is connected in the correct sequence to the three line conductors and the indicator will show the sequence as either correct or incorrect. Once the correct sequence is established at the origin this should be the same at every point in the installation.

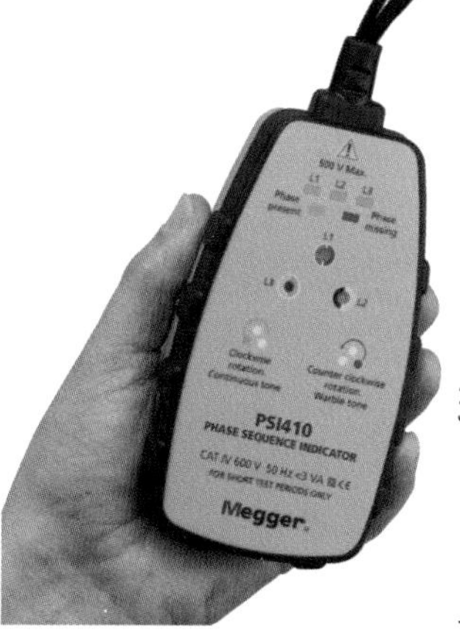

Image courtesy of Megger

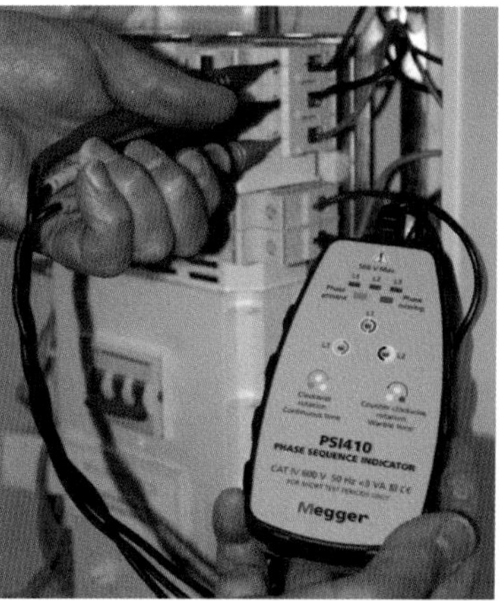

Figure 5.22 *Typical phase sequence tester*

Note

Many instrument manufacturers use colour codes other than those used in the fixed wiring, the most common being the Red, Yellow (or white) and Blue of the old UK colours. If this is the case then the corresponding fixed wiring colours are:

Colour comparison	
New colours	**Old colours**
Brown	Red
Black	Yellow (or white)
Grey	Blue

This phase sequencing throughout the installation is important for a number of reasons including:

- Operation of three phase machines: the phase sequence determines direction
- Load distribution: Where single phase loads are connected to remote distribution boards the load balancing will have been determined by the designer and incorrect sequence may seriously affect this balance
- Circuits on the same phase: where single phase circuits in a particular location are supplied from different distribution boards, e.g. lighting, power and general socket outlets and dedicated computer sockets, then incorrect phase sequencing may result in adjacent equipment being supplied on different phases of the supply.

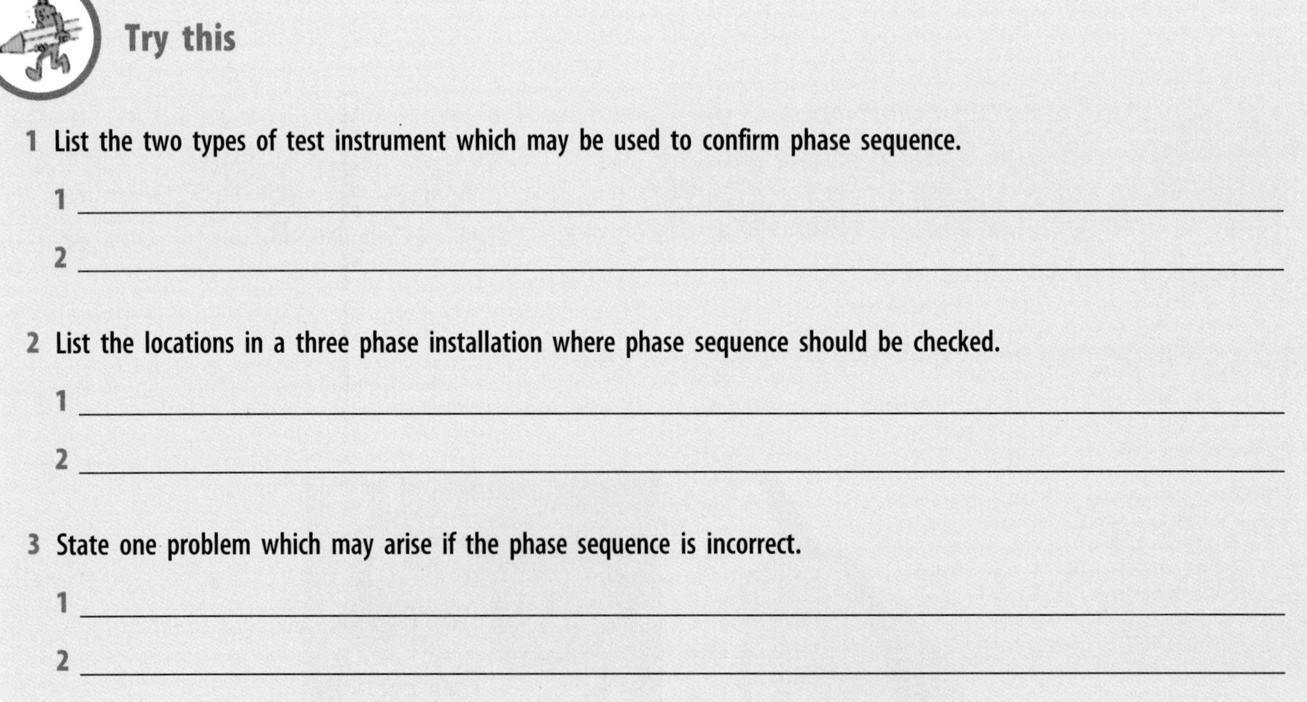

Try this

1 List the two types of test instrument which may be used to confirm phase sequence.

1 ______________________

2 ______________________

2 List the locations in a three phase installation where phase sequence should be checked.

1 ______________________

2 ______________________

3 State one problem which may arise if the phase sequence is incorrect.

1 ______________________

2 ______________________

Functional testing

Functional testing is the final process where the actual operation of the equipment is checked. This does not involve any test instruments and some of the function checks will have been completed during the inspection and testing process so far.

The inspector needs to confirm the correct operation and function of such equipment as:

- Switchgear
- Controls
- Isolators
- Interlocks.

The manual operation of isolators and circuit breakers are generally confirmed during the testing process when isolation is confirmed and then circuits are energized. The other controls, isolators and similar equipment need to be confirmed once the other testing has been completed.

Voltage drop

BS 7671 includes a requirement, where necessary, to confirm the installation complies with the voltage drop requirements. It then goes on to say that this is not normally required during initial verification.

Voltage drop within an installation is the result of the resistance of the conductors supplying the equipment and the load current which is carried by the cables. The higher the conductor resistance and/or the load current the greater the voltage drop will be.

If we apply basic principles we can see that voltage drop is a product of load and resistance which we know results in power ($P = I^2 R$). So voltage drop may be considered as an indication of power loss. This power loss is dissipated as heat which means that the cable will be operating at a higher temperature as a result of excessive voltage drop. This may also result in the malfunction of the equipment.

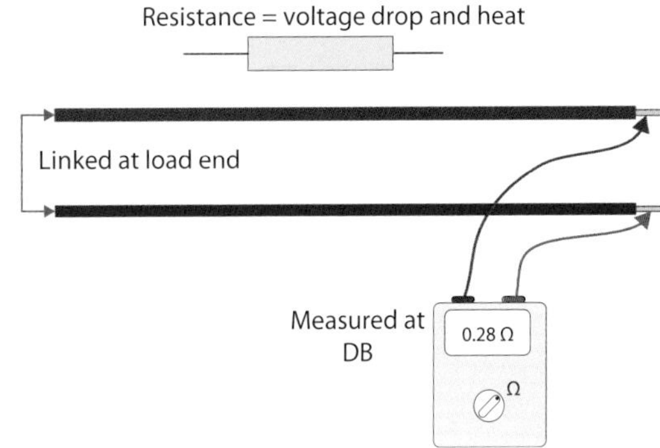

Figure 5.23 *Voltage drop*

There are two options for determining the voltage drop of a circuit.

Calculation: this is carried out using calculations such as the use of diagrams or graphs of maximum cable length against load current. These need to identify the different conductor cross-sectional areas and percentage voltage drops for given nominal voltages, conductor temperatures and wiring systems. These may be obtained from the cable manufacturer for the particular cable used.

The calculation method is not a common method used on site and the use of measurement is more practical. This does not involve measuring voltage directly and the measurement process requires some calculation on the part of the inspector.

Measurement: To determine the voltage drop requirement has been complied with by measurement involves measuring circuit resistance and then calculating voltage drop using circuit resistance, load current and a correction factor for conductor temperature.

Let's consider the process for a single phase radial power circuit, supplied from the public distribution system and operating at 230 V with a load current I_b of 20 A. The circuit is supplied from a distribution board at the origin of the installation.

The process for this measurement is very similar to the $R_1 + R_2$ test used for continuity of cpc, only this time we use the line and neutral conductor $R_1 + R_n$.

Using a low resistance ohmmeter, which is in calibration and has been checked for condition and function, null the test leads.

Safely isolate and lock off the circuit and then link line and neutral conductors together at the furthest point of the circuit and measure the conductor resistance line to neutral at the distribution board (alternatively this could be linked at the distribution board (DB) and measured at the furthest point). This produces a reading of 0.28 Ω.

Now calculate the voltage drop using the formula Voltage drop = $(R_1 + R_n) \times I_b \times 1.2$ with the 1.2 factor used to compensate for the difference in the conductor temperature under normal operating conditions and at the time of testing.

For our example we have Voltage drop = $0.28 \times 20 \times 1.2 = 6.72$ V.

Now we need to determine whether the voltage drop meets the requirements. BS 7671 provides maximum values for voltage drop in consumer's installations in Table 4Ab.

Task

Familiarize yourself with the contents of BS 7671 Table 4Ab before you continue with this chapter.

From Table 4Ab we can see that the maximum permitted voltage drop is 5 per cent of the nominal supply voltage, which in this case is 230 V.

The maximum permissible voltage drop for this circuit is 5 per cent × 230 V = 11.5 V.

The calculated voltage drop is 6.72 V which is less than 11.5 V and so the circuit is acceptable.

Remember

The maximum permitted voltage drop is measured from the origin of the installation to every point of utilization. If there are distribution circuits included then the voltage drop for all the cables supplying the equipment must be taken into account.

Try this

1 Calculate the maximum permitted voltage drop, in volts, for circuits supplied from the public distribution system supplying:

a A 230 V lighting circuit.

____

____

____

b A 230 V power circuit.

____

____

____

c A 400 V three phase heating load.

____

____

____

2 State the two methods of determining voltage drop.

1 ____

____

2 ____

____

Part 6 Documentation and client liaison

Documentation

On completion of the inspection, testing and commissioning of the electrical installation we have to provide the client with all the appropriate documentation. This will include the Electrical Installation Certificate, the Schedules of Inspections and the Schedules of Test Results, much of which we completed during the inspection and testing process.

Note

More detailed information on the forms of certification are contained in the next chapter of this studybook.

We will also need to ensure that the client is provided with the other relevant information to enable the installation to be used, adjusted and maintained during its working life. This information will include:

Design information: the details of the design of the electrical installation should be passed to the client as this shows the methods used to ensure the installation has been designed to the requirements of BS 7671.

Certification: there may be certification provided for items of equipment which have been installed, often referred to as certificates of conformity. These show that suitable equipment has been installed and would also be needed by the client in the event of a problem with an item of equipment.

Manufacturers' installation and operation instructions: These will be required in order for the client to maintain and adjust the equipment such as time clocks, thermostats and presence sensors. These will also be necessary for the equipment to be maintained correctly.

Having detailed the requirements for inspection, testing and commissioning the electrical installation, we need to consider the ways in which we keep the customer and client safe and informed throughout the process.

Some of the requirements have been considered during the inspection and testing process but it is worth summarizing these requirements. As initial verification takes place on alterations and additions to existing installations as well as brand new installations we do need to consider all these situations.

Safety

The considerations for the safety of the client include:

- Safe isolation of the installation, circuits and equipment is essential for the safety of the inspector, the client and the users of the installation. It is particularly important to make sure that any exposed live parts of the electrical installation are isolated when they are not under the immediate control of the inspector, i.e. when they are actually being worked on. Do not wander off to fetch tools and the like leaving such equipment unattended.
- Areas where work is being carried out should be identified and clear warning signs and labels placed to advise people of the dangers. Signs placed at the entrances to the building will warn visitors and staff alike as they come into the building that electrical work is being carried out.
- The labelling of isolators and switchgear which are locked off for the purposes of inspection and testing, to advise people that work is being carried out, is an important consideration. It informs people why the circuit or equipment is not functioning and does not allow re-energizing by unauthorized persons.
- Using suitable test procedures can significantly reduce the danger to others. We discussed in Chapter 4 of this studybook, the process for testing continuity of ring final circuits from a socket outlet rather than the distribution board. As an example, that process allows the test to be completed on a circuit which is isolated and locked off and any exposed parts will be isolated and under

the control of the inspector whilst the test is undertaken at every socket.

- Simple checks to confirm that all covers are on and all barriers and enclosures are complete, the equipment is connected and secure before energizing a circuit or installation to make sure that it is safe to energize is a simple but essential step to be taken in all circumstances.

Keeping the client informed

It is important to keep the client informed of the activities and progress during the inspection, testing and commissioning.

Obtaining permission from the client to isolate the installation or circuits is an important part of the liaison between the client and the inspector. The inspector needs the permission from the client or responsible person before any existing circuits are isolated from the supply. The responsible person can identify when and for how long these circuits can be isolated and any preparatory work to be carried out by the staff such as closing down IT equipment and computers. There may be ongoing processes which cannot be stopped midway and so the inspector will need to agree a suitable time for the work.

Progress reports should be given to the client to inform them of the progress on site. There may be fixed completion dates and the client will need to know whether these are going to be met. It is also possible that, should the work be ahead of schedule, the client will be able to carry out their enabling work, such as furniture and fittings, earlier and so ease their own preparation timetable.

If the work is falling behind schedule or there are problems which need to be put right before the commissioning can be completed, the client needs to be advised as soon as possible so that their programme can be adjusted and a mutually agreed plan of action put in place.

Labelling

In an ideal world the inspection, testing and commissioning of the electrical installation would be completed before any of the installation is placed into service. In reality during the commissioning process it may be desirable, or necessary, for parts of the installation or equipment to be put into service before the whole process is completed. For example, there may be a need to make the power available for other services such as HVAC earlier so that their specialist commissioning can take place. During this stage it is important to identify any electrical circuits, systems and equipment which have not yet been commissioned.

Try this

The installation of a new shower circuit has been carried out and the initial verification and commissioning has been completed.

List the documents which will need to be passed to the client now the works are complete.

____

____

____

Try this: Crossword

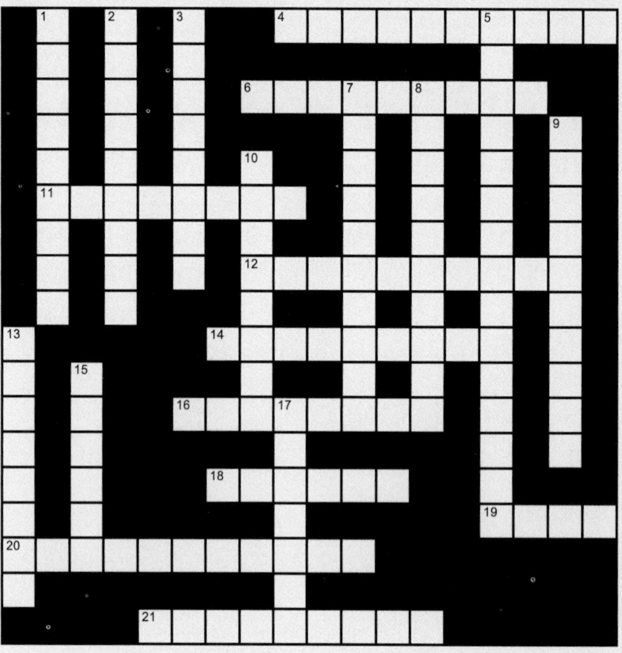

Across

4 One of these is used for every test (10)

6 A snappy lead connector this clip (9)

11 One of these is where conductors are connected (8)

12 R_A is this for 2 down (10)

14 After testing Z_e we must ... the earthing conductor (9)

16 Where an RCD is located here it will need to be an 'S' type (8)

18 This type of inspection is used to confirm polarity (6)

19 Z_e is the external earth fault ... impedance (4)

20 Test instruments must have this in date when testing (11)

21 The circuit will be this to measure Z_s (9)

Down

1 If any test equipment is this it should not be used (9)

2 The installation connection to earth in a TT system (9)

3 This conductor is disconnected for Z_e (8)

5 This type of instrument needs to be set for each test carried out (15)

7 Test results must be verified to confirm this (10)

8 Further from the origin than 16 across (10)

9 This will precede all the testing of a new installation (10)

1 These may need to be removed to access live terminals (8)

13 The order of tests (8)

15 A type of circuit and tyre (6)

17 What the inspector carries out when 9 down is completed (7)

Congratulations, you have completed this chapter of the studybook. Complete the self assessment questions before continuing to Chapter 6.

SELF ASSESSMENT

Circle the correct answers.

1 An earth fault loop impedance tester may be used to measure the resistance of an installation earth electrode where the installation forms part of a TT system and is:

a. Less than 100 A
b. In a remote location
c. Protected by an RCD
d. Surrounded by metalled ground

2 The DNO declared maximum value of Z_e for a TN-S system is:

a. 0.35 Ω
b. 0.8 Ω
c. 2.0 Ω
d. 21 Ω

3 The current used when measuring earth fault loop impedance need not exceed:

a. 30 A
b. 25 A
c. 20 A
d. 15 A

4 The measured earth fault loop impedance of a radial circuit must be carried out at:

a. Every point on the circuit
b. The point closest to the origin
c. The point furthest from the origin
d. Any convenient point on the circuit

5 In order to compare the measured value of earth fault loop impedance Z_s with the tabulated values given in BS 7671, the inspector must:

a. Make a direct comparison of the measured and tabulated figures
b. Apply a multiplying factor of 0.8 to the measured values
c. Apply a multiplying factor of 0.8 to the tabulated values
d. Divide the tabulated values by a factor of 0.8

6 The maximum test current to be applied to a 300 mA RCD installed to provide fire protection is:

a. 1500 mA
b. 300 mA
c. 100 mA
d. 30 mA

7 When determining voltage drop compliance the formula Voltage drop $= (R_1 + R_n) \times I_b \times 1.2$ is used. In this formula the 1.2 figure is used to:

a. Allow a margin of safety
b. Allow for changes in the load current
c. Compensate for errors in the measurement
d. Compensate for the change in conductor temperature

8 Three types of documented information may be provided to the client following the commissioning of an electrical installation. These include design information, manufacturer's operating instructions and:

a. Forms of certification
b. Contract documents
c. Bills of sale
d. Quotations

6 Certificates and documentation

RECAP

Before you start work on this chapter, complete the exercise below to ensure that you remember what you learned earlier.

- The correct incoming supply ______________ to the installation must be confirmed before any ________ testing is undertaken.
- For electrical installations protected by an ________ and forming part of a ________ system we can measure R_A using an ______________________________ tester.
- BS 7671 states that values of earth ______________ resistance above a value of ____________ may prove to be unreliable.
- The test to confirm Z_e is carried out to confirm that the ____________ path provided by the ____________ is present and that the ____________ value is within the ______________ limits.
- The DNO declared maximum earth ___________ loop values for the ___________ distribution network are ____________ for a TN-S system and ____________ for a TN-C-S system.
- The details of Z_e are recorded on the Electrical ________________ Certificate in the Supply ____________________ and Earthing ____________________ section.
- A test of Z_s is carried out at the ____________ point on every ____________ circuit and every ____________ socket outlet on ____________ final circuits.

- The expected value of Z_s for a ______________________ can be determined using the ______________________ values in the formula Z_s = _______ + R_1 _______.
- To compensate for the ______________________ between conductor ______________________ at the time of testing and the normal operating ______________________ of the conductor, a multiplier of ______ is applied to the BS 7671 ______________________ values.
- A test to establish PFC is carried out in order to ensure that the ______________________ devices can ______________________ disconnect the prospective fault current which is likely to ______________________ at the ______________________ at which they are ______________________.
- Where three phase supply is provided the PFC will be determined by the highest ______________________ between line and ______________________ at the ______________________ of the installation multiplied by ______________________.
- An RCD ≤ ______________________ should be tested at three test currents of ½ × $I_{\Delta n}$, 1 × $I_{\Delta n}$ and ______________________.
- An RCD rated more than ______________________ does not require the ______________________ test to be carried out.
- The correct operation of RCDs in series can be achieved by using an ______________________ RCD ______________________.
- A 30 mA RCD to BS EN 61009 should operate within ______________________ when tested at ______________________.
- The final test on an RCD is the ______________________ of the ______________________ test button.
- Confirmation of ______________________ sequence is carried out at the ______________________ of the installation and at every three phase ______________________ board and ______________________.
- Voltage drop may be determined using the formula Voltage drop = __________ × ______ × __________.

LEARNING OBJECTIVES

On completion of this chapter you should be able to:

- Explain the purpose of and relationship between:
  - An Electrical Installation Certificate
  - A Minor Electrical Installation Works Certificate

- Schedule of Inspections
- Schedule of Test Results.

- State the information that must be contained within:
  - An Electrical Installation Certificate
  - A Minor Electrical Installation Works Certificate
  - Schedule of Inspections
  - Schedule of Test Results.
- Describe the certification process for a completed installation and identify the responsibilities of different relevant personnel in relation to the completion of the certification process.
- Explain the procedures and requirements, in accordance with the Requirements for Electrical Installations and IET Guidance Note 3 and where appropriate customer/client requirements for the recording and retention of completed:
  - Electrical Installation Certificates
  - Minor Electrical Installation Works Certificates
  - Schedules of Inspections
  - Schedules of Test Results.

Part 1 Forms of certification

This chapter considers the forms of certification used for the initial verification of electrical installation work. This includes the purpose, use, completion and content of the forms together with the advice given to the client regarding these forms.

The forms of certification used throughout this studybook are produced by the Electrical Contractors Association (ECA). Completed samples of these forms of certification for initial verification are shown in Appendix 1 of this studybook.

Whilst working through this chapter you will need to refer to BS 7671, Requirements for electrical installations and IET Guidance Note 3 (GN3) Inspection and Testing.

We have mentioned various sections of the forms and certification in Chapters 4 and 5 of this studybook when recording the test results. To consider the certification and verification process we first need to understand the forms of certification and where they are used.

Minor Electrical Installation Works Certificate (MEIWC)

This certificate, often referred to as simply the Minor Works Certificate, has some particular requirements for its use. The standard form in BS 7671 and IET Guidance Note 3, Inspection and Testing may be used where an alteration or addition is:

- Made to a single circuit
- Does not include a new circuit.

Where alteration or addition work is carried out on a number of circuits a MEIWC will need to be issued for each circuit involved. The reason for this is that the standard form contains a provision for recording the details of one circuit only. Some of the industry bodies produce certificates modelled on the standard form which allow more than one circuit to be recorded on a single MEIWC.

Remember

The standard forms contained in BS 7671 contain the minimum information that needs to be recorded. Other forms of certification may be used providing they contain no less information than the standard forms.

The ECA version of the MEIWC provides the facility to record the details and results for up to three circuits. The layout of this certificate has been altered to allow the required details to be entered for each circuit.

The MEIWC is intended to allow alterations and additions to a single circuit to be certificated without the need for an Electrical Installation Certificate to be issued. The alteration or addition, and any part of the existing electrical installation which affects that particular circuit, must comply with the requirements of BS 7671. There is not a requirement for the whole of the installation to be updated to the current requirements. The relevant information for the work carried out to a circuit can be recorded on the MEIWC and any comments on the existing installation are also recorded.

The MEIWC may also be used to certificate the like-for-like replacement of electrical accessories and equipment. It is not an ideal form for this activity but does allow the electrician to record the tests carried out, together with the results and any comments on the existing installation. This provides evidence that, following its replacement, the particular item of equipment was safe for use.

Note

The MEIWC must not be used for the replacement of a distribution board, consumer unit or similar items.

There is guidance for completing the certificate provided in the form of a note advising on the use of this particular form.

MINOR ELECTRICAL INSTALLATION WORKS CERTIFICATE NOTES:

The Minor Works Certificate is intended to be used for additions and alterations to an installation that do not extend to the provision of new circuit. Examples include the addition of socket-outlets or lighting points to an existing circuit, the relocation of a light switch etc. This Certificate may also be used for the replacement of equipment such as accessories or luminaires, but not for the replacement of distribution boards or similar items. Appropriate inspection and testing, however, should always be carried out irrespective of the extent of the work undertaken.

Courtesy of the ECA

Figure 6.1 *The advisory note on the use of the MEIWC*

MINOR ELECTRICAL INSTALLATION WORKS CERTIFICATE FOR UP TO THREE CIRCUITS

ECA

(REQUIREMENTS FOR ELECTRICAL INSTALLATIONS BS 7671 (IET WIRING REGULATIONS))

To be used only for minor electrical work which does not include the provision of a new circuit

Certificate number: MW001234 **Member number:**

PART 1: DESCRIPTION OF MINOR WORKS

1. Description of the minor works: Addition of three spotlights in the office reception area
2. Location / address: The Centre, Coppice Lane, Closetown, Cutcounty, NC7 4 HP
3. Date minor works completed: -- July 20--
4. Details of departures, if any, from BS 7671:2008: NONE

PART 2: INSTALLATION DETAILS

1. System earthing arrangement: TN-C-S ✓ TN-S TT
2. Method of fault protection: ADS
3. Protective device for the modified circuit:
   1 Type: BS EN 60898 Type B Rating: 10 A
   2 Type: Rating: A
   3 Type: Rating: A

Comments on existing installation, including adequacy of earthing and bonding arrangements (see 132.16)

Unable to access main protective bonding connection to the water installation pipe work due to boxing in

Line/neutral insulation resistance not measured due to nature and number of existing connected loads

PART 3: ESSENTIAL TESTS

		Continuity ✓ or Ω (fill 1 col. only)		Insulation resistance MΩ			Polarity	Zs	RCD (if applicable)	
CCT No	Circuit description	$R_1 + R_2$	R_2	Line / neutral	Line / earth	Neutral / earth	✓	Ω	1 x IΔn	5 x IΔn
1	Reception area lighting	1.2		LIM	198	198	✓	1.35	N/A	N/A
2										
3										

PART 4: DECLARATION

I / We CERTIFY that the works do not impair the safety of the existing installation, that the said works have been designed, constructed, inspected and tested in accordance with BS 7671:2008 (IET Wiring Regulations), amended to 2011 (date) and that the said works, to the best of my / our knowledge and belief, at the time of my / our inspection complied with BS 7671 except as detailed in Part 1 above.

Contractor's name: James Douglas
Signature: James Douglas
For and on behalf of: J D Installations Ltd
Position: Proprietor
Address: Unit 6, Gambols Estate, Neartown, Cutcounty, NT5 8LR
Date: -- July 20---

Courtesy of the ECA

Figure 6.2 *ECA Minor Electrical Installation Work Certificate*

Electrical installation certificate (EIC)

The Electrical Installation Certificate (EIC) is the form used to certify any new circuit or electrical installation.

It may be used to certify:

- A new installation
- An alteration to an electrical installation or circuit
- An addition to an electrical installation or circuit.

The BS 7671 requirement to certificate every new circuit necessitates the issue of an EIC. As we have already established, alterations and additions to an existing circuit can be certificated using a MEIWC. As the number of circuits, which are altered or added to, increases so do the number of MEIWCs which need to be issued. Additionally, as more circuits are altered, more changes are being made to the installation. A view would need to be taken as to the continuing compliance of the existing installation following a number of alterations and/or additions.

The information provided on the EIC relates to the supply characteristics and earthing arrangements and details of the installation, together with the details of those competent persons responsible for the design, construction and inspection and testing. As we shall see later in this studybook it does not include details of inspection and testing or any circuit results. In order to complete the information necessary to confirm the installation complies with the requirements of the design and BS 7671, the certificate must be accompanied by two additional documents. These documents are:

- The Schedule of Inspections
- The Schedule of Test Results.

These additional documents, which for complex installations may run to many pages, must be attached to the certificate in order for the certificate to be valid.

Task

Using the standard MEIWC form in BS 7671 compare this with the ECA version shown in Appendix 1 of this studybook.

ELECTRICAL INSTALLATION CERTIFICATE BS 7671:2008 ECA
THREE SIGNATURE Certificate number: 49781 Member number: (optional) Sheet 1 of 6

DETAILS OF THE CLIENT
Dr. T David, 281 Percival Street, Coldsworthy, CW8 9TS

INSTALLATION ADDRESS
481 High Street, Nearby, Cutcounty, NC1 2 HS

DESCRIPTION AND EXTENT OF THE INSTALLATION Tick boxes as appropriate
Description of installation: Rewire of a domestic property
Extent of installation covered by this Certificate: The rewiring and installation of circuits as described in the attached continuation sheet, but excluding the central heating controls installed by others.
(Use continuation sheet if necessary) See continuation sheet no. 3 and 4
New installation ✓
Addition to an existing installation
Alteration to an existing installation

FOR DESIGN
I/We being the person(s) responsible for the design of the electrical installation (as indicated by my/our signatures below), particulars of which are described above, having exercised reasonable skill and care when carrying out the design, hereby CERTIFY that the design work of which I/we have been responsible is, to the best of my/our knowledge and belief, in accordance with BS 7671:2008 amended to 2011 (date) except for departures, if any, detailed as follows.

Details of departures from BS 7671 (regulation 120.3 and 133.5)
None

The extent of liability of the signatory or signatories is limited to the work described above as the subject of this Certificate.
For the DESIGN of the installation: **Where there is mutual responsibility for the design
Signature *Donald Smith* Date -- June 20-- Name (CAPITALS) DONALD SMITH Designer No. 1
Signature N/A Date Name (CAPITALS) Designer No. 2**

FOR CONSTRUCTION
I/We being the person(s) responsible for the construction of the electrical installation (as indicated by my/our signatures below), particulars of which are described above, having exercised reasonable skill and care when carrying out the construction, hereby CERTIFY that the construction work of which I/we have been responsible is, to the best of my/our knowledge and belief, in accordance with BS 7671:2008 amended to 2011 (date) except for departures, if any, detailed as follows.

Details of departures from BS 7671 (regulation 120.3 and 133.5)
None

The extent of liability of the signatory or signatories is limited to the work described above as the subject of this Certificate.
For the CONSTRUCTION of the installation:
Signature *James Douglas* Date -- July 20-- Name (CAPITALS) JAMES DOUGLAS Constructor

FOR INSPECTION & TESTING
I/We being the person(s) responsible for the inspection & testing of the electrical installation (as indicated by my/our signatures below), particulars of which are described above, having exercised reasonable skill and care when carrying out the inspection & testing, hereby CERTIFY that the work of which I/we have been responsible is, to the best of my/our knowledge and belief, in accordance with BS 7671:2008 amended to 2011 (date) except for departures, if any, detailed as follows.

Details of departures from BS 7671 (regulation 120.3 and 133.5)
None

The extent of liability of the signatory or signatories is limited to the work described above as the subject of this Certificate.
For the INSPECTION & TESTING of the installation:
Signature *James Douglas* Date -- July 20-- Name (CAPITALS) JAMES DOUGLAS Inspector

NEXT INSPECTION
I/We the designer(s), recommend that this installation is further inspected and tested after an interval of not more than 10 years / ~~months~~

C-EICE4-ECA REV V1 Aug 2011

Sheet 2 of 6

PARTICULARS OF SIGNATORIES TO THE ELECTRICAL INSTALLATION CERTIFICATE
Designer (No. 1)
Name Donald Smith Company DS Electrical Consultants
Address The Centre, Coppice Lane, Closetown, Cutcounty
Postcode NC7 4 HP Tel 07858196200
Designer (No. 2)
Name N/A Company
Address
Postcode Tel
Constructor
Name James Douglas Company J D Installations Ltd
Address Unit 6, Gambols Estate, Neartown, Cutcounty
Postcode NT5 8LR Tel 0800468924
Inspector
Name James Douglas Company J D Installations Ltd
Address Unit 6, Gambols Estate, Neartown, Cutcounty
Postcode NT5 8LR Tel 0800468924

SUPPLY CHARACTERISTICS AND EARTHING ARRANGEMENTS Tick boxes and enter details as appropriate

Earthing arrangements	Number and type of live conductors	Nature and type of supply parameters	Supply protective device
TN-S ✓	a.c. ✓ d.c.	Nominal voltage, U / $U_0^{(1)}$ 230 V	BS (EN) BS 88-3
TN-C-S	1-phase, 2-wire ✓ 2-wire	Nominal frequency, $f^{(1)}$ 50 Hz	
TT	2-phase, 3-wire 3-wire	Prospective fault current, $I_{pf}^{(2)}$ 0.48 kA	Type System C
TN-C	3-phase, 4-wire	External loop impedance, $Ze^{(2)}$ 0.60 Ω	
IT	Confirmation of supply polarity	Note: (1) by enquiry (2) by enquiry or measurement	Rated current 100 A

Alternative source of supply (as detailed on attached schedule)

PARTICULARS OF INSTALLATION REFERRED TO IN THE CERTIFICATE Tick boxes and enter details as appropriate

Means of earthing	Maximum demand		
Distributor's facility ✓	Maximum demand (load) 96 A kVA / Amps (delete as appropriate)		
	Details of installation earth electrode (*where applicable*)		
Installation earth electrode	Type (e.g. rod(s), tape, etc.) N/A	Location N/A	Electrode resistance to earth N/A Ω

Main protective conductors
Earthing conductor material Copper csa 16 mm² Continuity and connection verified ✓
Main protective bonding conductors material Copper csa 10 mm² Continuity and connection verified ✓
To incoming water and/~~or~~ gas service To other elements: N/A
Main switch or circuit-breaker
BS, type and no. of poles BS EN60947-3 (2 pole) Current rating 100 A Voltage rating 400 V V
Location Consumer unit in utility room Fuse rating or setting N/A A
Rated residual operating current $I_{\Delta n}$ N/A mA, and operating time of ms (at $I_{\Delta n}$) (Applicable only where an RCD is suitable and is used as a main circuit-breaker)

COMMENTS ON EXISTING INSTALLATION (in the case of an addition or alteration see Section 633)
None

SCHEDULES
The attached Schedules are part of this document and the Certificate is valid only when they are attached to it.
1 Schedules of Inspections and 1 Schedules of Test Results are attached.
(Enter quantities of Schedules attached.)

C-EICE4-ECA REV V1 Aug 2011

Courtesy of the ECA

Figure 6.3 *Electrical Installation Certificate*

Schedule of Inspections

The Schedule of Inspections which accompanies the EIC details the items and requirements for the installation. The inspector will complete this schedule following the inspection and will indicate whether the items were acceptable or not applicable to that particular installation.

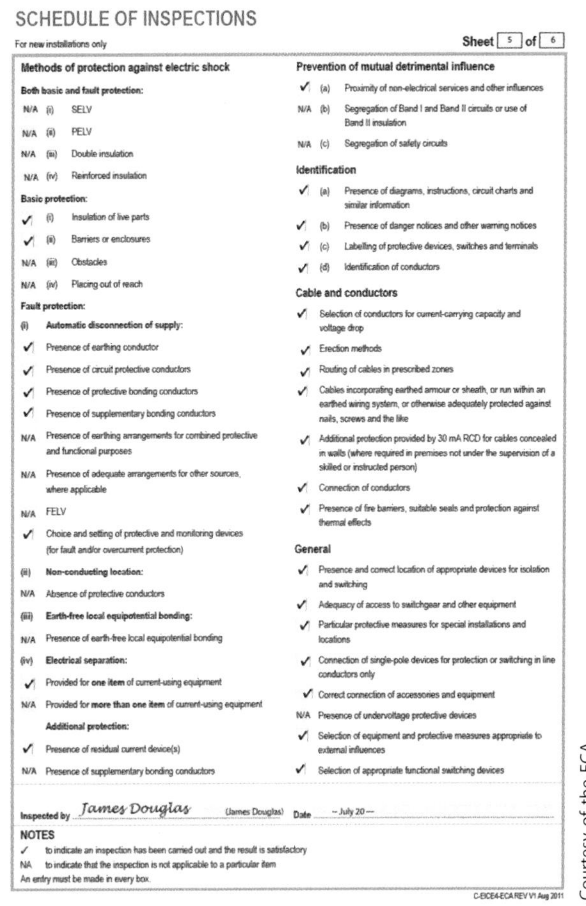

SCHEDULE OF INSPECTIONS
For new installations only Sheet 5 of 6

Methods of protection against electric shock

Both basic and fault protection:
N/A (i) SELV
N/A (ii) PELV
N/A (iii) Double insulation
N/A (iv) Reinforced insulation

Basic protection:
✓ (i) Insulation of live parts
✓ (ii) Barriers or enclosures
N/A (iii) Obstacles
N/A (iv) Placing out of reach

Fault protection:
(i) **Automatic disconnection of supply:**
✓ Presence of earthing conductor
✓ Presence of circuit protective conductors
✓ Presence of protective bonding conductors
✓ Presence of supplementary bonding conductors
N/A Presence of earthing arrangements for combined protective and functional purposes
N/A Presence of adequate arrangements for other sources, where applicable
N/A FELV
✓ Choice and setting of protective and monitoring devices (for fault and/or overcurrent protection)
(ii) **Non-conducting location:**
N/A Absence of protective conductors
(iii) **Earth-free local equipotential bonding:**
N/A Presence of earth-free local equipotential bonding
(iv) **Electrical separation:**
✓ Provided for **one item** of current-using equipment
N/A Provided for **more than one item** of current-using equipment
Additional protection:
✓ Presence of residual current device(s)
N/A Presence of supplementary bonding conductors

Prevention of mutual detrimental influence
✓ (a) Proximity of non-electrical services and other influences
N/A (b) Segregation of Band I and Band II circuits or use of Band II insulation
N/A (c) Segregation of safety circuits

Identification
✓ (a) Presence of diagrams, instructions, circuit charts and similar information
✓ (b) Presence of danger notices and other warning notices
✓ (c) Labelling of protective devices, switches and terminals
✓ (d) Identification of conductors

Cable and conductors
✓ Selection of conductors for current-carrying capacity and voltage drop
✓ Erection methods
✓ Routing of cables in prescribed zones
✓ Cables incorporating earthed armour or sheath, or run within an earthed wiring system, or otherwise adequately protected against nails, screws and the like
✓ Additional protection provided by 30 mA RCD for cables concealed in walls (where required in premises not under the supervision of a skilled or instructed person)
✓ Connection of conductors
✓ Presence of fire barriers, suitable seals and protection against thermal effects

General
✓ Presence and correct location of appropriate devices for isolation and switching
✓ Adequacy of access to switchgear and other equipment
✓ Particular protective measures for special installations and locations
✓ Connection of single-pole devices for protection or switching in line conductors only
✓ Correct connection of accessories and equipment
N/A Presence of undervoltage protective devices
✓ Selection of equipment and protective measures appropriate to external influences
✓ Selection of appropriate functional switching devices

Inspected by *James Douglas* (James Douglas) Date -- July 20 --

NOTES
✓ to indicate an inspection has been carried out and the result is satisfactory
NA to indicate that the inspection is not applicable to a particular item
An entry must be made in every box.

C-EICE4-ECA REV V1 Aug 2011

Courtesy of the ECA

Figure 6.4 *Schedule of Inspections*

Schedule of Test Results

The Schedule of Test Results details the information relating to the distribution board and circuits of the installation. A minimum of one Schedule of Test Results should be produced for each distribution board. Depending on the complexity of the installation more than one Schedule of Test Results may be required and continuation sheets are available for the schedule. The information includes the circuit details and the results of the tests carried out on each circuit.

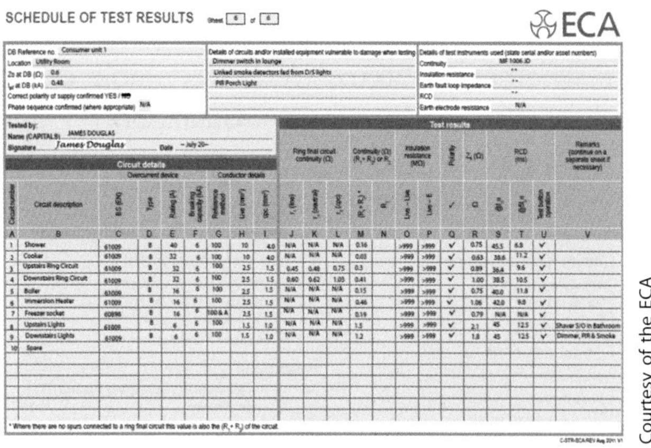

SCHEDULE OF TEST RESULTS Sheet 6 of 6 — ECA

DB Reference no. Consumer unit 1
Location Utility Room
Zs at DB (Ω) 0.6
I_{pf} at DB (kA) 0.48
Correct polarity of supply confirmed YES / NO
Phase sequence confirmed (where appropriate) N/A

Details of circuits and/or installed equipment vulnerable to damage when testing:
Dimmer switch in lounge
Linked smoke detectors fed from D/S lights
PIR Porch Light

Details of test instruments used (state serial and/or asset numbers):
Continuity MF 1006 JD
Insulation resistance "
Earth fault loop impedance "
RCD "
Earth electrode resistance N/A

Tested by:
Name (CAPITALS) JAMES DOUGLAS
Signature *James Douglas* Date – July 20–

Circuit number	Circuit description	BS (EN)	Type	Rating (A)	Breaking capacity (kA)	Reference method	Live (mm²)	cpc (mm²)	r_1 (line)	r_n (neutral)	r_2 (cpc)	$(R_1 + R_2)$*	R_2	Live – Live	Live – E	Polarity ✓	Z_s Ω	RCD (ms) @$I_{\Delta n}$	RCD (ms) @$5I_{\Delta n}$	Test button operation	Remarks (continue on a separate sheet if necessary)
A	B	C	D	E	F	G	H	I	J	K	L	M	N	O	P	Q	R	S	T	U	V
1	Shower	61009	B	40	6	100	10	4.0	N/A	N/A	N/A	0.16		>999	>999	✓	0.75	45.5	6.8	✓	
2	Cooker	61009	B	32	6	100	10	4.0	N/A	N/A	N/A	0.03		>999	>999	✓	0.63	38.6	11.2	✓	
3	Upstairs Ring Circuit	61009	B	32	6	100	2.5	1.5	0.45	0.48	0.75	0.3		>999	>999	✓	0.89	36.4	9.6	✓	
4	Downstairs Ring Circuit	61009	B	32	6	100	2.5	1.5	0.60	0.62	1.03	0.41		>999	>999	✓	1.00	38.5	10.5	✓	
5	Boiler	61009	B	16	6	100	2.5	1.5	N/A	N/A	N/A	0.15		>999	>999	✓	0.75	40.0	11.8	✓	
6	Immersion Heater	61009	B	16	6	100	2.5	1.5	N/A	N/A	N/A	0.46		>999	>999	✓	1.06	42.0	9.8	✓	
7	Freezer socket	60898	B	16	6	100 & A	2.5	1.5	N/A	N/A	N/A	0.19		>999	>999	✓	0.79	N/A	N/A	✓	
8	Upstairs Lights	61009	B	6	6	100	1.5	1.0	N/A	N/A	N/A	1.5		>999	>999	✓	2.1	45	12.5	✓	Shaver S/O in Bathroom
9	Downstairs Lights	61009	B	6	6	100	1.5	1.0	N/A	N/A	N/A	1.2		>999	>999	✓	1.8	45	12.5	✓	Dimmer, PIR & Smoke
10	Spare																				

* Where there are no spurs connected to a ring final circuit this value is also the $(R_1 + R_2)$ of the circuit.

C-STR-ECA-REV Aug 2011 V1

Courtesy of the ECA

Figure 6.5 *Schedule of Test Results*

There is advice provided on the use and completion of the EIC in the form of a note.

ELECTRICAL INSTALLATION CERTIFICATE NOTES:

1 The Electrical Installation Certificate is to be used only for the initial certification of a new installation or for an addition or alteration to an existing installation where new circuits have been introduced.

It is not to be used for a Periodic Inspection, for which an Electrical Installation Condition Report form should be used. For an addition or alteration which does not extend to the introdution of new circuits a Minor Electrical Installation Works Certificate may be used.

The 'original' Certificate is to be given to the person ordering the work (Regulation 632.1). A duplicate should be retained by the contractor.

2 This Certificate is only valid if accompanied by the Schedule of Inspections and the Schedule(s) of Test Results.

3 The signatures appended are those of the persons authorised by the companies executing the work of design, construction and inspection and testing respectively. A signatory authorised to certify more than one category of work should sign in each of the appropriate places.

4 The time interval recommended before the first periodic inspection must be inserted (see IET Guidance Note 3 for gudiance).

5 The page numbers for each of the Schedules of Test Results should be indicated, together with the total number of sheets involved.

6 The maximum prospective value of fault current (I_{pf}) recorded should be the greater of either the prospective value of short-circuit current or the prospective value of earth fault current.

7 The proposed date for the next inspection should take into consideration the frequency and quality of maintenance that the installation can reasonably be expected to receive during its intended life and the period should be agreed between the designer, installer and other relevant parties.

Courtesy of the ECA

Figure 6.6 *The advisory note for the EIC*

Remember

An Electrical Installation Certificate is only valid when accompanied by the Schedule(s) of Inspections and the Schedule(s) of Test Results.

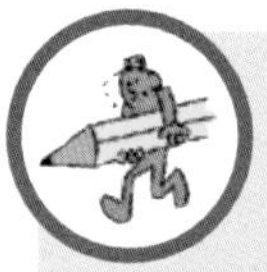

Try this

1 State the documents that would be used to certify the following works:

a An additional light to an office lighting circuit

____

b A electric shower circuit installed in a cricket club changing room

____

c Removing two sockets from a ring circuit to allow a wall to be removed

____

2 State the documents on which the following information is to be recorded:

a The person responsible for the design of the installation

____

b The $R_1 + R_2$ for a radial circuit

____

c The presence of a warning label at a main protective bonding connection

____

Part 2 Information recorded on forms of certification

A separate certificate should be issued, for each distinct installation, by the contractor who is responsible for the construction of the electrical installation. The certificate is issued to the person who ordered the work irrespective of whether they, or their client, have requested a certificate.

Having considered the forms used to certificate the electrical installation work we need to examine the information contained on each of these forms.

Minor Electrical Installation Works Certificate

As the MEIWC relates to alterations and additions to an existing single circuit the information recorded is significantly less than that required on the EIC. The certificate comprises four parts (Parts 1-4) and the content of each is as follows:

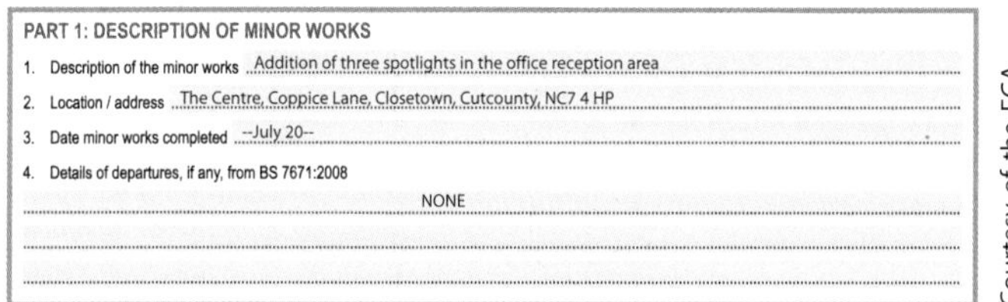

PART 1: DESCRIPTION OF MINOR WORKS

1. Description of the minor works Addition of three spotlights in the office reception area
2. Location / address The Centre, Coppice Lane, Closetown, Cutcounty, NC7 4 HP
3. Date minor works completed --July 20--
4. Details of departures, if any, from BS 7671:2008

NONE

Courtesy of the ECA

Figure 6.7 *Part 1: Description of minor works*

Part 1 is where the details of the minor works are recorded including:

- A description of the work
- The address and location
- The date on which the work was completed
- Details of any departures from BS 7671.

This last section relates to departures introduced in the design of the alteration or addition. These departures must result in an installation which is no less safe than it would be through full compliance with the requirements of BS 7671. It is extremely unlikely that there will be such a departure in general installations.

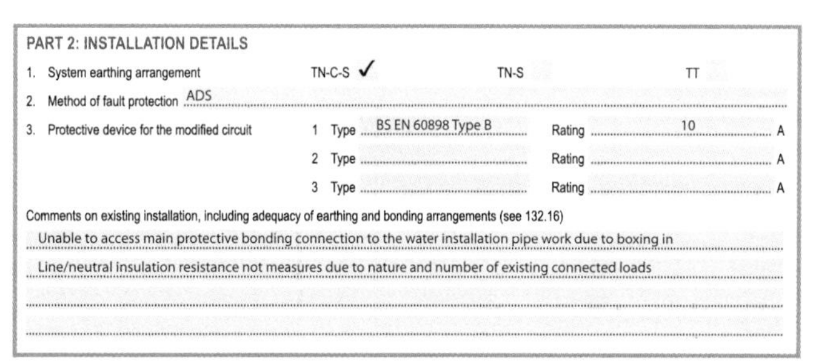

PART 2: INSTALLATION DETAILS

1. System earthing arrangement TN-C-S ✓ TN-S TT
2. Method of fault protection ADS
3. Protective device for the modified circuit
   1 Type BS EN 60898 Type B Rating 10 A
   2 Type Rating A
   3 Type Rating A

Comments on existing installation, including adequacy of earthing and bonding arrangements (see 132.16)

Unable to access main protective bonding connection to the water installation pipe work due to boxing in

Line/neutral insulation resistance not measures due to nature and number of existing connected loads

Courtesy of the ECA

Figure 6.8 *Part 2: Installation details*

In Part 2 the installation details are recorded and this includes the:

- System earthing arrangement
- Method of fault protection (generally automatic disconnection of supply ADS)
- Type and rating of the protective device for the circuit involved.

There is also a section for comments on the existing installation. This is where any observations or comments on the existing installation are made.

Areas of the installation which do not affect or are not affected by the alteration or addition do not have to be brought up to the current requirements. However, anything which we observe on the installation whilst carrying out the alteration or addition does have to be recorded on the certificate. This section may also be used to record any relevant comments on the installation. The sample certificate in Appendix 1 shows two such items of information:

- The inability to access the bonding connection to the water installation pipework
- An agreed limitation on testing insulation resistance between live conductors.

PART 3: ESSENTIAL TESTS

		Continuity ✓ or Ω (fill 1 col. only)		Insulation resistance M Ω			Polarity	Zs	RCD (if applicable)	
CCT No	Circuit description	$R_1 + R_2$	R_2	Line / neutral	Line / earth	Neutral / earth	✓	Ω	1 x IΔn	5 x IΔn
1	Reception area lighting	1.2		LIM	198	198	✓	1.35	N/A	N/A
2										
3										

Courtesy of the ECA

Figure 6.9 *Part 3: Essential tests*

Inspection and testing (initial verification), to confirm the compliance of the alteration or addition, must be carried out and the test results recorded. The extent of the testing does, to some extent, depend on the nature of the alteration or addition. The sample certificate shows that the only test not carried out was the insulation resistance test between live conductors. This is noted as being due to the number and type of luminaires already installed on the circuit. The extent of the interference with the existing installation and the risk of introducing faults during reassembly is the reason for this agreement made with the client to limit this test.

Note

The new wiring installed as part of the alteration and addition must be fully tested before being connected to the existing circuit. It is only when testing to confirm the status of the completed circuit after connection where the test between live conductors is omitted.

Remember

Any deviations or non-compliances which affect the alteration or addition to the circuit being worked on must be put right before the circuit is placed back in service.

PART 4: DECLARATION

I / We CERTIFY that the works do not impair the safety of the existing installation, that the said works have been designed, constructed, inspected and tested in accordance with BS 7671:2008 (IET Wiring Regulations), amended to ....2011................ (date) and that the said works, to the best of my / our knowledge and belief, at the time of my / our inspection complied with BS 7671 except as detailed in Part 1 above.

Contractor's name: James Douglas .... **Signature:** James Douglas ....

For and on behalf of: JD Installations Ltd .... **Position:** ....

Address: Unit 6, Gambols Estate, Neartown, Cutcounty, NTS 8LR .... **Date:** -- July 20 -- ....

....

....

Courtesy of the ECA

Figure 6.10 *Part 4: The declaration*

Part 4 is the declaration section where the competent person responsible for the alteration and addition is expected to sign to confirm that the electrical installation work is carried out:

- Does not impair the safety of the existing installation
- Has, to the best of the installer's knowledge and belief, been designed, constructed and inspected and tested in accordance with BS 7671 (except for any departures recorded on Part 1).

The remainder of the section contains information on the company and the particular individual responsible for the electrical work.

Note

There is no provision on the MEIWC to record the details of the client.

Electrical Installation Certificate

The Electrical Installation Certificate is available in two formats:

- The multiple signature version (often referred to as the long or three signature certificate)
- The single signature version (often referred to as the short certificate).

The information contained on these certificates is basically the same with the only difference being the declaration section.

We shall consider the multiple signature certificate as our example and then identify the difference between this and the single signature certificate.

The multiple signature certificate

DETAILS OF THE CLIENT
Dr. T David, 281 Percival Street, Coldsworthy, CW8 9TS

INSTALLATION ADDRESS
481 High Street, Nearby, Cutcounty, NC1 2 HS

Courtesy of the ECA

Figure 6.11 *EIC Details of client and the installation address*

The first two sections of the certificate relate to the details of the client, the name and address and the installation address, as these two may not be the same.

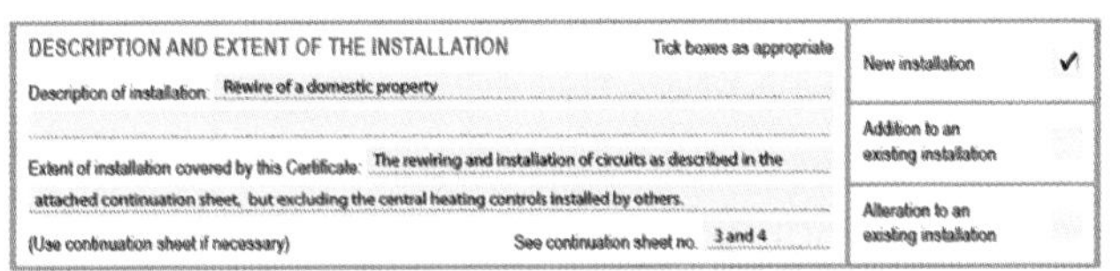

DESCRIPTION AND EXTENT OF THE INSTALLATION — Tick boxes as appropriate

Description of installation: Rewire of a domestic property

Extent of installation covered by this Certificate: The rewiring and installation of circuits as described in the attached continuation sheet, but excluding the central heating controls installed by others.

(Use continuation sheet if necessary) See continuation sheet no. 3 and 4

New installation	✓
Addition to an existing installation	
Alteration to an existing installation	

Courtesy of the ECA

Figure 6.12 *Description and extent of the installation*

The third section is where the description and the extent of the installation are recorded. This is a significant section as it declares what the signatories are actually responsible for. The description of the installation simply states what the installation is, such as the domestic rewire shown in the sample in Appendix 1. There are also three tick boxes to identify whether the work is:

- A new installation
- An addition to an existing installation
- An alteration to an existing installation.

Task

Compare the completed sample MEIWC contained in Appendix 1 of this study book with the example of a completed standard form contained in IET Guidance Note 3, Inspection and Testing.

There may be occasions where all three of the boxes are ticked.

Example: The owners of a semi-detached house are having the small box bedroom converted to an en suite shower room. As far as the electrical installation is concerned we have:

- New installation: the electric shower circuit
- Addition to the existing: the extractor fan and the shaver point added to the lighting circuit
- Alteration to existing: the removal of the socket outlets from the bedroom, altering the upstairs socket outlet circuit.

It is the extent of the installation which requires careful thought as this declares the work which is covered by the certificate and for which the signatories are responsible. The more detailed this description is the better, as it should leave no room for doubt about what the certificate covers.

In many cases there is insufficient space available on the form to detail the extent of the work and so continuation sheets are used. This section has space to refer to them by sheet number. The sample certificate in Appendix 1 makes reference to two sheets identified as pages 3 and 4 of the certificate.

Where work is carried out it is usual for the client to receive a quotation from the electrical contractor identifying the work that is proposed together with the cost involved. This quotation should contain details of precisely what is included and so for the rewire example this should itemise what is to be installed in each room. This is also contractually sound as there is then no question of what was included in the quotation. This listing, without any financial details, can be used as the continuation sheets for the extent of work on the certificate.

Each and every page of the certificate is numbered and once completed the total number of pages making up the certificate is added so numbering becomes, Sheet (or page) 1 of 6 for example. The continuation sheets form part of the certificate and so are included in the page numbering.

Remember

The extent of the installation declares the work covered by the Certificate. Statements such as 'whole house' are not appropriate as it actually identifies that everything in the electrical installation is covered. It will be very difficult to identify any additional work added on later by others as not being part of the original contractor's responsibility.

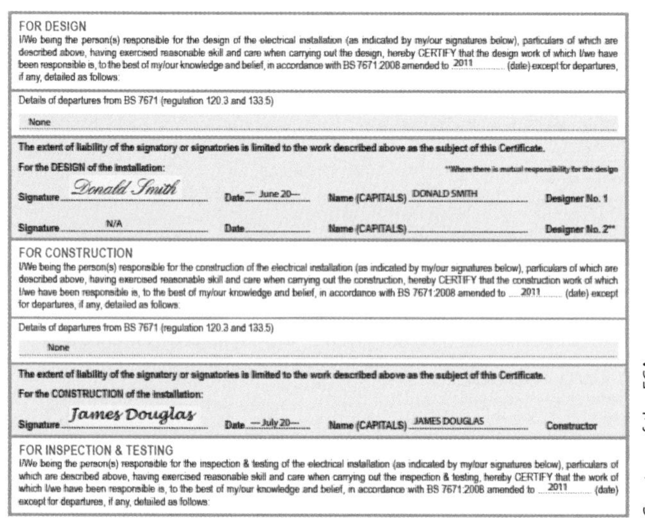

FOR DESIGN
I/We being the person(s) responsible for the design of the electrical installation (as indicated by my/our signatures below), particulars of which are described above, having exercised reasonable skill and care when carrying out the design, hereby CERTIFY that the design work of which I/we have been responsible is, to the best of my/our knowledge and belief, in accordance with BS 7671:2008 amended to 2011 (date) except for departures, if any, detailed as follows:

Details of departures from BS 7671 (regulation 120.3 and 133.5)

None

The extent of liability of the signatory or signatories is limited to the work described above as the subject of this Certificate.

For the DESIGN of the installation: **Where there is mutual responsibility for the design

Signature Donald Smith **Date** — June 20— **Name (CAPITALS)** DONALD SMITH **Designer No. 1**

Signature N/A **Date** **Name (CAPITALS)** **Designer No. 2****

FOR CONSTRUCTION
I/We being the person(s) responsible for the construction of the electrical installation (as indicated by my/our signatures below), particulars of which are described above, having exercised reasonable skill and care when carrying out the construction, hereby CERTIFY that the construction work of which I/we have been responsible is, to the best of my/our knowledge and belief, in accordance with BS 7671:2008 amended to 2011 (date) except for departures, if any, detailed as follows:

Details of departures from BS 7671 (regulation 120.3 and 133.5)

None

The extent of liability of the signatory or signatories is limited to the work described above as the subject of this Certificate.

For the CONSTRUCTION of the installation:

Signature James Douglas **Date** — July 20— **Name (CAPITALS)** JAMES DOUGLAS **Constructor**

FOR INSPECTION & TESTING
I/We being the person(s) responsible for the inspection & testing of the electrical installation (as indicated by my/our signatures below), particulars of which are described above, having exercised reasonable skill and care when carrying out the inspection & testing, hereby CERTIFY that the work of which I/we have been responsible is, to the best of my/our knowledge and belief, in accordance with BS 7671:2008 amended to 2011 (date) except for departures, if any, detailed as follows:

Courtesy of the ECA

Figure 6.13 *The declarations*

The multi-signature has three declaration sections one for each activity:

- Design
- Construction
- Inspection and testing.

I/We being the person(s) responsible for the construction of the electrical installation (as indicated by my/our signatures below), particulars of which are described above, having exercised reasonable skill and care when carrying out the construction, hereby CERTIFY that the construction work of which I/We have been responsible is, to the best of my/our knowledge and belief, in accordance with BS 7671:2008 amended to.........2011..........(date) except for departures, if any, detailed as follows:

Courtesy of the ECA

Figure 6.14 *Generic declaration for the construction*

In each section there is a statement which only varies according to the particular discipline and a generic version is shown in Figure 6.14.

The design declaration has the facility to record the details of two designers. It is not uncommon for complex installations to have the design of the distribution circuits, the location of distribution boards and the positioning of luminaires, accessories and equipment carried out by a consultant. The design of the final circuits is often left to the contractor carrying out the electrical installation to allow for variation in site conditions and cable routes.

Each of the signatories accepts the responsibility and makes the declaration for their part of the design, not the whole design, and so responsibility is shared. There is only the facility for one person to be responsible for the construction or the inspection and testing.

It is permissible for one person to be responsible for more than one activity, for example both the construction, and inspection and testing. Where this is the case, that person should complete both the relevant declarations.

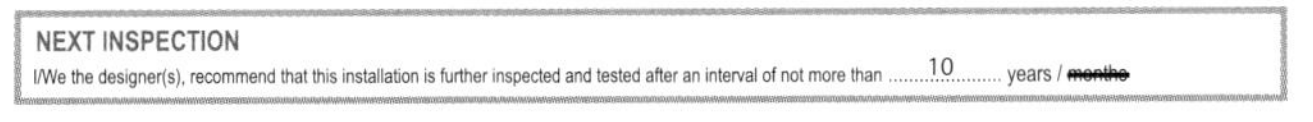

NEXT INSPECTION

I/We the designer(s), recommend that this installation is further inspected and tested after an interval of not more than ....10......... years / ~~months~~

Courtesy of the ECA

Figure 6.15 *Next inspection*

The final section on the first page of the certificate relates to the next inspection of the installation. BS 7671 states that all electrical installations should be periodically inspected and tested. It is the designer's responsibility to recommend the interval to the first of these periodic inspections based upon their knowledge of:

- The type of installation and equipment
- The use and operation of the installation
- The frequency and quality of maintenance
- Any external influences to which it is subjected.

IET Guidance Note 3 provides some guidance on the interval to the first periodic inspection in Table 3.2.

Task

Familiarize yourself with the content of Table 3.2 in IET Guidance Note 3 before you continue with this chapter.

PARTICULARS OF SIGNATORIES TO THE ELECTRICAL INSTALLATION CERTIFICATE

Designer (No. 1)
Name Donald Smith Company DS Electrical Consultants
Address The Centre, Coppice Lane, Closetown, Cutcounty
Postcode NC7 4 HP Tel 07858196200

Designer (No. 2)
Name N/A Company
Address
Postcode Tel

Constructor
Name James Douglas Company J D Installations Ltd
Address Unit 6, Gambols Estate, Neartown, Cutcounty
Postcode NT5 8LR Tel 0800468924

Inspector
Name James Douglas Company J D Installations Ltd
Address Unit 6, Gambols Estate, Neartown, Cutcounty
Postcode NT5 8LR Tel 0800468924

Courtesy of the ECA

Figure 6.16 *Particulars of the signatories*

On the first page of the EIC those competent persons responsible for the design, construction and inspection and testing signed their respective declarations. This first section on page 2 contains the details of those signatories. It includes the name of the signatory, the name and address of their company together with the company telephone number.

SUPPLY CHARACTERISTICS AND EARTHING ARRANGEMENTS — Tick boxes and enter details as appropriate

Earthing arrangements		Number and type of live conductors				Nature and type of supply parameters	Supply protective device
TN-S	✓	a.c.	✓	d.c.		Nominal voltage, U / U_0[1] 230 V	BS (EN) BS 88-3
TN-C-S		1-phase, 2-wire	✓	2-wire		Nominal frequency, f[1] 50 Hz	
TT		2-phase, 3-wire		3-wire		Prospective fault current, I_{pf}[2] 0.48 kA	Type System C
TN-C		3-phase, 4-wire				External loop impedance, Ze[2] 0.60 Ω	
IT		Confirmation of supply polarity				Note: (1) by enquiry, (2) by enquiry or measurement	Rated current 100 A

Alternative source of supply (as detailed on attached schedule)

Figure 6.17 *Supply characteristics and earthing arrangements*

The Supply Characteristics and Earthing Arrangements section contains information under four main headings where the particular characteristics of the supply for the installation being certificated are recorded. The main headings and the information within them are:

- Earthing arrangements (e.g. TT, TN-S, TN-C-S, TNC or IT)
- Number and type of live conductors (ac or dc, 1 phase – 2 wire, 3 phase – 4 wire, etc.)
- Nature and type of supply parameters (voltage, frequency, PFC and Z_e)
- Supply protective device (BS EN type and rating).

PARTICULARS OF INSTALLATION REFERRED TO IN THE CERTIFICATE — Tick boxes and enter details as appropriate

Means of earthing
Distributor's facility ✓
Installation earth electrode

Maximum demand
Maximum demand (load) 96 A kVA / Amps (delete as appropriate)

Details of installation earth electrode *(where applicable)*
Type (e.g. rod(s), tape, etc.) N/A — Location N/A — Electrode resistance to earth N/A Ω

Main protective conductors
Earthing conductor — material Copper — csa 16 mm² — Continuity and connection verified ✓
Main protective bonding conductors — material Copper — csa 10 mm² — Continuity and connection verified ✓
To incoming water and/or gas service — To other elements: N/A

Main switch or circuit-breaker
BS, type and no. of poles BS EN60947-3 (2 pole) — Current rating 100 A — Voltage rating 400 V V
Location Consumer unit in utility room — Fuse rating or setting N/A A
Rated residual operating current $I_{\Delta n}$ N/A mA, and operating time of ms (at $I_{\Delta n}$) (Applicable only where an RCD is suitable and is used as a main circuit-breaker)

COMMENTS ON EXISTING INSTALLATION (in the case of an addition or alteration see Section 633)
None

Figure 6.18 *Particulars of the installation referred to in the certificate*

The particulars of the installation section includes a number of items.

Means of earthing: the method of providing a connection to earth for the installation is recorded (distributor's facility or installation earth electrode).

Maximum demand: the maximum demand for the installation to be certified is recorded here in either kVA or Amperes.

Details of the installation earth electrode: the details of the type, location and resistance of the earth electrode, where this is the means of earthing, are recorded in this section.

Main protective conductors: the details of the material and csa of the earthing and any main protective bonding conductors are recorded here. The extraneous conductive parts to which the bonding is connected are also recorded.

Main switch or circuit breaker: the information relating to the main switch for the installation includes the BS type and number of poles, current and voltage rating and its location. Where the main switch is a fused switch or circuit breaker the fuse rating or setting is recorded. If the main switch for the installation is an RCD, as is often the case with a TT installation, the $I_{\Delta n}$ rating and its operating time at the 1 × $I_{\Delta n}$ test current are also recorded in this section.

Comments on the existing installation: where a circuit or circuits are added to an existing electrical installation these circuits must comply with BS 7671. Any deviations or departures observed on the existing installation are to be recorded for the benefit of the recipient of the certificate. This section will not apply where the installation is completely new but should not be left blank and so the comments are recorded as 'none' in such cases.

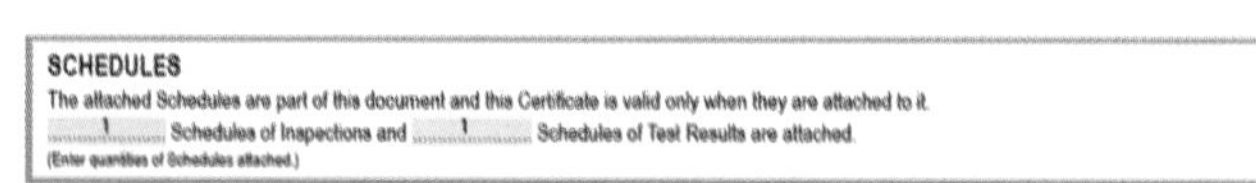
SCHEDULES
The attached Schedules are part of this document and this Certificate is valid only when they are attached to it.
1 Schedules of Inspections and 1 Schedules of Test Results are attached.
(Enter quantities of Schedules attached.)

Figure 6.19 *Schedules*

This final section advises that the certificate is only valid when the Schedule(s) of Inspections and Schedule(s) of Test Results are attached. The number of each of the schedules is recorded here to allow the recipient to identify the number of schedules that should be present.

Task

Familiarize yourself with the content of the completed sample multi-signature EIC in Appendix 1 of this study book before you continue with this chapter.

The Single Signature Certificate

The single signature certificate contains the same information as the multiple signature certificate but there are some conditions attached to its use.

The certificate may only be issued where the same person is responsible for the design, construction and inspection and testing of the electrical installation.

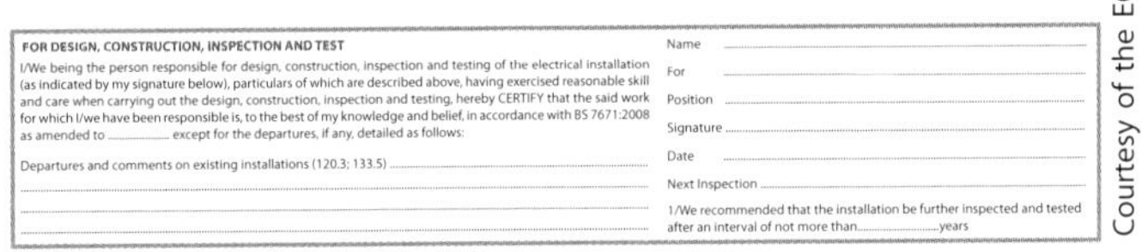

FOR DESIGN, CONSTRUCTION, INSPECTION AND TEST

I/We being the person responsible for design, construction, inspection and testing of the electrical installation (as indicated by my signature below), particulars of which are described above, having exercised reasonable skill and care when carrying out the design, construction, inspection and testing, hereby CERTIFY that the said work for which I/we have been responsible is, to the best of my knowledge and belief, in accordance with BS 7671:2008 as amended to .... except for the departures, if any, detailed as follows:

Departures and comments on existing installations (120.3; 133.5) ....

Name ....
For ....
Position ....
Signature ....
Date ....
Next Inspection ....

1/We recommended that the installation be further inspected and tested after an interval of not more than.......... years

Courtesy of the ECA

Figure 6.20 *The declaration from the single signature EIC*

Because the same person is responsible for all three activities the declarations have been combined to include the design, construction and inspection and testing in a single declaration requiring just one signature.

Note

The single signature certificate is a shortened form of the EIC and may only be used where the same person is responsible for the design, construction and inspection and testing of the electrical installation.

Schedule of Inspections

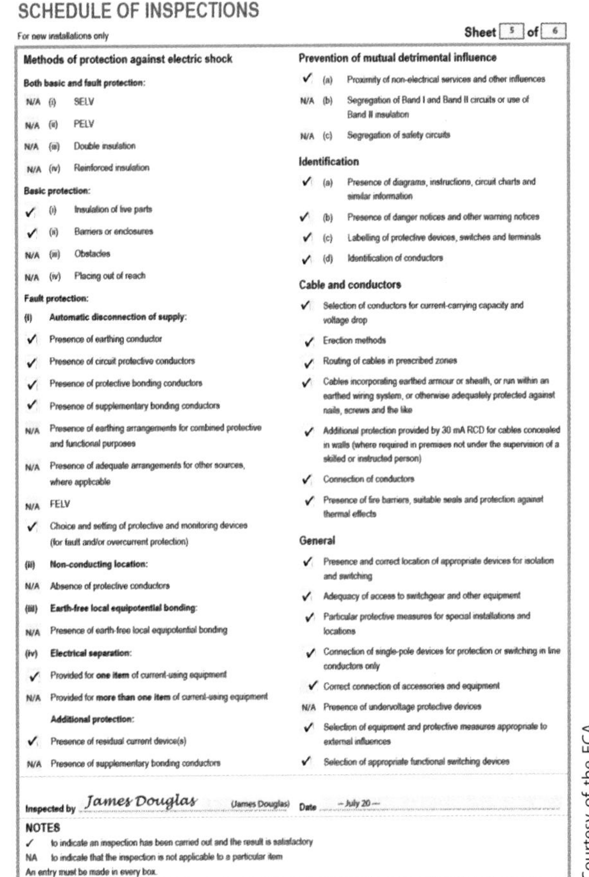

SCHEDULE OF INSPECTIONS

For new installations only — Sheet 5 of 6

Methods of protection against electric shock

Both basic and fault protection:
N/A (i) SELV
N/A (ii) PELV
N/A (iii) Double insulation
N/A (iv) Reinforced insulation

Basic protection:
✓ (i) Insulation of live parts
✓ (ii) Barriers or enclosures
N/A (iii) Obstacles
N/A (iv) Placing out of reach

Fault protection:
(i) **Automatic disconnection of supply:**
✓ Presence of earthing conductor
✓ Presence of circuit protective conductors
✓ Presence of protective bonding conductors
✓ Presence of supplementary bonding conductors
N/A Presence of earthing arrangements for combined protective and functional purposes
N/A Presence of adequate arrangements for other sources, where applicable
N/A FELV
✓ Choice and setting of protective and monitoring devices (for fault and/or overcurrent protection)
(ii) **Non-conducting location:**
N/A Absence of protective conductors
(iii) **Earth-free local equipotential bonding:**
N/A Presence of earth-free local equipotential bonding
(iv) **Electrical separation:**
✓ Provided for **one item** of current-using equipment
N/A Provided for **more than one item** of current-using equipment

Additional protection:
✓ Presence of residual current device(s)
N/A Presence of supplementary bonding conductors

Prevention of mutual detrimental influence
✓ (a) Proximity of non-electrical services and other influences
N/A (b) Segregation of Band I and Band II circuits or use of Band II insulation
N/A (c) Segregation of safety circuits

Identification
✓ (a) Presence of diagrams, instructions, circuit charts and similar information
✓ (b) Presence of danger notices and other warning notices
✓ (c) Labelling of protective devices, switches and terminals
✓ (d) Identification of conductors

Cable and conductors
✓ Selection of conductors for current-carrying capacity and voltage drop
✓ Erection methods
✓ Routing of cables in prescribed zones
✓ Cables incorporating earthed armour or sheath, or run within an earthed wiring system, or otherwise adequately protected against nails, screws and the like
✓ Additional protection provided by 30 mA RCD for cables concealed in walls (where required in premises not under the supervision of a skilled or instructed person)
✓ Connection of conductors
✓ Presence of fire barriers, suitable seals and protection against thermal effects

General
✓ Presence and correct location of appropriate devices for isolation and switching
✓ Adequacy of access to switchgear and other equipment
✓ Particular protective measures for special installations and locations
✓ Connection of single-pole devices for protection or switching in line conductors only
✓ Correct connection of accessories and equipment
N/A Presence of undervoltage protective devices
✓ Selection of equipment and protective measures appropriate to external influences
✓ Selection of appropriate functional switching devices

Inspected by *James Douglas* (James Douglas) Date – July 20 –

NOTES
✓ to indicate an inspection has been carried out and the result is satisfactory
NA to indicate that the inspection is not applicable to a particular item
An entry must be made in every box.

Courtesy of the ECA

Figure 6.21 *Schedule of Inspections*

The options for completing the Schedule of Inspections are the entry of either:

- A tick (inspected and correct)
- N/A (not applicable to the particular installation being inspected).

Any applicable items which are not correct must be put right before the installation can be certificated and placed in service.

The Schedule of Inspections is used to record the results of the inspection process. As there are a large number of items to be inspected the results are grouped under main, sub and item headings.

Remember

This schedule relates to inspection only and not to testing. When carrying out the inspection we are confirming that, by inspection, the requirements for each applicable item have been met. So, for example, the presence of cpcs is first by inspection to confirm they are present at each point on the circuit. At the testing stage we then confirm they are continuous and connect all points on the circuit to the MET.

The whole of the left-hand column relates to methods of protection against electric shock which is identified in the main heading in bold at the top of the column. There are then a number of sub-headings for the methods of providing this protection including:

Both basic and fault protection: this includes SELV, PELV, double insulation and reinforced insulation. All these methods will provide both basic and fault protection. However, they are all special methods when applied to an installation and are unlikely to be used in a domestic environment.

Basic protection: this includes insulation of live parts and barriers and enclosures both of which are common to all electrical insulations. It also includes obstacles and placing out of reach both of which are not common and only used in special circumstances. They are not suitable for domestic installations.

Fault protection: this is further divided into four sub-headings which are:

- i Automatic disconnection of supply
- ii Non-conducting location
- iii Earth-free equipotential bonding
- iv Electrical separation.

Of these methods the non-conducting location, earth-free equipotential bonding and electrical separation for more than one item of equipment, are specialized installations and can only be used where the installation is under the control of skilled or instructed persons.

Automatic disconnection of supply is by far the most common method of fault protection and the items listed under this apply to almost every electrical installation.

Fault protection:

(i)	**Automatic disconnection of supply:**
✓	Presence of earthing conductor
✓	Presence of circuit protective conductors
✓	Presence of protective bonding conductors
N/A	Presence of supplementary bonding conductors
N/A	Presence of earthing arrangements for combined protective and functional purposes
N/A	Presence of adequate arrangements for other sources, where applicable
N/A	FELV
✓	Choice and setting of protective and monitoring devices (for fault and/or overcurrent protection)

Courtesy of the ECA

Figure 6.22 *ADS checklist*

Electrical separation: identifies two scenarios, one of which is for a single item of equipment. This may be appropriate where a shaver socket outlet is installed in a room containing a bath or shower. This type of socket is only permitted in that location when it is supplied through an isolating transformer and so the method of protection is appropriate for that location.

The final sub-heading in the left-hand column is:

Additional protection: this is where either protection by RCD or supplementary bonding has been installed to provide additional protection as defined in BS 7671.

Note

Supplementary bonding appears in both ADS and additional protection. In ADS this applies where supplementary bonding is required by BS 7671, generally in special locations such as swimming pools and so on. The additional protection entry is where supplementary bonding has been used because the earth fault loop impedance was too high to provide disconnection within the prescribed time (additional protection).

Task

Familiarize yourself with the 'Methods of protection against electric shock' check list in the Schedule of Inspections in Appendix 1 of this studybook before continuing with this chapter.

The right-hand column of the Schedule of Inspections consists of four main headings.

Prevention of mutual detrimental influence

This heading relates to the effects of electrical and non-electrical services on the electrical installation and vice versa. Non-electrical services include gas, water, oil, steam and chilled water pipework. The inspection is carried out to confirm that the electrical installation will not be adversely affected by the proximity of any of the other services in the premises.

Segregation of Band I and Band II circuits will apply where any Band I circuits are installed and these include data, telephone and television circuits and other circuits operating at ≤ 50 V ac or ≤ 120 V dc.

Segregation of safety services relates specifically to the separation of the electrical installation from the designated safety services as described in BS 7671.

Identification

All installations will require the inspection to confirm that all the diagrams, charts and labels are present, the protective devices, switches and terminals are correctly labelled and the conductors are correctly identified.

Figure 6.23 *All labels are in place*

Cables and conductors

The items under this heading refer to the inspection requirements for the cables and conductors and some of these items need a little clarification as to how they are applied.

Selection of conductors for current carrying capacity and voltage drop: is an inspection to confirm that the cables and conductors which are installed:

- Are the correct csa as detailed in the designer's specification
- Are compatible with the I_n rating of the protective device (conductor current carrying capacity $\geq I_n$).

Erection methods: apply to all cable installations and the inspection is to confirm that the cables and conductors have been installed in accordance with the requirements of BS 7671, i.e. correctly fixed and supported and so on.

Routing of cables in the prescribed zones: The 'prescribed zones' refer to the locations in which cables concealed within walls can be installed. Therefore this only applies where cables are concealed within the walls of the building.

Figure 6.24 *Routing of cables in prescribed zones*

The next two items are only applicable where cables are routed in the prescribed zones and so that inspection box is ticked.

Cables incorporating etc. refers to the methods prescribed in BS 7671 for cables to afford suitable protection against penetration by nails or screws and the associated risk of electric shock. If any of these options are used then the inspector must confirm that they are in place and so place a tick in the check box to confirm this.

Additional protection by 30 mA RCD etc. refers to the alternative option which is given in BS 7671. If the cables are not of a type or installed in compliance with the previous requirement then they must be protected by an RCD as defined in BS 7671.

Either or both of these options may be used in an electrical installation and the appropriate inspection must be carried out to confirm the requirements have been met.

Where there are no cables concealed within the walls of the premises all three of these checkboxes will be marked N/A.

Connection of conductors: requires an inspection to confirm all terminations are mechanically sound and correctly terminated.

Presence of fire barriers, suitable seals and protection against thermal effects: Wherever the cables or containment systems of the electrical installation pass through a fire barrier the barrier must be reinstated to the same level of protection as the surrounding material. This inspection checkbox is used once this requirement is confirmed. If no fire barriers are breached by the electrical installation this would be marked as N/A.

Remember

The ceilings within a dwelling, for example, are a minimum of a 30 minute fire barrier and any penetrations through these are to be suitably reinstated.

General

Includes the general requirements which apply beyond those already mentioned above and most of these are self explanatory. There are three which will benefit from some further explanation.

Presence and correct location of appropriate devices for isolation and switching: this refers to the isolation and switching for the electrical control of the installation. It includes the main isolator, circuit breakers, remote isolators and the like. It does not include functional switching used by the client and users of the installation.

Particular protective measures for special installations and locations: is applicable to those installations and locations which are included in Part 7 of BS 7671 such as rooms containing a bath or shower.

Presence of undervoltage protection: this generally relates to particular circuits such as those supplying electric motors where a contactor is included in the control circuit. When the voltage falls below a set level the contactor will automatically disconnect the supply to the equipment.

Finally the Schedule of Inspections is signed and dated by the inspector.

Schedule of Test Results

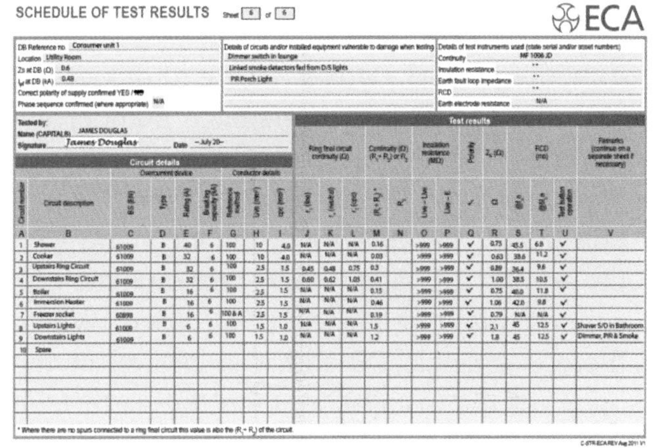

SCHEDULE OF TEST RESULTS Sheet 6 of 6 ECA

DB Reference no. Consumer unit 1
Location Utility Room
Zs at DB (Ω) 0.6
I_{pf} at DB (kA) 0.48
Correct polarity of supply confirmed YES
Phase sequence confirmed (where appropriate) N/A

Details of circuits and/or installed equipment vulnerable to damage when testing
Dimmer switch in lounge
Linked smoke detectors fed from D/S lights
PIR Porch Light

Details of test instruments used (state serial and/or asset numbers)
Continuity MF 1006 JD
Insulation resistance **
Earth fault loop impedance **
RCD **
Earth electrode resistance N/A

Tested by:
Name (CAPITALS) JAMES DOUGLAS
Signature James Douglas Date – July 20–

A	B	C	D	E	F	G	H	I	J	K	L	M	N	O	P	Q	R	S	T	U	V
Circuit number	Circuit description	BS (EN)	Type	Rating (A)	Breaking capacity (kA)	Reference method	Live (mm²)	cpc (mm²)	r_1 (line)	r_n (neutral)	r_2 (cpc)	(R_1+R_2)*	R_2	Live – Live	Live – E	✓	Ω	@$I_{\Delta n}$	@$5I_{\Delta n}$	Test button operation	Remarks (continue on a separate sheet if necessary)
1	Shower	61009	B	40	6	100	10	4.0	N/A	N/A	N/A	0.16		>999	>999	✓	0.73	43.5	6.8	✓	
2	Cooker	61009	B	32	6	100	10	4.0	N/A	N/A	N/A	0.03		>999	>999	✓	0.63	38.6	11.2	✓	
3	Upstairs Ring Circuit	61009	B	32	6	100	2.5	1.5	0.45	0.48	0.75	0.3		>999	>999	✓	0.89	36.4	9.6	✓	
4	Downstairs Ring Circuit	61009	B	32	6	100	2.5	1.5	0.60	0.62	1.05	0.41		>999	>999	✓	1.00	38.5	10.5	✓	
5	Boiler	61009	B	16	6	100	2.5	1.5	N/A	N/A	N/A	0.15		>999	>999	✓	0.75	40.0	11.8	✓	
6	Immersion Heater	61009	B	16	6	100	2.5	1.5	N/A	N/A	N/A	0.46		>999	>999	✓	1.06	42.0	9.8	✓	
7	Freezer socket	60898	B	16	6	100 & A	2.5	1.5	N/A	N/A	N/A	0.19		>999	>999	✓	0.79	N/A	N/A	✓	
8	Upstairs Lights	61009	B	6	6	100	1.5	1.0	N/A	N/A	N/A	1.5		>999	>999	✓	2.1	45	12.5	✓	Shaver S/O in Bathroom
9	Downstairs Lights	61009	B	6	6	100	1.5	1.0	N/A	N/A	N/A	1.2		>999	>999	✓	1.8	45	12.5	✓	Dimmer, PIR & Smoke
10	Spare																				

* Where there are no spurs connected to a ring final circuit this value is also the $(R_1 + R_2)$ of the circuit.

C-STR-ECA REV Aug 2011 V1

Figure 6.25 *Schedule of Test Results*

Courtesy of the ECA

In the previous chapters we identified the individual sections of the Schedule of Test Results where the results of each test would be recorded. We will not consider these again here but look at the other areas of the schedule and the information to be entered.

DB Reference no. Consumer unit 1	Details of circuits and/or installed equipment vulnerable to damage when testing	Details of test instruments used (state serial and/or asset numbers)
Location Utility Room	Dimmer switch in lounge	Continuity MF 1006 JD
Zs at DB (Ω) 0.6	Linked smoke detectors fed from D/S lights	Insulation resistance **
I_{pf} at DB (kA) 0.48	PIR Porch Light	Earth fault loop impedance **
Correct polarity of supply confirmed YES		RCD **
Phase sequence confirmed (where appropriate) N/A		Earth electrode resistance N/A

Figure 6.26 *The top section of the Schedule of Test Results*

Courtesy of the ECA

Task

Familiarize yourself with the second column check list in the Schedule of Inspections in Appendix 1 of this studybook before continuing with this chapter.

In the top section of the Schedule of Test Results the general information is recorded which includes:

Distribution board details: where the location and distribution board reference number are recorded together with the earth fault loop impedance and PFC measured at the distribution board. The polarity of the incoming supply to the DB and, where appropriate, the correct phase sequence is recorded. Where there is a single DB and it is located at the origin of the installation, then the earth fault loop impedance and PFC will be the same as those recorded on the EIC. Where the DB is remote from the origin then the values at the DB are to be recorded.

Details of circuits and/or installed equipment vulnerable to damage when testing: is where information on equipment which requires special consideration during the testing process is noted. This relates primarily to damage resulting from the application of test voltages, particularly when carrying out insulation resistance testing. Such items include electronic equipment and timers, smoke alarms, photocells and so on.

Details of test instruments used: it is important to record the serial or company asset number of the test instrument(s) used for the tests recorded on the schedule. This will allow the same test instrument to be used for any subsequent tests carried out or confirmation of recorded values. Should an instrument be found to be faulty at the ongoing accuracy checks the record will allow the contractor to identify the installations which have been tested using that particular test instrument.

Tested by:
Name (CAPITALS) James Douglas
Signature *James Douglas* Date -- July 20 --

Courtesy of the ECA

Figure 6.27 *Name and signature of the inspector with the date of the tests*

The inspector is required to print their name and sign the schedule and record the date on which the tests were undertaken.

Circuit details

Circuit details								
		Overcurrent device				Conductor details		
Circuit number	Circuit description	BS (EN)	Type	Rating (A)	Breaking capacity (kA)	Reference method	Live (mm²)	cpc (mm²)
A	B	C	D	E	F	G	H	I
1	Shower	61009	B	40	6	100	10	4.0
2	Cooker	61009	B	32	6	100	10	4.0
3	Upstairs Ring Circuit	61009	B	32	6	100	2.5	1.5
4	Downstairs Ring Circuit	61009	B	32	6	100	2.5	1.5
5	Boiler	61009	B	16	6	100	2.5	1.5
6	Immersion Heater	61009	B	16	6	100	2.5	1.5
7	Freezer socket	60898	B	16	6	100 & A	2.5	1.5
8	Upstairs Lights	61009	B	6	6	100	1.5	1.0
9	Downstairs Lights	61009	B	6	6	100	1.5	1.0
10	Spare							

* Where there are no spurs connected to a ring final circuit this value is also the $(R_1 + R_2)$ of the circuit.

Courtesy of the ECA

Figure 6.28 *Circuit details*

The first nine columns comprise the circuit details and contain information which is necessary for the inspector to be able to carry out the inspection and testing. The columns are:

- Circuit number: identifies the circuit by unique number

- Circuit description: what the circuit supplies such as upstairs lights or office power
- The overcurrent device:
  - BS or BSEN number
  - Type
  - Rating A (I_n)
  - Breaking capacity in kA
- Conductor details:
  - Reference method
  - Live (csa in mm^2)
  - cpc (csa in mm^2).

As we can see the information contained in these sections of the Schedule of Test Results is necessary for the inspection and testing to be carried out safely.

Task

Familiarize yourself with the completed sample of the Schedule of Test Results in Appendix 1 of this study book before continuing with this chapter.

Try this

Using the information contained in IET Guidance Note 3 and referring to the Schedule of Test Results shown in Figure 6.29, identify SIX results which would require investigation and correction before the installation can be placed in service.

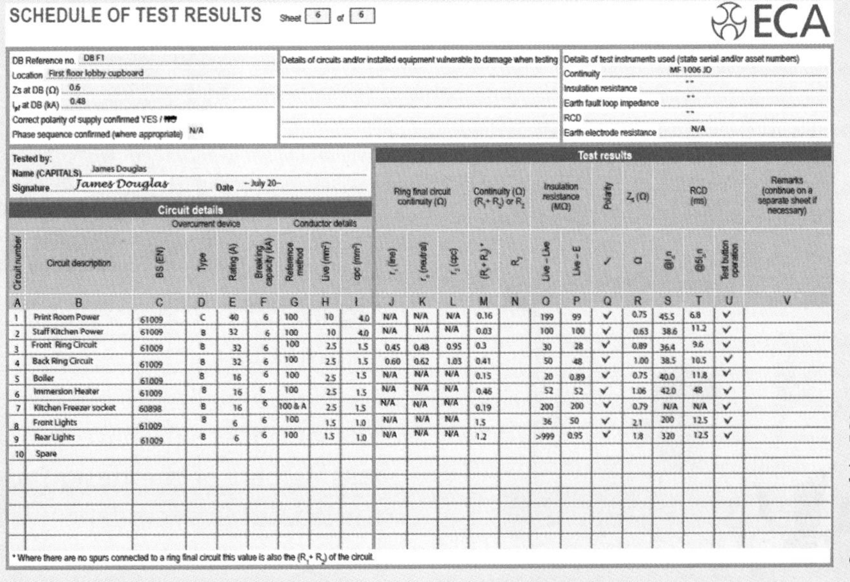

SCHEDULE OF TEST RESULTS Sheet 6 of 6 ECA

DB Reference no. DB F1
Location First floor lobby cupboard
Zs at DB (Ω) 0.6
I_{pf} at DB (kA) 0.48
Correct polarity of supply confirmed YES / ~~NO~~
Phase sequence confirmed (where appropriate) N/A

Details of circuits and/or installed equipment vulnerable to damage when testing

Details of test instruments used (state serial and/or asset numbers)
Continuity MF 1006 JD
Insulation resistance "
Earth fault loop impedance "
RCD "
Earth electrode resistance N/A

Tested by:
Name (CAPITALS) James Douglas
Signature *James Douglas* Date – July 20–

Circuit number	Circuit description	BS (EN)	Type	Rating (A)	Breaking capacity (kA)	Reference method	Live (mm^2)	cpc (mm^2)	r_1 (line)	r_n (neutral)	r_2 (cpc)	(R_1+R_2)*	R_2	Live – Live	Live – E	Polarity ✓	Z_s Ω	RCD @$I_{\Delta n}$	RCD @$5I_{\Delta n}$	Test button operation	Remarks (continue on a separate sheet if necessary)
	Circuit details								Test results												
		Overcurrent device				Conductor details			Ring final circuit continuity (Ω)			Continuity (Ω) (R_1+R_2) or R_2		Insulation resistance (MΩ)		Polarity	Z_s (Ω)	RCD (ms)			
A	B	C	D	E	F	G	H	I	J	K	L	M	N	O	P	Q	R	S	T	U	V
1	Print Room Power	61009	C	40	6	100	10	4.0	N/A	N/A	N/A	0.16		199	99	✓	0.75	45.5	6.8	✓	
2	Staff Kitchen Power	61009	B	32	6	100	10	4.0	N/A	N/A	N/A	0.03		100	100	✓	0.63	38.6	11.2	✓	
3	Front Ring Circuit	61009	B	32	6	100	2.5	1.5	0.45	0.48	0.95	0.3		30	28	✓	0.89	36.4	9.6	✓	
4	Back Ring Circuit	61009	B	32	6	100	2.5	1.5	0.60	0.62	1.03	0.41		50	48	✓	1.00	38.5	10.5	✓	
5	Boiler	61009	B	16	6	100	2.5	1.5	N/A	N/A	N/A	0.15		20	0.89	✓	0.75	40.0	11.8	✓	
6	Immersion Heater	61009	B	16	6	100	2.5	1.5	N/A	N/A	N/A	0.46		52	52	✓	1.06	42.0	48	✓	
7	Kitchen Freezer socket	60898	B	16	6	100 & A	2.5	1.5	N/A	N/A	N/A	0.19		200	200	✓	0.79	N/A	N/A	✓	
8	Front Lights	61009	B	6	6	100	1.5	1.0	N/A	N/A	N/A	1.5		36	50	✓	2.1	200	12.5	✓	
9	Rear Lights	61009	B	6	6	100	1.5	1.0	N/A	N/A	N/A	1.2		>999	0.95	✓	1.8	320	12.5	✓	
10	Spare																				

* Where there are no spurs connected to a ring final circuit this value is also the (R_1+R_2) of the circuit.

Courtesy of the ECA

Figure 6.29 *Identify the results which require investigation and correction*

Part 3 The certification process

Having looked at the forms of certification and the information that is to be contained on them we need to consider the actual process of certification for a completed installation. We will go through the process on the basis that the responsibilities for the design, construction and inspection and testing are all attributed to different individuals.

Remember

The certificate is issued by the person responsible for the construction of the installation as only they can confirm the compliance of the construction.

The designer will have completed the design before the installation was carried out. Part of that process will be to confirm that the design meets the requirements of BS 7671. If there are any departures from BS 7671 in the design the designer must ensure that the installation will be no less safe than it would be by compliance with BS 7671.

As we discussed earlier the designer will be required to complete the declaration for the design on the Electrical Installation Certificate.

Figure 6.30 *The designer is responsible for the design*

During the construction stage the person responsible for the construction is responsible for confirming that the construction of the installation meets the requirements of BS 7671 and the Building Regulations. This is usually done by regular inspection throughout the construction stage and checking that the installed equipment meets the design specification and is suitably installed.

During the construction the person responsible for the inspection and testing of the installation should also be involved in inspection, and where appropriate testing, of the installation. In this way both the constructor and the inspector are able to confirm the compliance of the construction.

Figure 6.31 *The installer is responsible for the construction*

The designer will have provided the circuit details as part of the design and the installation is carried out in accordance with these details. The constructor is then responsible for producing the Electrical Installation Certificate and the circuit details on the Schedule of Test Results. At this point the constructor can sign their declaration and pass the certificate to the inspector.

The inspector carries out the final inspection and then, providing the inspection is satisfactory, the testing of the installation. The verification process is then undertaken by the inspector, often during the testing, to confirm that the installation meets the design specification and BS 7671.

Figure 6.32 *The inspector is responsible for the inspection, testing and verification*

Providing the results of the inspection and testing are verified as acceptable and the installation is compliant the inspector will complete the Schedule(s) of Inspections and the Schedule(s) of Test Results. The inspector then signs the declaration for the inspection and testing of the installation and the certificate is returned to the constructor. The constructor will confirm that the inspection, testing and declaration section has been correctly completed.

It is often at this stage that the certificate is passed to the designer for the design declaration to be signed. At this point the designer has the opportunity to review the results of the inspection and testing and to confirm the compliance of the installation. The designer can then complete the declaration and enter the recommended interval to the next inspection.

Each signatory takes responsibility for their particular activity but there is an obligation on each party to notify any discrepancies which become apparent during their part of the work.

Once the Electrical Installation Certificate is completed, and all the declarations are completed, the certificate is ready to be passed to the client together with all the other relevant documentation for the operation and maintenance of the installation.

Contractor's certificate records and retention

The contractor is responsible for keeping a record of the forms of certification issued for the electrical installations they have undertaken. Each certificate should be allocated a unique number which is recorded on the certificate and the contractor's register. The register should record, as a minimum, the certificate number and details of the client and the date of issue.

JD Installations Ltd			
Electrical Installation Certificate Register			
Certificate no.	Client details	Installation address	Issue date
EIC 012345	Dr T David	481 High Street, Nearby, NC1 2HS	--July 20--

Figure 6.33 *Typical certificate register*

A certificate register would be required for both the EIC and the MEIWC and these may be kept electronically.

The contractor is expected to keep a copy of Electrical Installation Certificates issued for each installation carried out. The proprietary pads of certificates generally contain an original and copy certificate, normally no carbon required (NCR), so that an original certificate can be passed to the client and the copy retained by the contractor.

For complex installations it is common for all the client's documents to be produced and provided to the client electronically. Where certificates are produced electronically the contractor's copy may also be kept as an electronic copy, whilst written copies may be scanned and stored electronically.

The length of time for which the contractor keeps copies of certificates should be for at least the period of the warranty for the installation. Paper versions of certificates may require considerable storage space, whereas the electronic versions require very little physical space. The advantage of electronic storage is that the certificates can be kept, with very little space requirement, for an indefinite period so that a record is available at any time.

Clients' certification documents and retention

The standard forms in BS 7671 include guidance for the recipients of the forms of certification which should be attached to the certificate which is given to the client.

ELECTRICAL INSTALLATION CERTIFICATE GUIDANCE FOR RECIPIENTS
(to be appended to the Certificate)

This safety Certificate has been issued to confirm that the electrical installation work to which it relates has been designed, constructed, inspected and tested in accordance with British Standard 7671 (the IET Wiring Regulations).

You should have received an 'original' Certificate and the contractor should have retained a duplicate. If you were the person ordering the work, but not the owner of the installation, you should pass this Certificate, or a full copy of it including the schedules, immediately to the owner.

The 'original' Certificate should be retained in a safe place and be shown to any person inspecting or undertaking further work on the electrical installation in the future. If you later vacate the property, this Certificate will demonstrate to the new owner that the electrical installation complied with the requirements of British Standard 7671 at the time the Certificate was issued. The Construction (Design and Management) Regulations require that, for a project covered by those Regulations, a copy of this Certificate, together with its schedules, is included in the project health and safety documentation.

For safety reasons the electrical installation will need to be inspected at appropriate intervals by a competent person. The maximum time interval recommended before the next inspection is stated on Page 1 under 'Next Inspection'.

This Certificate is intended to be issued only for a new electrical installation or for new work associated with an addition or alteration to an existing installation. It should not have been issued for the inspection of an existing electrical installation. An 'Electrical Installation Condition Report' should be issued for such an inspection.

Courtesy of the ECA

Figure 6.34 *EIC guidance for recipients*

When the documents are handed over to the client it is important to ensure that the client is aware of their responsibilities in regards to the certificate. It is not sufficient to simply rely on the printed guidance and so the advice should be given directly to the client whenever possible.

Figure 6.35 *Suitable advice must be given to the client*

The client should be made aware of the printed guidance and the key points outlined to ensure that they are aware of the significance of the certificate. These key points include:

- The certificate is the evidence that the electrical installation has been designed, constructed and inspected and tested in accordance with the requirements of BS 7671 and confirms the installation is safe for use.
- If the client is not the owner of the installation then the original certificate or a full copy of the certificate including the schedules should be passed to the owner without delay.
- The original certificate should be kept in a safe place and shown to anyone undertaking work or inspection and testing of the installation.
- Should ownership of the property change, the certificate should be passed to the new owner as proof that the installation complied with the edition of BS 7671 current at the time the installation was carried out.
- The certificate should remain with the installation throughout its lifetime as reference to establish whether deterioration of the installation has occurred.

MINOR ELECTRICAL INSTALLATION WORKS CERTIFICATE GUIDANCE FOR RECIPIENTS

(to be appended to the Certificate)

This Certificate has been issued to confirm that the electrical installation work to which it relates has been designed, constructed, inspected and tested in accordance with British Standard 7671 (the IET Wiring Regulations).

You should have received an original Certificate and the contractor should have retained a duplicate. It you were the person ordering the work, but not the owner of the installation, you should pass this Certificate, or a copy of it, to the owner. A separate Certificate should have been received for each existing circuit on which minor works have been carried out. This Certificate is not appropriate if you requested the contractor to undertake more extensive installation work, for which you should have received an Electrical Installation Certificate.

The Certificate should be retained in a safe place and be shown to any person inspecting or undertaking further work on the electrical installation in the future. If you later vacate the property, this Certificate will demonstrate to the new owner that the minor electrical installation work carried out complied with the requirements of British Standard 7671 at the time the Certificate was issued.

Courtesy of the ECA

Figure 6.36 *MEIWC guidance for recipients*

The Electrical Installation Certificate and the Schedule(s) of Inspection and Schedule(s) of Test Results provide the client with evidence to satisfy the requirements of the EWR that the installation has been installed so it is safe for use. It also forms the basis for the subsequent periodic inspection of the installation where the information is used to determine any deterioration of the installation.

The keeping of EICs, MEIWCs and subsequent Electrical Installation Condition Reports (EICRs) throughout the life of the installation allows changes in the installation condition and compliance to be monitored. It also provides evidence that the electrical installation is being maintained which is a requirement of the EWR.

Task

1 You have designed and constructed the rewiring of a domestic bungalow and the installation work is now complete. Produce a simple flow chart to show the process of initial verification from the beginning of the process through to handing over the appropriate documents to the client.

2 Produce a bullet point list of the information and advice you will give the client when handing over the completed EIC for the rewire of the bungalow.

- ____________________
- ____________________
- ____________________
- ____________________
- ____________________
- ____________________
- ____________________
- ____________________
- ____________________
- ____________________

Congratulations, you have now completed Chapter 6 of this studybook. Complete the self assessment questions before continuing to the end test.

SELF ASSESSMENT

Circle the correct answers.

1 A minor works certificate does **NOT** include a record of:

a. System earthing arrangement
b. External earth fault loop impedance
c. Circuit protective device
d. Circuit earth fault loop impedance

2 The tick boxes used to identify the use of an Electrical Installation Certificate do **NOT** include:

a. A new installation
b. An alteration to an existing installation
c. An addition to an existing installation
d. A replacement of an accessory

3 When the same individual is responsible for the design, construction and inspection and testing of an installation the most appropriate form of certification to issue is:

a. Single signature EIC
b. Schedule of Inspections
c. Multi-signature EIC
d. MEIWC

4 The minimum number of pages that will be issued for an EIC to be valid is:

a. 2
b. 3
c. 4
d. 5

5 The value of PFC is recorded on the:

a. EIC and the MEIWC
b. EIC and Schedule of Inspections
c. EIC and Schedule of Test Results
d. MEIWC and the Schedule of Test Results

Appendix 1: Certificates

MINOR ELECTRICAL INSTALLATION WORKS CERTIFICATE FOR UP TO THREE CIRCUITS

(REQUIREMENTS FOR ELECTRICAL INSTALLATIONS BS 7671 (IET WIRING REGULATIONS))

To be used only for minor electrical work which does not include the provision of a new circuit

Certificate number: MW001234 **Member number:**

PART 1: DESCRIPTION OF MINOR WORKS

1. Description of the minor works: Addition of three spotlights in the office reception area
2. Location / address: The Centre, Coppice Lane, Closetown, Cutcounty, NC7 4 HP
3. Date minor works completed: -- July 20---
4. Details of departures, if any, from BS 7671:2008

NONE

PART 2: INSTALLATION DETAILS

1. System earthing arrangement: TN-C-S ✓ TN-S TT
2. Method of fault protection: ADS
3. Protective device for the modified circuit
   1 Type: BS EN 60898 Type B Rating: 10 A
   2 Type: Rating: A
   3 Type: Rating: A

Comments on existing installation, including adequacy of earthing and bonding arrangements (see 132.16)

Unable to access main protective bonding connection to the water installation pipe work due to boxing in

Line/neutral insulation resistance not measured due to nature and number of existing connected loads

PART 3: ESSENTIAL TESTS

CCT No	Circuit description	Continuity ✓ or Ω (fill 1 col. only)		Insulation resistance M Ω			Polarity	Zs	RCD (if applicable)	
		$R_1 + R_2$	R_2	Line / neutral	Line / earth	Neutral / earth	✓	Ω	1 x IΔn	5 x IΔn
1	Reception area lighting	1.2		LIM	198	198	✓	1.35	N/A	N/A
2										
3										

PART 4: DECLARATION

I / We CERTIFY that the works do not impair the safety of the existing installation, that the said works have been designed, constructed, inspected and tested in accordance with BS 7671:2008 (IET Wiring Regulations), amended to 2011 (date) and that the said works, to the best of my / our knowledge and belief, at the time of my / our inspection complied with BS 7671 except as detailed in Part 1 above.

Contractor's name: James Douglas **Signature:** James Douglas

For and on behalf of: J D Installations Ltd **Position:** Proprietor

Address: Unit 6, Gambols Estate, Neartown, Cutcounty, NT5 8LR **Date:** -- July 20---

C-MW3-ECA REV V1 Aug 2011

Courtesy of the ECA

MINOR ELECTRICAL INSTALLATION WORKS CERTIFICATE NOTES:

The Minor Works Certificate is intended to be used for additions and alterations to an installation that do not extend to the provision of a new circuit. Examples include the addition of socket-outlets or lighting points to an existing circuit, the relocation of a light switch etc. This Certificate may also be used for the replacement of equipment such as accessories or luminaires, but not for the replacement of distribution boards or similar items. Appropriate inspection and testing, however, should always be carried out irrespective of the extent of the work undertaken.

MINOR ELECTRICAL INSTALLATION WORKS CERTIFICATE GUIDANCE FOR RECIPIENTS

(to be appended to the Certificate)

This Certificate has been issued to confirm that the electrical installation work to which it relates has been designed, constructed, inspected and tested in accordance with British Standard 7671 (the IET Wiring Regulations).

You should have received an original Certificate and the contractor should have retained a duplicate. It you were the person ordering the work, but not the owner of the installation, you should pass this Certificate, or a copy of it, to the owner. A separate Certificate should have been received for each existing circuit on which minor works have been carried out. This Certificate is not appropriate if you requested the contractor to undertake more extensive installation work, for which you should have received an Electrical Installation Certificate.

The Certificate should be retained in a safe place and be shown to any person inspecting or undertaking further work on the electrical installation in the future. If you later vacate the property, this Certificate will demonstrate to the new owner that the minor electrical installation work carried out complied with the requirements of British Standard 7671 at the time the Certificate was issued.

ELECTRICAL INSTALLATION CERTIFICATE BS 7671:2008 THREE SIGNATURE

Certificate number: 49781 Member number: (optional) **Sheet** 1 **of** 6

DETAILS OF THE CLIENT

Dr. T David, 281 Percival Street, Coldsworthy, CW8 9TS

INSTALLATION ADDRESS

481 High Street, Nearby, Cutcounty, NC1 2 HS

DESCRIPTION AND EXTENT OF THE INSTALLATION

Tick boxes as appropriate

Description of installation: Rewire of a domestic property

Extent of installation covered by this Certificate: The rewiring and installation of circuits as described in the attached continuation sheet, but excluding the central heating controls installed by others.

(Use continuation sheet if necessary) See continuation sheet no. 3 and 4

New installation	✓
Addition to an existing installation	
Alteration to an existing installation	

FOR DESIGN

I/We being the person(s) responsible for the design of the electrical installation (as indicated by my/our signatures below), particulars of which are described above, having exercised reasonable skill and care when carrying out the design, hereby CERTIFY that the design work of which I/we have been responsible is, to the best of my/our knowledge and belief, in accordance with BS 7671:2008 amended to 2011 (date) except for departures, if any, detailed as follows:

Details of departures from BS 7671 (regulation 120.3 and 133.5)

None

The extent of liability of the signatory or signatories is limited to the work described above as the subject of this Certificate.

For the DESIGN of the installation: ****Where there is mutual responsibility for the design**

Signature Donald Smith **Date** --- June 20--- **Name (CAPITALS)** DONALD SMITH **Designer No. 1**

Signature N/A **Date** **Name (CAPITALS)** **Designer No. 2****

FOR CONSTRUCTION

I/We being the person(s) responsible for the construction of the electrical installation (as indicated by my/our signatures below), particulars of which are described above, having exercised reasonable skill and care when carrying out the construction, hereby CERTIFY that the construction work of which I/we have been responsible is, to the best of my/our knowledge and belief, in accordance with BS 7671:2008 amended to 2011 (date) except for departures, if any, detailed as follows:

Details of departures from BS 7671 (regulation 120.3 and 133.5)

None

The extent of liability of the signatory or signatories is limited to the work described above as the subject of this Certificate.

For the CONSTRUCTION of the installation:

Signature James Douglas **Date** --- July 20--- **Name (CAPITALS)** JAMES DOUGLAS **Constructor**

FOR INSPECTION & TESTING

I/We being the person(s) responsible for the inspection & testing of the electrical installation (as indicated by my/our signatures below), particulars of which are described above, having exercised reasonable skill and care when carrying out the inspection & testing, hereby CERTIFY that the work of which I/we have been responsible is, to the best of my/our knowledge and belief, in accordance with BS 7671:2008 amended to 2011 (date) except for departures, if any, detailed as follows:

Details of departures from BS 7671 (regulation 120.3 and 133.5)

None

The extent of liability of the signatory or signatories is limited to the work described above as the subject of this Certificate.

For the INSPECTION & TESTING of the installation:

Signature James Douglas **Date** --- July 20--- **Name (CAPITALS)** JAMES DOUGLAS **Inspector**

NEXT INSPECTION

I/We the designer(s), recommend that this installation is further inspected and tested after an interval of not more than 10 years / ~~months~~

C-EICE4-ECA REV V1 Aug 2011

Courtesy of the ECA

Sheet 2 of 6

PARTICULARS OF SIGNATORIES TO THE ELECTRICAL INSTALLATION CERTIFICATE

Designer (No. 1)

Name: Donald Smith — Company: DS Electrical Consultants

Address: The Centre, Coppice Lane, Closetown, Cutcounty

Postcode: NC7 4 HP — Tel: 07858196200

Designer (No. 2)

Name: N/A — Company:

Address:

Postcode: — Tel:

Constructor

Name: James Douglas — Company: J D Installations Ltd

Address: Unit 6, Gambols Estate, Neartown, Cutcounty

Postcode: NT5 8LR — Tel: 0800468924

Inspector

Name: James Douglas — Company: J D Installations Ltd

Address: Unit 6, Gambols Estate, Neartown, Cutcounty

Postcode: NT5 8LR — Tel: 0800468924

SUPPLY CHARACTERISTICS AND EARTHING ARRANGEMENTS

Tick boxes and enter details as appropriate

Earthing arrangements	Number and type of live conductors	Nature and type of supply parameters	Supply protective device
TN-S ✓	a.c. ✓ d.c.	Nominal voltage, U / U_0 (1) 230 V	BS (EN) BS 88-3
TN-C-S	1-phase, 2-wire ✓ 2-wire	Nominal frequency, f (1) 50 Hz	
TT	2-phase, 3-wire 3-wire	Prospective fault current, I_{pf} (2) 0.48 kA	Type System C
TN-C	3-phase, 4-wire	External loop impedance, Ze (2) 0.60 Ω	
IT	Confirmation of supply polarity	Note: (1) by enquiry. (2) by enquiry or measurement	Rated current 100 A

Alternative source of supply (as detailed on attached schedule)

PARTICULARS OF INSTALLATION REFERRED TO IN THE CERTIFICATE

Tick boxes and enter details as appropriate

Means of earthing

Distributor's facility ✓

Installation earth electrode

Maximum demand

Maximum demand (load) 96 A kVA / Amps (delete as appropriate)

Details of installation earth electrode *(where applicable)*

Type (e.g. rod(s), tape, etc.)	Location	Electrode resistance to earth
N/A	N/A	N/A Ω

Main protective conductors

Earthing conductor — material Copper — csa 16 mm^2 — Continuity and connection verified ✓

Main protective bonding conductors — material Copper — csa 10 mm^2 — Continuity and connection verified ✓

To incoming water and/or gas service — To other elements: N/A

Main switch or circuit-breaker

BS, type and no. of poles BS EN60947-3 (2 pole) — Current rating 100 A — Voltage rating 400 V V

Location Consumer unit in utility room — Fuse rating or setting N/A A

Rated residual operating current $I_{\Delta n}$ N/A mA, and operating time of ms (at $I_{\Delta n}$) (Applicable only where an RCD is suitable and is used as a main circuit-breaker)

COMMENTS ON EXISTING INSTALLATION (in the case of an addition or alteration see Section 633)

None

SCHEDULES

The attached Schedules are part of this document and this Certificate is valid only when they are attached to it.

1 Schedules of Inspections and 1 Schedules of Test Results are attached.

(Enter quantities of Schedules attached.)

C-EICE4-ECA REV V1 Aug 2011

ELECTRICAL INSTALLATION CERTIFICATE NOTES:

1 The Electrical Installation Certificate is to be used only for the initial certification of a new installation or for an addition or alteration to an existing installation where new circuits have been introduced.

It is not to be used for a Periodic Inspection, for which an Electrical Installation Condition Report form should be used. For an addition or alteration which does not extend to the introduction of new circuits a Minor Electrical Installation Works Certificate may be used.

The 'original' Certificate is to be given to the person ordering the work (Regulation 632.1). A duplicate should be retained by the contractor.

2 This Certificate is only valid if accompanied by the Schedule of Inspections and the Schedule(s) of Test Results.

3 The signatures appended are those of the persons authorised by the companies executing the work of design, construction and inspection and testing respectively. A signatory authorised to certify more than one category of work should sign in each of the appropriate places.

4 The time interval recommended before the first periodic inspection must be inserted (see IET Guidance Note 3 for guidance).

5 The page numbers for each of the Schedules of Test Results should be indicated, together with the total number of sheets involved.

6 The maximum prospective value of fault current (I_{pf}) recorded should be the greater of either the prospective value of short-circuit current or the prospective value of earth fault current.

7 The proposed date for the next inspection should take into consideration the frequency and quality of maintenance that the installation can reasonably be expected to receive during its intended life and the period should be agreed between the designer, installer and other relevant parties.

ELECTRICAL INSTALLATION CERTIFICATE GUIDANCE FOR RECIPIENTS

(to be appended to the Certificate)

This safety Certificate has been issued to confirm that the electrical installation work to which it relates has been designed, constructed, inspected and tested in accordance with British Standard 7671 (the IET Wiring Regulations).

You should have received an 'original' Certificate and the contractor should have retained a duplicate. If you were the person ordering the work, but not the owner of the installation, you should pass this Certificate, or a full copy of it including the schedules, immediately to the owner.

The 'original' Certificate should be retained in a safe place and be shown to any person inspecting or undertaking further work on the electrical installation in the future. If you later vacate the property, this Certificate will demonstrate to the new owner that the electrical installation complied with the requirements of British Standard 7671 at the time the Certificate was issued. The Construction (Design and Management) Regulations require that, for a project covered by those Regulations, a copy of this Certificate, together with its schedules, is included in the project health and safety documentation.

For safety reasons the electrical installation will need to be inspected at appropriate intervals by a competent person. The maximum time interval recommended before the next inspection is stated on Page 1 under 'Next Inspection'.

This Certificate is intended to be issued only for a new electrical installation or for new work associated with an addition or alteration to an existing installation. It should not have been issued for the inspection of an existing electrical installation. An 'Electrical Installation Condition Report' should be issued for such an inspection.

SCHEDULE OF INSPECTIONS

For new installations only

Sheet 5 **of** 6

Methods of protection against electric shock

Both basic and fault protection:

N/A (i) SELV

N/A (ii) PELV

N/A (iii) Double insulation

N/A (iv) Reinforced insulation

Basic protection:

✓ (i) Insulation of live parts

✓ (ii) Barriers or enclosures

N/A (iii) Obstacles

N/A (iv) Placing out of reach

Fault protection:

(i) Automatic disconnection of supply:

✓ Presence of earthing conductor

✓ Presence of circuit protective conductors

✓ Presence of protective bonding conductors

✓ Presence of supplementary bonding conductors

N/A Presence of earthing arrangements for combined protective and functional purposes

N/A Presence of adequate arrangements for other sources, where applicable

N/A FELV

✓ Choice and setting of protective and monitoring devices (for fault and/or overcurrent protection)

(ii) Non-conducting location:

N/A Absence of protective conductors

(iii) Earth-free local equipotential bonding:

N/A Presence of earth-free local equipotential bonding

(iv) Electrical separation:

✓ Provided for **one item** of current-using equipment

N/A Provided for **more than one item** of current-using equipment

Additional protection:

✓ Presence of residual current device(s)

N/A Presence of supplementary bonding conductors

Prevention of mutual detrimental influence

✓ (a) Proximity of non-electrical services and other influences

N/A (b) Segregation of Band I and Band II circuits or use of Band II insulation

N/A (c) Segregation of safety circuits

Identification

✓ (a) Presence of diagrams, instructions, circuit charts and similar information

✓ (b) Presence of danger notices and other warning notices

✓ (c) Labelling of protective devices, switches and terminals

✓ (d) Identification of conductors

Cable and conductors

✓ Selection of conductors for current-carrying capacity and voltage drop

✓ Erection methods

✓ Routing of cables in prescribed zones

✓ Cables incorporating earthed armour or sheath, or run within an earthed wiring system, or otherwise adequately protected against nails, screws and the like

✓ Additional protection provided by 30 mA RCD for cables concealed in walls (where required in premises not under the supervision of a skilled or instructed person)

✓ Connection of conductors

✓ Presence of fire barriers, suitable seals and protection against thermal effects

General

✓ Presence and correct location of appropriate devices for isolation and switching

✓ Adequacy of access to switchgear and other equipment

✓ Particular protective measures for special installations and locations

✓ Connection of single-pole devices for protection or switching in line conductors only

✓ Correct connection of accessories and equipment

N/A Presence of undervoltage protective devices

✓ Selection of equipment and protective measures appropriate to external influences

✓ Selection of appropriate functional switching devices

Inspected by *James Douglas* (James Douglas) Date – July 20 –

NOTES

✓ to indicate an inspection has been carried out and the result is satisfactory

NA to indicate that the inspection is not applicable to a particular item

An entry must be made in every box.

C-EICE4-ECA REV V1 Aug 2011

Courtesy of the ECA

SCHEDULE OF TEST RESULTS

Sheet 6 of 6

ECA

DB Reference no. Consumer unit 1
Location Utility Room
Zs at DB (Ω) 0.6
I_{pf} at DB (kA) 0.48
Correct polarity of supply confirmed YES / ~~NO~~
Phase sequence confirmed (where appropriate) N/A

Details of circuits and/or installed equipment vulnerable to damage when testing
Dimmer switch in lounge
Linked smoke detectors fed from D/S lights
PIR Porch Light

Details of test instruments used (state serial and/or asset numbers)
Continuity MF 1006 JD
Insulation resistance " "
Earth fault loop impedance " "
RCD " "
Earth electrode resistance N/A

Tested by:
Name (CAPITALS) JAMES DOUGLAS
Signature *James Douglas* **Date** -- July 20--

Circuit details

Circuit number	Circuit description	Overcurrent device: BS (EN)	Type	Rating (A)	Breaking capacity (kA)	Conductor details: Reference method	Live (mm²)	cpc (mm²)
A	B	C	D	E	F	G	H	I
1	Shower	61009	B	40	6	100	10	4.0
2	Cooker	61009	B	32	6	100	10	4.0
3	Upstairs Ring Circuit	61009	B	32	6	100	2.5	1.5
4	Downstairs Ring Circuit	61009	B	32	6	100	2.5	1.5
5	Boiler	61009	B	16	6	100	2.5	1.5
6	Immersion Heater	61009	B	16	6	100	2.5	1.5
7	Freezer socket	60898	B	16	6	100 & A	2.5	1.5
8	Upstairs Lights	61009	B	6	6	100	1.5	1.0
9	Downstairs Lights	61009	B	6	6	100	1.5	1.0
10	Spare							

Test results

Circuit number	Ring final circuit continuity (Ω): r_1 (line)	r_n (neutral)	r_2 (cpc)	Continuity (Ω) (R_1+R_2) or R_2: (R_1+R_2)*	R_2	Insulation resistance (MΩ): Live – Live	Live – E	Polarity ✓	Z_s (Ω)	RCD (ms): $@I_{\Delta n}$	$@5I_{\Delta n}$	Test button operation	Remarks (continue on a separate sheet if necessary)
A	J	K	L	M	N	O	P	Q	R	S	T	U	V
1	N/A	N/A	N/A	0.16		>999	>999	✓	0.75	45.5	6.8	✓	
2	N/A	N/A	N/A	0.03		>999	>999	✓	0.63	38.6	11.2	✓	
3	0.45	0.48	0.75	0.3		>999	>999	✓	0.89	36.4	9.6	✓	
4	0.60	0.62	1.03	0.41		>999	>999	✓	1.00	38.5	10.5	✓	
5	N/A	N/A	N/A	0.15		>999	>999	✓	0.75	40.0	11.8	✓	
6	N/A	N/A	N/A	0.46		>999	>999	✓	1.06	42.0	9.8	✓	
7	N/A	N/A	N/A	0.19		>999	>999	✓	0.79	N/A	N/A	✓	
8	N/A	N/A	N/A	1.5		>999	>999	✓	2.1	45	12.5	✓	Shaver S/O in Bathroom
9	N/A	N/A	N/A	1.2		>999	>999	✓	1.8	45	12.5	✓	Dimmer, PIR & Smoke
10													

* Where there are no spurs connected to a ring final circuit this value is also the $(R_1 + R_2)$ of the circuit.

C-STR-ECA REV Aug 2011 V1

Courtesy of the ECA

ELECTRICAL INSTALLATION CERTIFICATE
BS 7671:2008 – single signature

Certificate number: ....

Member number: .... (optional)

ECA

DETAILS OF CLIENT:

INSTALLATION ADDRESS:

JOB NUMBER (optional)

Sheet .... of ....

DESCRIPTION AND EXTENT OF INSTALLATION COVERED BY THIS CERTIFICATE

New installation ☐ Addition ☐ Alteration ☐

FOR DESIGN, CONSTRUCTION, INSPECTION AND TEST

I/We being the person responsible for design, construction, inspection and testing of the electrical installation (as indicated by my signature below), particulars of which are described above, having exercised reasonable skill and care when carrying out the design, construction, inspection and testing, hereby CERTIFY that the said work for which I/we have been responsible is, to the best of my knowledge and belief, in accordance with BS 7671:2008 as amended to .... except for the departures, if any, detailed as follows:

Departures and comments on existing installations (120.3; 133.5) ....

Name ....

For ....

Position ....

Signature ....

Date ....

Next Inspection ....

I/We recommend that the installation be further inspected and tested after an interval of not more than .... years.

SUPPLY CHARACTERISTICS AND EARTHING ARRANGEMENTS

Nominal voltage U/Uo V

Prospective fault current, Ipf .... kA

Frequency F .... Hz

External loop impedance, Ze .... Ohms

Alternative source of supply ☐ a.c. ☐ d.c. ☐

Number and type of live conductors

.... 1-phase, 2-wire

.... 3-phase, 3-wire

.... 4-phase, 4-wire

Supply protective device characteristics

Type/BS (EN) ....

Rated Current .... A

Earthing arrangements

TN-S

TN-C-S

TT

Other ....

Distributor's facility

Installation earth electrode

Type .... (Rod, plate, tape, etc.)

Location ....

Resistance .... Ohms

PARTICULARS OF INSTALLATION REFERRED TO IN THIS CERTIFICATE

Maximum demand

kVA / Amps

....

Main switch or circuit breaker

BS .... Current rating .... A

Type .... No. of poles ....

Location ....

Voltage Rating .... V Fuse rating or setting .... A

RCD trip time .... ms RCD $I_{\Delta n}$ .... mA

(Applicable only where RCD is suitable and is used as a main circuit breaker)

Location of main protective bonding connections

Earthing conductor

Copper

Steel

Aluminium

Main protective conductors

CSA .... mm²

Connections verified

Main protective bonding conductor

Copper

Steel

Aluminium

CSA .... mm²

Connections verified

Main bonding:

Water Gas Other

C-EICE3-ECA REV V1 Aug 2011

Courtesy of the ECA

ELECTRICAL INSTALLATION CERTIFICATE NOTES:

1. The Electrical Installation Certificate is to be used only for the initial certification of a new installation or for an addition or alteration to an existing installation where new circuits have been introduced.

   It is not to be used for a Periodic Inspection, for which an Electrical Installation Condition Report form should be used. For an addition or alteration which does not extend to the introduction of new circuits, a Minor Electrical Installation Works Certificate may be used.

   The 'original' Certificate is to be given to the person ordering the work (Regulation 632.1). A duplicate should be retained by the contractor.

2. This Certificate is only valid if accompanied by the Schedule of Inspections and the Schedule(s) of Test Results.
3. The signatures appended are those of the persons authorised by the companies executing the work of design, construction and inspection and testing respectively. A signatory authorised to certify more than one category of work should sign in each of the appropriate places.
4. The time interval recommended before the first periodic inspection must be inserted (see IET Guidance Note 3 for guidance).
5. The page numbers for each of the Schedules of Test Results should be indicated, together with the total number of sheets involved.
6. The maximum prospective value of fault current (I_{pf}) recorded should be the greater of either the prospective value of short-circuit current or the prospective value of earth fault current.
7. The proposed date for the next inspection should take into consideration the frequency and quality of maintenance that the installation can reasonably be expected to receive during its intended life and the period should be agreed between the designer, installer and other relevant parties.

Courtesy of the ECA

ELECTRICAL INSTALLATION CERTIFICATE GUIDANCE FOR RECIPIENTS

(to be appended to the Certificate)

This safety Certificate has been issued to confirm that the electrical installation work to which it relates has been designed, constructed, inspected and tested in accordance with British Standard 7671 (the IET Wiring Regulations).

You should have received an 'original' Certificate and the contractor should have retained a duplicate. If you were the person ordering the work, but not the owner of the installation, you should pass this Certificate, or a full copy of it including the schedules, immediately to the owner.

The 'original' Certificate should be retained in a safe place and be shown to any person inspecting or undertaking further work on the electrical installation in the future. If you later vacate the property, this Certificate will demonstrate to the new owner that the electrical installation complied with the requirements of British Standard 7671 at the time the Certificate was issued. The Construction (Design and Management) Regulations require that, for a project covered by those Regulations, a copy of this Certificate, together with its schedules, is included in the project health and safety documentation.

For safety reasons the electrical installation will need to be inspected at appropriate intervals by a competent person. The maximum time interval recommended before the next inspection is stated on Page 1 under 'Next Inspection'.

This Certificate is intended to be issued only for a new electrical installation or for new work associated with an addition or alteration to an existing installation. It should not have been issued for the inspection of an existing electrical installation. An 'Electrical Installation Condition Report' should be issued for such an inspection.

SCHEDULE OF INSPECTIONS

ECA

NOTES:

✓ to indicate an inspection has been carried out and the result is satisfactory
N/A to indicate that the inspection is not applicable to a particular item

NOTE – items on the right are seldom relevant in a domestic setting

Sheet ☐ of ☐

METHODS OF PROTECTION AGAINST ELECTRIC SHOCK

Basic protection:

- ☐ (i) Insulation of live parts
- ☐ (ii) Barriers or enclosures

Fault protection:

(i) Automatic disconnection of supply:

- ☐ Presence of earthing conductor
- ☐ Presence of circuit protective conductors
- ☐ Presence of protective bonding conductors
- ☐ Presence of supplementary bonding conductors
- ☐ Choice of setting of protective and monitoring devices (for fault and/or overcurrent protection)

Additional protection:

- ☐ Presence of residual current device(s)
- ☐ Presence of supplementary bonding conductors

PREVENTION OF MUTUAL DETRIMENTAL INFLUENCE

- ☐ (a) Proximity to non-electrical services and other influences
- ☐ (b) Segregation of Band I and Band II circuits or use of Band II insulation

IDENTIFICATION

- ☐ (a) Presence of diagrams, instructions, circuit charts and similar information
- ☐ (b) Presence of danger notices and other warning notices
- ☐ (c) Labelling of protective devices, switches and terminals
- ☐ (d) Identification of conductors

CABLES AND CONDUCTORS

- ☐ Selection of conductors for current-carrying capacity and voltage drop
- ☐ Erection methods
- ☐ Routing of cables in prescribed zones
- ☐ Cables incorporating earthed armour or sheath, or run within an earthed wiring system, or otherwise adequately protected against nails, screws and the like

CABLES AND CONDUCTORS (continued)

- ☐ Additional protection provided by 30 mA RCD for cables concealed in walls (where required in premises not under the supervision of a skilled or instructed person)
- ☐ Connection of conductors
- ☐ Presence of fire barriers, suitable seals and protection against thermal effects

GENERAL

- ☐ Presence of correct location of appropriate devices for isolation and switching
- ☐ Adequacy of access to switchgear and other equipment
- ☐ Particular protective measures for special installations and locations
- ☐ Connection of single-pole devices for protection or switching in line conductors only
- ☐ Correct connection of accessories and equipment
- ☐ Selection of equipment and protective measures appropriate to external influences
- ☐ Selection of appropriate functional switching devices

ADDITIONAL SCHEDULE OF ITEMS INSPECTED (where applicable)

- ☐ SELV
- ☐ PELV
- ☐ Double insulation
- ☐ Reinforced insulation
- ☐ Obstacles
- ☐ Placing out of reach
- ☐ Presence of earthing arrangements for combined protective and functional purposes
- ☐ Presence of adequate arrangements for alternative source(s), where applicable
- ☐ FELV
- ☐ Absence of protective conductors
- ☐ Presence of earth-free local equipotential bonding
- ☐ Electrical separation provided for **one item** of current-using equipment
- ☐ Electrical separation provided for **more than one item** of current-using equipment
- ☐ Segregation of safety circuits
- ☐ Presence of undervoltage protective devices

C-EICE3-ECA REV V1 Aug 2011

Courtesy of the ECA

SCHEDULE OF TEST RESULTS

Sheet ☐ of ☐

ECA

DB Reference no.	Details of circuits and/or installed equipment vulnerable to damage when testing	Details of test instruments used (state serial and/or asset numbers)
Location	......	Continuity ......
Zs at DB (Ω)	......	Insulation resistance ......
I_{pf} at DB (kA)	......	Earth fault loop impedance ......
Correct polarity of supply confirmed YES / NO	......	RCD ......
Phase sequence confirmed (where appropriate)	......	Earth electrode resistance ......

Tested by:
Name (CAPITALS) ......
Signature ...... Date ......

Circuit details									Test results												
		Overcurrent device				Conductor details			Ring final circuit continuity (Ω)			Continuity (Ω) $(R_1 + R_2)$ or R_2		Insulation resistance (MΩ)		Polarity	Z_s (Ω)	RCD (ms)			Remarks (continue on a separate sheet if necessary)
Circuit number	Circuit description	BS (EN)	Type	Rating (A)	Breaking capacity (kA)	Reference method	Live (mm²)	cpc (mm²)	r_1 (line)	r_n (neutral)	r_2 (cpc)	$(R_1 + R_2)$ *	R_2	Live – Live	Live – E	✓	Ω	@$I_{\Delta}n$	@$5I_{\Delta}n$	Test button operation	
A	B	C	D	E	F	G	H	I	J	K	L	M	N	O	P	Q	R	S	T	U	V

* Where there are no spurs connected to a ring final circuit this value is also the $(R_1 + R_2)$ of the circuit.

C-STR-ECA REV Aug 2011 V1

Courtesy of the ECA

End test

Tick the correct answer

1. When confirming safe isolation the Approved Voltage Indicator will need to be proved:

☐ a. Only after use

☐ b. Only before use

☐ c. Before and after use

☐ d. At each stage of the testing

2. An inspector has safely isolated a sub distribution board supplying power to the third floor of a large office block. As a result of this action there will be no disruption to the:

☐ a. Customers

☐ b. Sales staff

☐ c. Office manager

☐ d. Inspector

3. When confirming safe isolation of a three phase and neutral isolator, the total number of tests to be made is:

☐ a. 3

☐ b. 4

☐ c. 7

☐ d. 10

4. When confirming correct polarity of the incoming supply the instrument to be used is:

☐ a. An ammeter

☐ b. A continuity tester

☐ c. A loop impedance tester

☐ d. An approved voltage indicator

5. A periodic inspection is carried out on:

☐ a. A new installation

☐ b. A new power circuit

☐ c. An existing installation

☐ d. A circuit before placing in service

6. Inspection of a new installation is carried out:

☐ a. After testing

☐ b. With the installation isolated

☐ c. With the installation energized

☐ d. Once the commissioning has been completed

7. The standard forms of certification can be found in BS 7671 in Appendix:

☐ a. 6

☐ b. 7

☐ c. 8

☐ d. 9

8. The document issued on completion of a periodic inspection is a:

- ☐ a. Periodic Inspection Report
- ☐ b. Electrical Installation Certificate
- ☐ c. Electrical Installation Condition Report
- ☐ d. Minor Electrical Installation Works Certificate

9. The Electricity at Work Regulations require an installation i) to be inspected and tested regularly and ii) records of the results of the inspections kept. In regards to these statements:

- ☐ a. Both statements i) and ii) are correct
- ☐ b. Statement i) only is correct
- ☐ c. Statement ii) only is correct
- ☐ d. Both statements are incorrect

10. Which of the following human senses would be best used to check whether a circuit breaker is correctly rated for the circuit it supplies:

- ☐ a. Sight
- ☐ b. Touch
- ☐ c. Taste
- ☐ d. Hearing

11. The correct colour for the line conductors of a single phase circuit is:

- ☐ a. Blue
- ☐ b. Grey
- ☐ c. Black
- ☐ d. Brown

12. Flat profile twin and circuit protective conductor cables without mechanical protection concealed within the walls of a dwelling should be inspected to ensure that they are within the prescribed zones and protected by a:

- ☐ a. 15 mA circuit breaker
- ☐ b. 30 mA residual current device
- ☐ c. BS 88-3 fuse
- ☐ d. Type C circuit breaker

13. The inspection of appropriate devices for isolation and switching would include a:

- ☐ a. Time switch
- ☐ b. Main isolator
- ☐ c. Light switch
- ☐ d. Photocell

14. The earthing conductor of an installation should be inspected during the initial verification. Which of the following would NOT be considered in this inspection?

- ☐ a. The type of material
- ☐ b. The cross-sectional area of the conductor
- ☐ c. The connection of the conductor
- ☐ d. The location of the main earthing terminal

15. The HSE guidance document for test equipment used by electricians is GS:

- ☐ a. 36
- ☐ b. 38
- ☐ c. 86
- ☐ d. 83

16. When testing continuity the resistance of the test leads should be nulled or:

- ☐ a. Subtracted from the test results
- ☐ b. Added to the test results
- ☐ c. Less than 0.01 Ω
- ☐ d. Ignored

17. The Method 2 long lead continuity test must be used when measuring continuity of:

- ☐ a. Ring final circuits
- ☐ b. Circuit protective conductors
- ☐ c. Conductor insulation resistance
- ☐ d. Main protective bonding conductors

18. A radial circuit which is 25 m long is installed using conductors with resistances: line 7.41 mΩ/m and circuit protective conductor 7.41 mΩ/m at 20 °C. The expected $R_1 + R_2$ measured value for this circuit is:

- ☐ a. 0.59 Ω
- ☐ b. 0.37 Ω
- ☐ c. 0.18 Ω
- ☐ d. 0.15 Ω

19. During Step 1 of a ring final circuit continuity test the following results were obtained: r_1= 0.45, r_n= 0.44 and r_2= 0.74. The expected test value at each socket outlet when the line and circuit protective conductor are correctly cross connected is:

- ☐ a. 0.11 Ω
- ☐ b. 0.22 Ω
- ☐ c. 0.29 Ω
- ☐ d. 0.59 Ω

20. An insulation resistance test between live conductors of a number of circuits produced the following results: 10 MΩ, 100 MΩ, 50 MΩ and 30 MΩ. The insulation resistance when measured between live conductors at the distribution board with all these circuits connected is:

- ☐ a. 190 MΩ
- ☐ b. 47.5 MΩ
- ☐ c. 10 MΩ
- ☐ d. 6 MΩ

21. An insulation resistance test is to be carried out on an addition to an existing circuit which has electronic control devices. Before the test is undertaken the electronic control devices must be:

- ☐ a. Linked out
- ☐ b. Turned on
- ☐ c. Disconnected
- ☐ d. Isolated

22. A single pole protective device has been incorrectly connected in the neutral conductor only of a radial circuit. Should a fault to earth occur on the circuit the effect will be that the device will:

- ☐ a. Only function if the fault current is twice the I_n of the device
- ☐ b. Operate but the circuit will remain live
- ☐ c. Operate and safely isolate the circuit
- ☐ d. Fail to operate

23. The maximum earth electrode resistance for an electrical installation protected by a 300 mA residual current device is:

- ☐ a. 1667 Ω
- ☐ b. 500 Ω
- ☐ c. 167 Ω
- ☐ d. 100 Ω

24. Measurement of earth electrode resistance may be carried out using an earth fault loop impedance tester where:

1) The installation forms part of a TT system

2) The installation is protected by a 30 mA residual current device

- ☐ a. Only statement 1) is correct
- ☐ b. Only statement 2) is correct
- ☐ c. Both statements 1) and 2) are correct
- ☐ d. Both statements 1) and 2) are incorrect

25. The Distribution Network Operator maximum declared Z_e for a TN-C-S system is:

- ☐ a. 21 Ω
- ☐ b. 2.0 Ω
- ☐ c. 0.8 Ω
- ☐ d. 0.35 Ω

26. The measured earth fault loop impedance of a ring final circuit should be taken at:

- ☐ a. Every accessible point on the circuit
- ☐ b. Any convenient point on the circuit
- ☐ c. The point furthest from the origin
- ☐ d. The point closest to the origin

27. When carrying out tests on a residual current device:

1) Pressing the test button on the residual current device is the same as carrying out the electrical tests

2) A 30 mA residual current device should trip at a 15 mA test current

- ☐ a. Only statement 1) is correct
- ☐ b. Only statement 2) is correct
- ☐ c. Both statements are correct
- ☐ d. Neither statement is correct

28. A 10 mA residual current device is installed to protect socket outlets in a school laboratory. When testing this residual current device the maximum test currents to be applied are:

- ☐ a. 10 mA, 20 mA and 50 mA
- ☐ b. 5 mA, 10 mA and 50 mA
- ☐ c. 5 mA and 10 mA
- ☐ d. 10 mA and 50 mA

29. Voltage drop may be confirmed using measurement. This involves measuring the:

- ☐ a. Resistance of circuit line and neutral conductors
- ☐ b. $R_1 + R_2$ for the circuit at the furthest point
- ☐ c. Earth fault loop impedance of the circuit
- ☐ d. Voltage at the origin and the load

30. To ensure the safety of the users of the installation the inspector should:

- ☐ a. Clearly identify areas where testing is taking place
- ☐ b. Leave all covers off whilst live testing is carried out
- ☐ c. Isolate the supply for the duration of the testing process
- ☐ d. Wear high visibility clothing to be readily noticed

31. A Minor Electrical Installation Works Certificate can NOT be used to certify:

- ☐ a. An additional socket outlet added to a radial circuit
- ☐ b. The replacement of a broken socket outlet
- ☐ c. An alteration to an existing power circuit
- ☐ d. The installation of a lighting circuit

32. A Minor Electrical Installation Works Certificate includes details of the:

- ☐ a. Type of system
- ☐ b. Client
- ☐ c. Prospective fault current
- ☐ d. Z_e

33. The Electrical Installation Certificate is issued by the:

- ☐ a. Designer
- ☐ b. Constructor
- ☐ c. Inspector
- ☐ d. Client

34. Any deviations found during the initial verification must be:

- ☐ a. Recorded on the certificate
- ☐ b. Notified to the client without delay
- ☐ c. Recorded and sent to the client with the certificate
- ☐ d. Corrected before the installation can be placed in service

35. An alteration or addition to an installation must comply with the current requirements of BS 7671 and must:

- ☐ a. Allow for further alterations at a later date
- ☐ b. Not reduce the safety of the existing installation
- ☐ c. Bring the current installation to the current requirements of BS 7671
- ☐ d. Be recorded only on a Minor Electrical Installation Works Certificate

36. An Electrical Installation Certificate which does not have a Schedule of Inspections and a Schedule of Test Results attached is:

- ☐ a. A legal document
- ☐ b. Completed
- ☐ c. Not valid
- ☐ d. Valid

37. The two documents on which the prospective fault current is to be recorded are the Electrical Installation Certificate and the:

- ☐ a. Minor Electrical Installation Works Certificate
- ☐ b. Commissioning certificate
- ☐ c. Schedule of Test Results
- ☐ d. Schedule of Inspections

38. The number of signatories on a full Electrical Installation Certificate is:

- ☐ a. 4
- ☐ b. 3
- ☐ c. 2
- ☐ d. 1

39. The client is required to retain the Electrical Installation Certificate in a safe place:

- ☐ a. Until the requirements of BS 7671 are amended
- ☐ b. For the lifetime of the electrical installation
- ☐ c. 12 Months
- ☐ d. 3 Years

40. The forms of certification passed to the client must include a written copy of the:

- ☐ a. Contractor's contact details
- ☐ b. Guidance for installers
- ☐ c. Original contract
- ☐ d. Guide for recipients

Answer section

Chapter 1

SELF ASSESSMENT Page 16

1 a. Use of the installation will be restricted
2 a. Have control of the isolated part of the installation
3 b. Confirm the AVI is functioning
4 c. 4 mm
5 d. Be supervised by a competent person

Chapter 2

Recap Page 18

- near system reasonably danger
- live unreasonable all dead
- shock fatal injury
- client disruption
- safe permission client
- Approved all GS 38
- safe live live earth
- regularly tested competent
- law equipment safety correctly instructions
- glasses risk arcing

SELF ASSESSMENT Page 32

1 a. Is safe to put into service
2 b. An existing electrical installation
3 c. 3
4 c. Voltage
5 a. A metallic conductor

Try this: Crossword Page 31

							1 U	N	S	2 A	F	E		
3 I	N	I	T	I	4 A	L				L			5 I	
N					P		6 P			T			N	
J					P		E			E			S	
U					R		R			R			P	
7 R	I	S	K		O		M		8 D	A	N	G	E	R
Y					V		I			T			C	
		9 P		10 C	E	R	T	I	F	I	C	11 A	T	12 E
		E			D					O		D		X
13 M		R					14 R			N		D		P
E		I					E					I		O
T		O		15 C	O	M	P	E	16 T	E	N	T		S
H		D					O		E			I		E
O		I					R		S			O		
17 D	O	C	U	M	E	N	T	A	T	I	O	N		

Chapter 3

Recap Page 33

- new design safe service
- existing complies current safe remain
- existing current whole not current
- inspection experience
- constructed maintained use

- Minor Certificate Certificate Inspections Test Results
- connected Diversity type
- earthing rating origin
- TT TN-S TN-C-S
- charts vulnerable designation live cpc protective

Task Page 40

1 Connection of conductors (sequence)
2 Correct identification of conductors
3 Correct cross-sectional area of conductors
4 Connection of single-pole switches in the line conductor only
5 Correct overcurrent device type and rating
6 Labelling of the circuits
7 Insulation is the correct length
8 All connections tight
9 Protective conductors correctly sleeved
10 There are no exposed conductors showing

SELF ASSESSMENT Page 51

1 c. Taste
2 a. Erected
3 a. Labelled 'Safety electrical connection do not remove'
4 c. Present at every point on the circuit
5 b. Segregated

Progress check

1 c. Obtain permission to isolate from the client
2 d. Will not function normally
3 b. A shock risk to the inspector
4 d. GS 38
5 c. All live conductors and earth
6 a. 2 mm
7 a. Initial Verification
8 d. Construction starts
9 d. 6
10 b. Electrical Installation Certificate
11 a. Bill of quantities
12 b. TN-C-S
13 b. Touch
14 a. Chapter 61
15 b. IET Guidance Note 3
16 c. Lid is correctly fitted
17 c. Coloured or numbered
18 a. Exposed and extraneous conductive parts
19 c. 150 mm
20 c. Light switch

Chapter 4

Recap Page 55

- relevant inspected
- sight smell systems
- Schedule Inspections
- key problems testing
- touch sight
- within building construction
- extraneous suitable label
- secure tight
- I_n current capacity type
- acceptable ☑ applicable installation
- acceptable corrected placed

Task Page 61

Calibration in date, not damaged, battery OK, instrument functions, leads and probes/clips comply with GS 38.

Try this Page 65

- Confirm circuit is isolated from the supply
- Link line and cpc at the distribution board
- Select a low resistance ohmmeter
- Confirm instrument and lead condition

- Confirm battery OK and instrument functions
- Null the test leads
- Test between line and cpc at every point on the circuit
- Record the highest reading as $R_1 + R_2$ for the circuit on the Schedule of Test Results
- Remove the line to cpc link.

Try this Page 67

- Obtain permission to isolate the supply
- Safely isolate and lock off the supply to the installation
- Select a low resistance ohmmeter and long test lead
- Confirm instrument and lead condition
- Confirm battery OK and instrument functions
- Null the test leads including the long lead
- Disconnect the main protective bonding conductor (e.g. at the distribution board)
- Connect the long test lead to the bonding conductor at the exposed conductive part
- Run the lead to the main earthing terminal and connect to the test instrument
- Connect other test lead to the disconnected main protective bonding conductor
- Test and record the result
- Disconnect the test instrument and long lead
- Reconnect the main protective bonding conductor.

Try this Page 70

$R_1 + R_2$ for 2.5 mm^2 with 1.5 mm^2 cpc = 19.51 mΩ/m $R_1 + R_2$ = mΩ/m x length so

$$\text{length} = \frac{1.3\,\Omega}{0.01951\,\Omega} = 66.63\,\text{m}$$

Try this Page 76

a $\dfrac{0.37 + 0.36}{4} = 0.18\,\Omega$

b $\dfrac{0.37 + 0.62}{4} = 0.25\,\Omega$

Try this Page 82

- Obtain permission to isolate the supply
- Safely isolate and lock off the supply to the installation
- Select an insulation resistance ohmmeter
- Confirm instrument and lead condition
- Confirm test leads comply with GS 38
- Confirm battery OK and instrument functions
- Select the 500 V test voltage
- Disconnect or isolate all loads and voltage sensitive equipment
- Link out any electronic or voltage operated controls
- All switches closed, all fuses in and circuit breakers in the on position
- Test between
  - All live conductors
  - All live conductors and earth
- Record the lowest result in each case
- Minimum acceptable value 1.0 MΩ.

Try this Page 88

1. All single pole protective and control devices are connected in the line conductors only
2. The centre pin of ES lampholders are connected to the line conductor only
3. All equipment and socket outlets are correctly connected.

Try this Page 93

a $R_A = \dfrac{141 + 146 + 137}{3} = 141.33\,\Omega$

b 5 per cent deviation = 7 Ω and all within this so OK

c $R_A(\max) = \dfrac{50}{0.1} = 500\,\Omega$ and 141 Ω is less than 500 Ω and it is also less than the recommended 200 Ω so it is OK

SELF ASSESSMENT Page 94

1 c. Low resistance ohmmeter
2 b. 0.37 Ω
3 a. Test leads are nulled
4 b. 500 V dc
5 d. The total length of the cable being tested
6 a. The line conductor
7 b. 3
8 b. 2

Chapter 5

Recap Page 95

- calibrated ongoing
- low ohmmeter nulled
- $R_1 + R_2$ long R_2
- 500 V dc 1.0 MΩ
- decreases increases decreases number parallel
- disconnected isolated linked out
- live live earth
- single switches protective line
- must generator
- two minimum three

Try this Page 100

- Seek permission to isolate
- Safely isolate and lock off the supply
- Disconnect the earthing conductor from the MET
- Select an earth fault loop impedance tester
- Confirm instrument is in calibration and not damaged
- Confirm test leads comply with GS 38
- Connect test instrument to
  - Disconnected earthing conductor
  - Incoming line terminal of the RCD
- Test and record the result
- Reconnect the earthing conductor to the MET
- Confirm test result is compliant.

Try this Page 108

- Locate the furthest socket outlet on the circuit
- Use a plug-in adapter or preparatory test lead
- Select an earth fault loop impedance tester
- Confirm instrument is in calibration and not damaged
- Confirm test leads comply with GS 38
- Connect test instrument
- Test and note the result
- Unplug the test instrument
- Confirm test result is compliant
- Record the result on the Schedule of Test Results.

Try this Page 111

- Obtain permission to isolate in order to access the main switch incoming supply terminals
- Select a PFC tester
- Confirm instrument is in calibration and not damaged
- Confirm test leads comply with GS 38
- Connect test instrument to the MET and the incoming line conductor
- Test and note the result as PEFC

- Connect test instrument to the incoming neutral and the incoming line conductor
- Test and note the result as PSCC
- Record the highest of the two values as the PFC for the installation on the EIC
- Confirm protective devices are I_{cn} rated ≥ PFC
- Reinstate the main switchgear.

Try this Page 116

- Obtain permission to isolate (the device will switch off)
- Select an RCD tester
- Confirm instrument is in calibration and not damaged
- Confirm test leads comply with GS 38
- Set the instrument to the 30 mA setting
- Set the test current to 150 mA ($5 \times I_{\Delta n}$)
- Connect test instrument to the MET and the outgoing line terminal of the RCD
- With the RCD switched on test at 0° and 180° resetting after each operation
- Record the highest of the two result as $5 \times I_{\Delta n}$ value
- Set the test current to 30 mA ($1 \times I_{\Delta n}$)
- Repeat the test at 0° and 180° resetting after each operation
- Record the highest of the two values as the $1 \times I_{\Delta n}$ value
- Set the test current to 15 mA ($\frac{1}{2} \times I_{\Delta n}$)
- Repeat the test at 0° and 180° where possible
- Disconnect the test instrument
- Operate the RCD integral test button
- Reinstate the supply.

Try this Page 121

1 a. 6.9 V
b. 11.5 V
c. 20 V

Try this: Crossword Page 124

SELF ASSESSMENT Page 125

1 c. Protected by an RCD
2 b. 0.8 Ω
3 b. 25 A
4 c. The point furthest from the origin
5 c. Apply a multiplying factor of 0.8 to the tabulated values
6 b. 300 mA
7 d. Compensate for the change in conductor temperature
8 a. Forms of certification

Chapter 6

Recap Page 126

- polarity live
- RCD TT earth fault loop impedance
- electrode 200 Ω
- earth DNO impedance declared
- fault public 0.8 Ω 0.35 Ω
- Installation Characteristics Arrangements

- furthest radial accessible ring
- circuit measured Z_e + R_2
- difference temperature temperature 0.8 tabulated
- protective safely occur point installed
- PSCC neutral origin two
- 30 mA 5 × $I_{\Delta n}$
- 30 mA 5 × $I_{\Delta n}$
- S type upstream
- 300 ms 1 × $I_{\Delta n}$
- operation integral
- phase origin distribution isolator
- $R_1 + R_n$ I_b 1.2

Try this Page 132

1 a. MEIWC or EIC
   b. EIC
   c. MEIWC or EIC

2 a. EIC
   b. Schedule of Test Results or MEIWR
   c. Schedule of Inspections

Try this Page 145

SCHEDULE OF TEST RESULTS Sheet 6 of 6

DB Reference no. DB F1 Location First floor lobby cupboard Zs at DB (Ω) 0.6 I_{pf} at DB (kA) 0.48 Correct polarity of supply confirmed YES / ~~NO~~ Phase sequence confirmed (where appropriate) N/A	Details of circuits and/or installed equipment vulnerable to damage when testing	Details of test instruments used (state serial and/or asset numbers) Continuity MF 1006 JD Insulation resistance " " Earth fault loop impedance " " RCD " " Earth electrode resistance N/A

Tested by:
Name (CAPITALS) James Douglas
Signature *James Douglas* Date – July 20–

Circuit details									Test results												
		Overcurrent device				Conductor details			Ring final circuit continuity (Ω)			Continuity (Ω) ($R_1 + R_2$) or R_2		Insulation resistance (MΩ)		Polarity	Z_s (Ω)	RCD (ms)			Remarks (continue on a separate sheet if necessary)
Circuit number	Circuit description	BS (EN)	Type	Rating (A)	Breaking capacity (kA)	Reference method	Live (mm²)	cpc (mm²)	r_1 (line)	r_n (neutral)	r_2 (cpc)	($R_1 + R_2$)*	R_2	Live – Live	Live – E	✓	Ω	@$I_{\Delta n}$	@$5I_{\Delta n}$	Test button operation	
A	B	C	D	E	F	G	H	I	J	K	L	M	N	O	P	Q	R	S	T	U	V
1	Print Room Power	61009	C	40	6	100	10	4.0	N/A	N/A	N/A	0.16		199	99	✓	(0.75)	45.5	6.8	✓	
2	Staff Kitchen Power	61009	B	32	6	100	10	4.0	N/A	N/A	N/A	0.03		100	100	✓	0.63	38.6	11.2	✓	
3	Front Ring Circuit	61009	B	32	6	100	2.5	1.5	0.45	0.48	(0.95)	0.3		30	28	✓	0.89	36.4	9.6	✓	
4	Back Ring Circuit	61009	B	32	6	100	2.5	1.5	0.60	0.62	1.03	0.41		50	48	✓	1.00	38.5	10.5	✓	
5	Boiler	61009	B	16	6	100	2.5	1.5	N/A	N/A	N/A	0.15		20	(0.89)	✓	0.75	40.0	11.8	✓	
6	Immersion Heater	61009	B	16	6	100	2.5	1.5	N/A	N/A	N/A	0.46		52	52	✓	1.06	42.0	(48)	✓	
7	Kitchen Freezer socket	60898	B	16	6	100 & A	2.5	1.5	N/A	N/A	N/A	0.19		200	200	✓	0.79	N/A	N/A	✓	
8	Front Lights	61009	B	6	6	100	1.5	1.0	N/A	N/A	N/A	1.5		36	50	✓	2.1	200	12.5	✓	
9	Rear Lights	61009	B	6	6	100	1.5	1.0	N/A	N/A	N/A	1.2		>999	(0.95)	✓	1.8	(320)	12.5	✓	
10	Spare																				

* Where there are no spurs connected to a ring final circuit this value is also the ($R_1 + R_2$) of the circuit.

Task Page 150

1

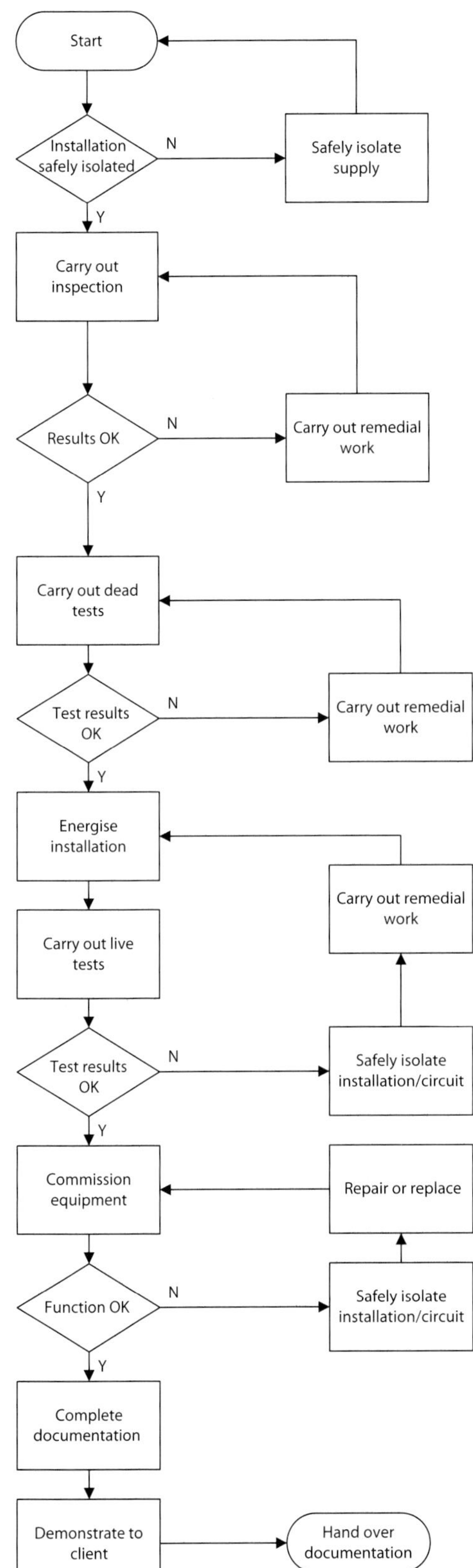

2
- Electrical Installation Certificate
- Schedule of Inspections
- Schedule of Test Results
- Manufacturer's installation and operating instructions
- Warranties
- Advice on operation of the installation (switching, thermostats, controllers, etc.)
- Advice on the purpose of the EIC
- Advice on the keeping of the IEC
- Actions in the event of a problem with the installation

SELF ASSESSMENT Page 151

1 b. External earth fault loop impedance
2 d. A replacement of an accessory
3 a. Single signature EIC
4 c. 4
5 c. EIC and Schedule of Test Results

End test

1 c. Before and after use
2 d. Inspector
3 d. 10
4 d. An Approved Voltage Indicator
5 c. An existing installation
6 b. With the installation isolated
7 a. 6
8 c. Electrical Installation Condition Report
9 d. Both statements are incorrect
10 a. Sight
11 d. Brown
12 b. 30 mA residual current device
13 b. Main isolator
14 d. The location of the main earthing terminal
15 b. 38
16 a. Subtracted from the test results
17 d. Main protective bonding conductors

18 b. 0.37 Ω
19 c. 0.29 Ω
20 d. 6 MΩ
21 a. Linked out
22 d. Fail to operate
23 c. 167 Ω
24 a. Only statement 1) is correct
25 d. 0.35 Ω
26 a. Every accessible point on the circuit
27 d. Neither statement is correct
28 b. 5 mA, 10 mA and 50 mA
29 a. Resistance of circuit line and neutral conductors
30 a. Clearly identify areas where testing is taking place
31 d. The installation of a lighting circuit
32 a. Type of system
33 b. Constructor
34 d. Corrected before the installation can be placed in service
35 b. Not reduce the safety of the existing installation
36 c. Not valid
37 c. Schedule of Test Results
38 b. 3
39 b. For the lifetime of the electrical installation
40 d. Guide for recipients

Glossary

ADS automatic disconnection of supply
AVI Approved Voltage Indicator

csa cross-sectional area
cpc circuit protective conductor

DB distribution board
DNO Distribution Network Operator

ECA The Electrical Contractors' Association
EIC Electrical Installation Certificate
EICR Electrical Installation Condition Report
ES Edison screw
EWR Electricity at Work Regulations

HSE Health and Safety Executive
HVAC heating, ventilation and air conditioning

IET Institution of Engineering and Technology
IP ingress protection
IT information technology

LED Light Emitting Diode
LV low voltage

MET main earthing terminal

NCR no carbon required
NICEIC The National Inspection Council for Electrical Installation Contracting

PEFC prospective earth fault current
PELV protective extra-low voltage
PFC prospective fault current
PIR passive infrared detector
PPE Personal protective equipment
PSCC prospective short circuit current

RCBO the residual current circuit breaker with overload protection
RCD residual current device

SELV separated extra-low voltage

TN-C-S a supply system in which the earth provision is provided by the DNO using a combined neutral and earth conductor within the supplier's network cables. The earth and neutral are then separated throughout the installation. These systems are referred to as TNC-S or PME systems
TN-S a supply system in which the earth provision is provided by the DNO using a separate metallic conductor provided by the DNO. This provision may be by connection to the metal sheath of the supply cable or a separate conductor within the supply cable
TT a supply system in which the DNO does not provide an earth facility. The installation's exposed and extraneous metalwork is connected to earth by a separate installation earth electrode and uses the general mass of earth as the return path

UPS Uninterruptable Power Supplies

Ventricular fibrillation where the heart rhythm is disrupted and results in irregular fluttering rather than the beat required to circulate blood around the body

Index: Electrical Installation Series – Inspection Testing and Commissioning